4.00

The

Canadian Contemporary Philosophy

Series

John King-Farlow
William R. Shea

Editors

Contemporary
Issues
in
Political
Philosophy

Contemporary
Issues
in
Political
Philosophy

William R. Shea
John King-Farlow

Editors

Science History Publications
New York · 1976

First published in the United States by
Science History Publications
a division of
Neale Watson Academic Publications, Inc.
156 Fifth Avenue, New York 10010

First Edition 1976
Designed *and* manufactured in the U.S.A.

Library of Congress Cataloging in Publication Data
Main entry under title:

Contemporary issues in political philosophy.

   (Canadian contemporary philosophy series)
   Bibliography: p.
   1. Political science--Addresses, essays, lec-
tures. I. Shea, William R.
JA39.C65   320   76-13836
ISBN 0-88202-156-7

Acknowledgement: The Editors gratefully acknowledge the secretarial
assistance made available to them through the courtesy of Dean Walter
Hitschfeld of McGill University.

To Jeanne, Maureen, and Philippe
for three generations of political discussions.

Contents

Introduction

WILLIAM R. SHEA

The essays in this book are intended to provide both the student of political philosophy and the general reader interested in political ideas with a representative sample of questions that are currently being debated. They make no attempt at exhaustiveness but aim at showing that philosophical positions, which may seem remote when encountered in textbooks, have a practical bearing on vital contemporary issues. The views expressed belong to a broad political spectrum and representative voices are heard from the right and the left as well as from the centre. The authors often disagree on the correct stance to adopt, but they are unanimous in denouncing the passive acquiescence that so often passes for rational assent. They write to inform but also to provoke and to challenge, and they make their case in clear and straightforward language that is refreshing to read.

In the first essay, Jan Narveson, one of Canada's foremost political philosophers, addresses himself to a question that is very much in the minds of Canadians wrestling with the rich cultural complexities of their country, and Americans reassessing their origins during the Bicentenary of the American Revolution: What is meant by nationhood. Professor Narveson provides a framework for subsequent discussions of the rights of individuals or groups within a nation. Michael McDonald shows how aboriginal rights can be meaningfully discussed in the perspective outlined by Narveson, and much of what he says will be found relevant not only to North American Indians but to native groups everywhere.

If nations are generally a minority, women are not. Yet, as Lorenne M.G. Clark argues in her persuasive essay on the rights of women, they are often treated as such. Just as the white man assumed that he was superior to the Red Indian, so the male took it for granted that he had justifiable grounds for considering himself superior to the female. If any such male lives through the onslaught of Ms. Clark, he will probably survive only as an intellectual fossil.

Conrad Black can rightly claim to belong to a minority for he is one of the small number of Canadian newspaper proprietors who find themselves threatened by a shift of power in the news media. He states, in uncompromisingly controversial terms, that journalists have banded together not to promote higher standards but to secure higher wages whatever the price to be paid by the nation as a whole. His statements cannot fail to provoke a lively discussion and to lead, one hopes, to a better awareness of the practical philosophy that should be implemented if our national press is to become genuinely democratic without falling prey to irresponsible pressure groups. Black believes that the public interest is best served under private ownership, which can be made accountable to Government, rather than under large unions that bully their way to power. Many will disagree with this assessment of the situation but no one will escape the challenge of Black's forceful prose.

In a more serene and detached tone of voice, Louise Marcil-Lacoste tells how she was involved as a professional philosopher in drafting the Quebec Bill of Rights. It is interesting to see how a real philosophical dialogue went on while the declaration was being revised and how genuinely philosophical considerations were brought to bear on the problem.

Dan Goldstick discusses, from a confessedly Communist standpoint, the right of nations to self-determination. Some readers may be surprised to see Professor Goldstick take such a strong stand on the question but, as Ivan Avakumic recently pointed out in his book *The Communist Party of Canada*, the Canadian Communist Party was profoundly influenced by the cultural configuration of our country, and its ethnic composition distinguishes it from most other Communist parties. Many immigrants to Western Canada between 1890 and the First World War came from the vast territories of the Russian Empire, and even if they were Ukrainians, Finns, or Jews, they were often fascinated by the Revolution that had changed their native land. They gravitated, through a kind of resurgent nationalism, towards the Communist Party and remained there because it provided a social life among people who spoke their language and shared their background. To date the Communist Party has not made much inroad into the wider population probably because the CCF and the NDP provide a movement wide enough to accommodate a variety of socialist attitudes. Dan Goldstick bears witness, however, to the fact that, like many other Canadian institutions, the Communist Party has a gift for survival and is alive to the current debate on the rights of nations.

Roger Beehler and George T. Monticone go beyond the realm of actual political problems to confront us with lessons from our nearest living relations, the apes. Some of the emotions and social interactions of chimpanzees closely resemble our own, and it is suggested that by observing them we can catch glimpses of human behaviour that would otherwise elude us. But although chimpanzees have a protracted childhood which lasts into their twelfth year, and the bond between mother and offspring is often maintained even after her children mature, there is one important way in which they differ from humans: The clarion call of women's liberation has not made itself heard in their

2

communities. Although kind to youngsters when they meet them, the males leave the females with the brunt of child-rearing while they disport themselves or move around on foraging expeditions. Lynda Lange and Mary O'Brien believe that too many men have not got very much beyond this stage, and their extended and closely-reasoned analysis of the inner contradictions of male supremacy are an important contribution to the philosophy of feminism.

The scene shifts again when Herman Tennessen fires a broadside at fashionable philosophical styles and suggests that the way out of tiresome philosophical disquisitions is to attend to the concrete facts of our existential situation. In this irreverent essay, philosophical positions are laughed off the stage wearing dunce hats labelled "the porcine fallacy" or "porcomania," speculative balloons are pricked, and the subtle arguments of linguistics philosophers are treated as gaudy baubles.

Robert Keyserlingk is also sceptical, but in a different way, of attempts to provide ideal solutions to our political ills. The projects for a brave new world that have been dangled before men's eyes for the last two centuries have produced little real emancipation. To revolutionary fervour, Keyserlingk would prefer orderly progress. He sees the fundamental right of man, as Edmund Burke put it in the eighteenth century, as "the right to decent, wise, just, responsible, stable government in the circumstances of a given time and place." Human rights are the result of experience, tradition, and compromise, and they are undermined by calls to build an impossible tomorrow.

But what is a free society? asks Anthony Mardiros in the concluding essay that many students may wish to read first. Freedom, for Mardiros, is a value that grows naturally out of humanism. Man truly knows himself only when he becomes aware of the creative possibilities of freedom. It is, in a sense, the defining quality of a man, a value to be preserved against both the ever-recurring temptation to anarchy on the one hand, and totalitariansim on the other.

Nationalism

JAN NARVESON

I

By 'nationalism,' for purposes of this essay, I mean the twin ideas (a) that it is at least morally legitimate and perhaps morally required that the government of one's nation should put the interests of the nation ahead of the interests of all others—should give it more importance than any other nation in its international dealings; and (b) that it is at least morally legitimate, and perhaps morally required, that the government of one's nation take various measures, in relation to its own citizens, to secure that *its* citizens and institutions are given some kinds of precedence over the people or institutions of other nations in dealings which enable such discriminations to be made, and to take measures with a view to keeping the idea or image of the nation "alive" in the minds and hearts of its citizens.

I am not directly concerned with another sense of the term in which it refers only to the doctrine that nations exist *at all* as legitimate entities. Many people probably believe that this second thesis, which is obviously presupposed by the first, is actually equivalent to it or implies it. But this is not true, as may be seen by an analogy between "individualism" and nationalism: Clearly it is one thing to say that individuals exist at all, are "legitimate" entities, and another to say that they have the moral right or even duty to prefer themselves to others, or to be constantly reminding themselves of their own identity and individuality. Perhaps they ought, but in any sense in which they might decide to do this, it is also possible for them to decide not to. And if it is possible for them either to do it or not do it, then the question whether they ought to do it can be raised; therefore it cannot be the same question as the one about their existence or legitimacy. Similarly, it would seem in principle to be possible for a nation to be impartial or self-effacing in the same way as some individuals sometimes are and are often enjoined to be. Logically, it would seem, a nation could, in its international behavior, be scrupulously impartial as between its own interests and those of others. Externally, it could concede disputed issues to the party which in its judgment had the strongest claim, irrespective of whether that party happened to be itself. And internally, it could be impartial between its own citizens and non-citizens—for example, it could make no tax distinctions between companies owned by foreigners and those owned by citizens, and it could allow all magazines and newspapers, wherever or by whomever published, to enjoy exactly the same mailing rates or circulation subsidies or non-subsidies.

There is, of course, some limit to this. A nation cannot make *absolutely* no distinctions of *any* kind between its citizens and non-citizens without ceasing to function altogether: Canada, for example, cannot decide to impose a tax on the people of, say, Stuttgart, Germany. But it conceivably could make no distinction between citizens and non-citizens among all those people who happen to come within its geographical boundaries, and could impose no restrictions on who may or may not come across those boundaries. It could abolish its national anthem, refrain from having national hockey teams, and in general do a great deal to down-play or even extinguish itself as an object of any considerable thought, loyalty, or affection on the part of its citizens. In these latter respects, nationalism is clearly going to be a matter of degree. A "nationalist" with respect to such matters is one who favors making a lot of such distinctions, or very strong distinctions, while someone who is not a "nationalist" favors making few or weak distinctions of those kinds. The question we will be considering in this essay, then, is whether "nationalism" is reasonable—whether one ought to be a "nationalist" in the senses defined above. Is it, for instance, morally legitimate for the Canadian Government to give tax money to Canadian symphony orchestras on condition that they frequently play the music of Canadian composers? Would it be legitimate for it to forbid the performance of non-Canadian works altogether? (If one wants to say 'yes' to the first but 'no' to the second, where and how do we draw the line between them?)

These questions very quickly raise a fundamental problem: What exactly constitutes a 'nation'? Thus far I have been talking as though Canada were a perfectly reasonable example of a "nation" for purposes of this inquiry; but in fact, various sub-regions and sub-groups have at one time or another been held to be nations, or to deserve to be considered as nations, with the implication that Canada, at least taken in its present legal entirety, is *not* one. Notoriously, there is the case of Quebec, but the Maritimes, British Columbia, the whole West, the North, have also all been the subject of nationalist aspirations (sometimes fantasies). Recently the representative of an Indian group in the MacKenzie valley has been quoted as saying to Mr. Justice Berger on his fact-and-opinion-gathering mission concerning proposed pipelines in those parts, "We are being destroyed. Your nation is destroying our nation." In what sense, then, is the term "nation" being used when such things are said, and what is the relation, or what ought to be the relation, between "nationhood" in that sense and in the more ordinary sense of the term? (When it is convenient to distinguish the two senses, if such

5

they are, I shall tend to use the term 'State' instead of 'nation' for what I have called the "more ordinary sense," and continue using 'nation' for the other sense. I will call the former the 'political' sense of the term, and the latter the 'cultural' sense, without meaning to prejudge any issues by so doing.) Note that in either sense of the term, however, the doctrines I described at the beginning are capable of being advocated and are, I think, just what are in question when nationalisms are espoused or denied: In either case, it is being claimed or denied that it is right for the "nation" in question to prefer itself or its members, to single itself out as having a greater claim on its members than other "nations" in various possible disputes, clashes, or, in general, situations where interests come into some sort of conflict.

I have said that we won't be directly concerned with the rather minimal sense of the term 'nationalism' in which it merely means that nations are legitimate, have the "right to exist." But it is clear that if nations are *not* even legitimate entities at all, then obviously they do not have the stronger rights which are raised in our question about national-ism. Now, a main reason why the idea of "cultural" nationalism is important in our inquiry is that proponents of such nationalisms believe that the "cultural" aspects of society make for a better, truer, or perhaps the only legitimate basis for a State. There is a sense that there is something arbitrary or artificial about States, and that leads to the suspicion that States are too insubstantial and contrived to have a reasonable right to exist. Whereas if those who are members of the State also have this other sort of nationality in common, then that is thought to be more satisfactory. And clearly, the question of what sort of thing makes a State legitimate at all will be closely related to the question of what it is about States that would make Nationalism in our strong sense a reasonable, or even a legitimate, attitude. We will begin the sub-stantive part of this essay, then, by considering briefly certain arguments about the legitimacy or illegitimacy of the State, with a view to seeing how such factors as cultural unity might bear on the matter. Only if such arguments can be reasonably countered, after all, is there much hope for nationalism. The plan of this essay, then, is to put nationalism on trial, as it were, and to see whether and in what degree it remains unscathed. And the first witnesses will testify against the nation, as a political entity, altogether.

II

The strongest enemy of the State as we know it is the proponent of what is now called "libertarianism," the belief that every individual has a natural right to do as he pleases and have what he likes, subject only to the restriction that he must respect everyone else's similar freedom. This

6

right is held to be supreme: Nothing else, including considerations of the general welfare, may override it. The right to liberty is taken to extend to property: Individuals may acquire previously unowned property (if any) as they are able, are entitled to whatever they can make, and may exchange as they can or give away as they please whatever they have legitimately acquired. Given these assumptions, short work is made of the modern State. It is allowed that a minimal State is needed, to prevent and punish violations of people's liberty, specifically, attacks on life, bodily security, property, or legitimate activities. But no further activities of the State are legitimate. Why? Because of coercion: To one or another degree, any State activity involves coercion, that is, forcing people to do what they may not want to. Laws of most kinds and taxes of all kinds are in that sense (allegedly) coercive; hence, says the libertarian, they are illegitimate. Any activities which require groups to carry them on must be carried on by voluntary groups, groups which the individual member is free to join or not join and, subject to the rules he has voluntarily accepted, to leave or stay as he pleases. The State is inherently unable to meet this requirement for legitimacy. Hence it must go, or at least all but its aforementioned police functions must go.

One way to try to meet the criticism of libertarians without rejecting their fundamental premises would be to make out that the State is, after all, a voluntary organization. It might be claimed that the citizens of a functioning modern State are voluntary members of it, in a number of ways. Immigrants, for instance, go there by choice and voluntarily assume citizenship. And even those who were born there may, after all, leave if they choose. By virtue of staying and taking advantage of the various benefits which the State makes available to its citizens, they may be considered voluntary members. And besides, the better modern States—like ourselves!—are all democracies. By having the vote, we actually rule over ourselves.

But none of these arguments, nor the sum of them, will satisfy the libertarian. In the first place, as has often been pointed out, people in many States are *not* permitted to leave as they wish; and even in those which do not have any legal prohibitions on the subject, it is not all that easy to just up and leave when one takes a notion to, especially because in order to go anywhere else you must get entrance permission from the other place, which is impossible in many cases, difficult in most, and even in the best cases is at very least a great nuisance. And as to having agreed by virtue of having taken advantage of benefits, even if there are any, this must be admitted to be a non-literal sense of 'agreed' on the most charitable construction. The State, to begin with, would make you obey its laws whether or not you actually got any benefits from its alleged sources of benefit. It may be a lousy deal from your point of view,

7

and certainly it's not as if you were ever asked to negotiate on the package. "He who accepts the benefits must shoulder the burdens," say the defenders of the State, but the State decides which and how many of each you are to get, and in the end you either go along or you get your teeth kicked in. What kind of voluntariness is that ? (Or as Robert Nozick has quipped, "Implicit consent isn't worth the paper it isn't written on!")

And as to democracy—that is worth a separate diatribe in itself. What democracy does is to ensure that the laws are made only by people who got elected, which means, getting more votes than any other candidate—not even a majority, usually. And what if it was a majority? So what? If you're in the minority, that means that you obey the laws which *their* representative makes—makes for everybody, not just for those voting for him. Furthermore, most of those voting either are, or might just as well be, idiots. What do they actually know about the candidate? What do they know about the issues? Practically nothing, in either case. Like as not, they voted for Smith because they liked his face on the campaign poster, or at best because he was at least a change from that fool Jones who preceded him in office. None of this makes it likely that good government will emerge, needless to say. But worse yet, none of it makes it likely that the rights of individuals will be respected in the result. It's unlikely, not just because governments thus elected cannot be expected to have any notion of individual rights, but for the still more serious reason that governments thus elected are almost certain to have the attitude that whatever the majority wants—i.e., whatever will keep them in office—is *ipso facto* right. Thus if, say, 40% of the voters are Roman Catholic, you may be sure that public moneys, extracted from non-Catholics as well as others, will in one way or another go to the support of Roman Catholic schools. Indeed, there's scarcely any indignity, any infringement on human rights, any monstrosity that could not be favored by an electoral majority at one time or another; so any governmental system predicated on the fantastic proposition that the support of a majority is enough to make something legitimate is simply bound to be an evil one.

This is a strong indictment, and one to take seriously. After all, who can doubt, in the words of J.S. Mill, that "If all mankind minus one were of the one opinion, and only one person were of the contrary opinion, mankind would be no more justified in silencing that one person than he, if he had the power, would be justified in silencing mankind"? Who can doubt that if some morning all but one member of a town were to get together and vote to crucify the remaining person, for no reason at all, then that person—even if his one vote were also allowed to count— would have been done a terrible wrong, rather than legitimately because legally (mis)used? Every reader will, I presume, find this absolutely obvious. But if so, then the idea that voting assures legitimacy must be firmly rejected. And if democracy is thought to be constituted by everyone's having the vote and all basic matters being decided by voting, then democracy is plainly suspect: at very least, inadequate as a foundation for the legitimate State. Certainly, then, the idea that a State is made into a voluntary organization by guaranteeing everybody the vote is fallacious.

Before attempting some more credible reply to the libertarian challenge, let us consider for a moment the possibility that cultural nationalism will help to prop up the legitimate State. A State, after all, is simply a collection of people, just any people, with a big line drawn around them and a central agency with the power to make people inside that line do what it says. Small wonder that there is a problem of legitimacy for such an entity. But suppose we don't draw the line around just anybody who happens to be in the neighborhood. Suppose instead that we draw it around all those who have the same language, the same religion, the same skin color, the same customs, and/or the same bringing-up: In short, suppose we draw the line around people who are truly a Nation instead of merely a happenstance lot of homo sapiens. Wouldn't this bring us at least a lot closer to the Voluntary State? For after all, by drawing the line in this way, we assure that we have people with a similar general outlook on life, similar attitudes about what should be done, and in short, an identity of *interest* lacking in the merely "political" State.

Certainly these are considerations that have been thought relevant by both theoreticians and statesmen for a very long time. At the Paris peace conference in 1918–19, for example, one of the "Fourteen Points" of President Wilson which were to form the basis of the peace was that "an independent Polish state should be erected which should include the territories inhabited by indisputably Polish populations," and much attention was devoted to seeing to it that national boundaries should be drawn around what really were nations. This in turn was based on the principle that territorial settlements should be made "in the interest and for the benefit of the populations concerned." We can well imagine what a great uproar there would be if it were decided, on grounds of administrative convenience, to splice eastern Ontario in with southwestern Quebec, or to chop off northern Maine and include it in with New Brunswick, the Gaspé, and Prince Edward Island to form a new province. It would simply be flying in the face of political reality to try to ignore the multiplicity of facts which I am lumping together under the heading of 'cultural nationality' in the course of practical world politics, difficult though it often is to identify and sort out the many groupings which emerge or which clamour for recognition.

But what sort of theory can reasonably underlie these practical recognitions, and how far does it get us in the face of the libertarian objections we began with? On the face of it, it is not clear that the situation is materially helped, and in some ways it may even be worsened, by obtruding cultural considerations into the picture. For consider—in the first place, it is difficult to identify precisely the areas around which to draw the requisite lines which turn culturally identified "nations" into States. In a geographical area there will invariably be some diversity: Any line that could be drawn would certainly fall short of enclosing precisely the culturally homogeneous "nation" we're after. This being so, as soon as it is drawn we may be certain that there will now be cultural minorities who are in danger of being oppressed by the cultural majority—for example, the English-speaking people of Quebec. And in the second place, the claim of a culturally homogeneous group to be a "voluntary" one must be looked upon with the darkest suspicions. For one thing, it is perhaps not entirely unfair to point out that the parent culture is foisted upon the children: *They* cannot be said to have "volunteered" to become cultural Arabs, Slavs, Quebeckers, or Inuits. But no doubt it will be said that children do not count, possibly on the ground that they do not have "wills" to be consulted on such matters. Letting that pass, there is the more serious difficulty that homogenous cultures maintain their homogeneity by all of the arbitrary measures we profess to disapprove when employed by our own governments. Tribes ostracize those who violate the tribal mores, nag and belittle those who question them, and generally toss Mill's "On Liberty" into the nearest cocked hat. So in respecting the cultural identities of those around whom we draw national boundaries, we are trading in one kind of oppression for another, or even combining the two into a still bigger bully: not just the majority, but the majority of Right-Thinking-Fellow-Tribesmen. We can forget about our cherished notions of civil liberties if we go in *this* direction. For now precisely the kind of discriminations which we think it wrong for officials or even civilians to exercise against one another—racial, linguistic, religious, and so on—are going to be reinstated; indeed, they are claimed to be the very basis of legitimacy from the beginning! Thus it is that contemporary liberals and radicals often find themselves in need of some rather fast footwork. On the one hand, they want to denounce their western liberal governments for violating the rights of various minorities, including natives; and then, on the other, they defend the right of those minorities, as groups, to deprive their own members of those very same rights. And isn't that even worse? Not to mention that culturally homogenous nations tend not to worry about democracy all that much anyway. Just as the Swiss used to argue that women didn't need the vote, since they'd just vote the same way as their husbands anyhow, so the dictator of a cultural "nation" can claim that the way *he* feels about an issue is the same as the way his People feel about it anyhow, so why bother with a vote? From the point of view of the aberrant individual(s) in a cultural Nation, then, this allegedly superior basis of nationhood may have all the disadvantages and none of such advantages as there are in plain old liberal democracy.

III

Having attempted to state the case against the State in a forcible, not to say outlandish, way, we must now see what there is to say on the other side. Of course, to justify the State, or at least to say what sort of State could be justified and how, has been the main task of political philosophy, and we can hardly expect to tackle that project in the few pages which are the most that we can devote to it here. Necessarily, then, my account will be very sketchy indeed. Nevertheless, I hope to say enough to lead us intelligibly toward a reasonable position on the main issue. The many threads left hanging, we can hope, will not too seriously enmesh the engine of argument, leaving it derailed or permanently sidetracked.

Let us begin by conceding the absolute minimum, namely the principles of libertarianism by which coercion is never justified except in order to prevent, punish, or exact compensation for unjustified acts of coercion. But even carrying on those functions, it turns out, will get one to some sort of State, some central agency which enforces all contracts, and punishes all malefactors. (For the details of the argument to that conclusion, see Robert Nozick's *Anarchy, State, and Utopia.*) Even the "Minimal State," as it is called, inevitably makes some people do what they don't want to do. Its justification is that this interference is absolutely and genuinely minimal, for if any less interference with liberty were made by the State—e.g., if there was no government at all, but only anarchy—then even more interference would be made, by other individuals whose coercive activities are now unrestrained.

This suggests a generalization of the criterion which the out-and-out libertarian would presumably be willing to accept in these matters, namely, that an institution is acceptable if for each affected person it would be chosen in preference to any practicable alternative. And it would seem that this criterion can be met if an institution advantageous to nearly everyone can undertake to compensate the rest for the disadvantage it visits on them. So long as the question of what constitutes an advantage is left to the individuals concerned to decide, proper operation of this criterion would seem not to violate anyone's liberty.

11

There is one basic point which may, however, require a parting of the ways with libertarianism, or at least an understanding of its reach. The libertarian allows coercion only in self-defense or defense of one's property and freedom of action. But what does it say of the person whose back is completely against the wall? Suppose that the free operation of the market, plus the parsimony or meanness of Mother Nature, leaves someone with only the alternatives of starvation or theft? Does the right to life, in the form of a right against society to provide the bare essentials of living, come into the picture here, or doesn't it? Libertarians tend to dodge this question by insisting that this would never happen in a truly libertarian society because people are basically nice if you give them a chance and wouldn't let people starve. But this is a dodge, obviously, and we must press the question. And in a way, it may not matter much what one says in theory on the point, for there are only two possibilities. Either we avoid a Hobbesian "state of war" with such persons by conceding the right to live, or else we fight the said war. There is no realistic alternative. When reduced to desperation, people will resort to violence, whether or not they have the "right" to do so. But if we choose the alternative of war, then we may well ask whether it is worth the price. That a war of the favored against the poor is in very poor moral taste to begin with, while perfectly true, is not really the deciding consideration. Forgetting altruism, isn't it irrational to risk one's life when a very marginal willingness to share would do the trick instead? And how about risking *other* people's lives? For we may be sure that in the terrible war of the classes, the poor will not be choosy who their victims will be; only collective security will work. And this gets us back to the State. Now, if protection against this source of coercion is a legitimate function of the State, then do we now have a more than minimal State, or don't we? We do, if compensation against starvation (to the unlucky poor) or against class war (to the favored ones) are legitimate kinds of "compensation." And how could they not be, faced rationally?

So a State at least slightly above the Minimum State (or if you prefer, a broadened realization of what constitutes the Minimum) seems justified by this method. But there is more, which is best seen by addressing ourselves briefly to the subject of compulsory State-operated health insurance. Here, thinks the libertarian, is a dandy example of injustice: You have to have the insurance, whether you want it or not, and you have to pay, whether you want to or not. A clear violation of liberty! But wait a minute—before swallowing this obvious-seeming indictment whole, let's have a look at the possibilities. Suppose, for instance, that if instead we have a wholly voluntary scheme, two things happen (not fanciful eventualities, to anyone who knows about these

12

matters): The available voluntary coverage is (a) far more expensive; and (b) far less comprehensive—if you're sick more than two months, the insurance company stops paying and *you* start. If you can't afford to pay, you're thrown out of the hospital on your tottering limbs. If you have your *choice* between voluntary and involuntary insurance, curiously enough, you will reasonably choose the involuntary variety. You know you won't like to pay. But you know that you'd like it even less to find yourself sick with a curable disease which you can't afford to have cured, and you die, leaving your family penniless, or motherless, or both.

What does it mean to say that you would *choose* the involuntary scheme if you had your *choice*? It's only a seeming paradox. We can voluntarily choose to put ourselves in a regime which will make a lot of things involuntary. We choose to take Chemistry 244, and then we have to do the assignments whether we like them or not, or fail the course. We choose to work at a certain job, and from then on must do, within reason, what our superior requires of us. And to get down to cases, we can choose to accept majority rule on many matters, after which we shall often find ourselves putting up with policies we didn't want. But with any luck, we shall *more* often, on the average, find ourselves enjoying policies we did want.

More generally, we find that in many conditions of life, such as that in which we have a fairly advanced industrial economy, we stand to benefit from being part of a system over which we have very little direct and immediate control. *Most* of us will be better off—*far* better off—by living under such a system. How about those who (think that they) are not? To satisfy the libertarian's requirement, we would need to compensate such people. How do we know whether this requirement has been satisfied? We may ask whether a rational political theory would accept the principle in the first place. But surely, in some form or other, it would, wouldn't it? After all, what the principle says is simply that any institutions which affect you must not affect you adversely, i.e., must not be such that you would not be at least indifferent as between their existing and their not existing. How can we fail to want this? How can a principle which says that all changes affecting the holder must be at least an acceptable deal for the holder fail to be accepted?

It hardly can. But deciding what falls within the ambit of relevant advantages and disadvantages is immensely difficult. My example about involuntary health insurance was designed to make two points. First, the one already made—that it will be overwhelmingly rational for nearly everyone to subscribe to such systems. But second, a more subtle and for present purposes more fundamental point, viz., that if you *proscribe* involuntary systems of the type described, then you seem to be depriving people of a possible choice; and it is not clear, any longer, that the people whose liberty has been "respected" by not imposing involuntary systems upon them have not now *deprived* the others, who are forbidden to enjoy the benefits of involuntary systems, of a rival possible liberty. Is the ideal of universally respecting everyone's liberty clear enough to be capable of coping with this kind of problem? I think not. Particularly not if, as is usually done, libertarianism is construed as a foundation for the free market. For in such markets, notoriously, the operations of some, the more efficient or more fortunately situated or whatever, can have drastic effects on the prospects of those in a worse competitive position, through no fault of the latter. Only the excuse that even the losers are somehow compensated would retrieve the free market (if it's retrievable!); but then, why won't it equally retrieve such things as involuntary health insurance?

The compensation requirement is a difficult one to size up because to compensate someone is to restore him to a previous state of well-being, the one prior to the incursion for which he is being compensated. This means we must have a "base-line," that is, some conception of how well off presumably disadvantaged people would have been without the disadvantage being imposed. If the notion of compensation is to be useful for social theory, then the base-line must be non-arbitrarily drawn at some prior state which was *just*. If X is in his favored situation only because of some injustice, done either by X or someone else, then theory can hardly call for compensating X. But what is the previous just situation prior to the State? The question seems unanswerable. In practice, it seems, we can do little better but hope to compensate people relative to their situation before our institutional innovation, whether or not we are assured they are altogether justly in that situation.

Two kinds of compensation are possible for those few who are disinclined to go along with an involuntary system despite its benefits. One way, as in both Canada and the U.K., is to make it possible for those who can afford it to have better inessentials—private hospital rooms with color TV's, perhaps—on a user-pay basis. Another is that there will be a range of involuntary systems from which the balance of benefits will swing their way instead. For example, well-maintained public highways are of much more benefit to the person who can afford a Lamborghini than to those who can only manage a bicycle; support of the arts is of much more benefit to the cultured than the uncultured. The system will be justified (not perfect—that's quite another matter) if nobody can honestly say that the total package of benefits is less than enough to compensate for the losses of liberty entailed, as compared with a base-line which, however difficult it may be to know just where to set it, must certainly involve a substantially more primitive condition of life. Such few, if any, as remain will either live by violence, in which case they cannot complain if they die by it or wind up incarcerated because of it, or will have to ponder the reflection that life on the terms they require would also require a great many others to live on terms that they would find intolerable. (Smith might relish the prospect of living like Robin Hood; all the others who would be reduced to serfdom in a system enabling such a life-style would have a quite different taste in their mouths.)

All of this is, of course, contingent on the assumption that involuntary systems really are necessary for many kinds of benefits. If, as some continue to imagine, we really could do as well or better with purely voluntary systems, this entire argument for the State would fall. But in that case, surely, good riddance to it! Does anyone still imagine that the State is something so lovable that we ought to stick by it in the absence of any benefits whatever?

IV

The foregoing argument does not do much for nationalism in the sense in which this essay is concerned with it. If it justifies the State, as I think it does, there are many things widely attributed to States which it does not justify. For example, it does not justify any duties to go off and assist in one's country's military adventures against others, unless in the strictest way necessary for self-defense. It does not endow the State with a right to make everybody speak the same language or accept the same religion, or live in the same kind of house; nor with the authority to halt the spread of marijuana, pornographic movies, tendencies to indulge in ermine coats, auto racing, zen buddhism, or even pop music and other aesthetic evils. It does not seem to make the State a fit object of loyalty or veneration. It most decidedly does not say, in the words of John F. Kennedy, "Ask not what your country can do for you; ask rather what you can do for your country." On the contrary, it seems to say that you certainly should ask your country what it can do for you, and you should look at the reply (if any) with jaundiced eye. Further, it is clear that the State, once in operation, is a tiger which few if any individuals have hold of, even by the tail. If it is allowed for a moment to believe, as most people apparently do, that it actually has the right to do more or less anything it pleases, including anything the electorate will permit it to do, then in a trice it will be off and doing it. And of course, what State has *not* indulged itself in this mythical legitimacy? Prominent among these sins are ones of marginal concern to us here, such as insensate bureaucracy. But also high on the list, it would seem, are all manifestations of nationalism in the sense defined.

15

Wrongly, however. For it is time to reflect on the matter of international relations. Nationalism, recall, was defined in this regard as the tendency to "put the interests of the nation ahead of the interests of all other nations." And it is not clear that the foregoing arguments show that nations may not do this. Even when a State is constituted merely by a rather arbitrary line drawn around a rather arbitrary collection of people, the very fact of its existence both enables it and causes it to have relations with other States which bear some comparison with the relations one individual can have with another individual. Out-and-out nationalism, along the lines of our definition, would be comparable to out-and-out egoism at the individual level. It is worth drawing out the comparison somewhat.

Ethical egoism is the doctrine that an individual ought to regard other persons entirely as "means to his own ends": that an action is the right one for X to do if and only if it on the whole brings maximum benefit to X, no matter what it may do to anyone else (all things considered, and in the long run). Without getting involved in the very real and perplexing difficulties of interpretation and understanding which this apparently simple characterization brings up, there is a classical problem with egoism which many have thought renders it a non-starter. If we accept the characterization of morality as the set of rules or principles by which everyone is to be guided, and to which one may appeal only if everyone may so appeal, then consider what egoism seems to entail. If, for instance, others find it in their interest simply to dispose of Mr. X, then X has no entitlement to any sort of protection on this principle. If what is right for you to do is whatever is in your interest, then the fact that what you propose is very contrary to mine will be quite irrelevant in my moral assessment of your action. I must, it seems, approve of actions contrary to my own interest. But how odd that, starting out with the idea of advancing my own interests alone, I end up with a morality which approves of others' thwarting me.

This will do, very briefly, as a statement of this well-known difficulty with egoism. We cannot pause to consider the innumerable counter-arguments, some rather ingenious, which have been advanced as a cure for this paradox. I do not, myself, think that there is any "cure" in the end, nor that one is needed, and will simply assume for the rest that this is so, noting only that most philosophers would probably agree with this assessment. If we are right, then what follows about international relations?

Well, what follows about individual relations? One important option is to say that in principle, one ought to count everyone's interests equally with one's own. There is unquestionably a great deal of abstract appeal about this idea. But it is quite unclear what it really means in practice. Does it, for instance, mean that competitive behavior, in which one attempts to promote one's own advantage against others, is always wrong? No, for various reasons, one of which is that competitions, such as races or games, are often enjoyable to all concerned: Everyone participating wants everyone to do his best, and enjoys the state of affairs in which each does so more than the alternative states even if one loses the game oneself and would have "won" had others not even been trying. No, because it is in many cases far more efficient for each to look after himself, and the net benefit to everyone, impartially considered, is greatest when each does so. Again, however, we cannot possibly discuss this option, which is pure utilitarianism, without getting hopelessly far afield. Enough to say that we can frame options to egoism which avoid the intolerable consequences of that theory, respect the restriction that the rules must be the same for everyone, and still allow individuals considerable leeway to pursue their own interests without too much regard for those of others. We will have restricted pursuit of self-interest, rather than unlimited pursuit.

Prima facie, then, the same will be true on the international level. If the State is held to have the right to pursue its interests without any intrinsic regard for what happens to others, then the universal acceptance of this morality is acquiescence in self-destruction. There have to be limitations imposed, therefore, and in the case of powerful nations they will almost inevitably have to be largely self-imposed. Exactly what the terms will be is not entirely clear, but minimally, we may expect, they will have to include a general condemnation and disavowal of aggressive war, and perhaps some obligation for rich nations to help nations in dire need. Here there may be room, then, for a certain amount of legitimate competition. But there is no room for the view that one's nation represents the Master Race to whom all others have the sacred (and enforceable) duty to knuckle under. And there is no room for the idea that whenever we can get away with it, we needn't bother about observing the same rules which we expect others to observe.

The major snag in this analogy is that States are not individuals. The morality of international dealings is necessarily a borrowing from the morality of individuals, who must remain the primary unit of ethical analysis; and so far as it goes, the borrowing works rather well. It works far less well when full account is taken of the fact that unlike individuals, States have members who are individuals and to whom they have moral relations as well. (What is it for a State, since it is not an individual, to have "moral relations" with anyone? While this question raises interesting puzzles about how to fix responsibility on an office as opposed to the individual who happens to be occupying the

17

office, etc., the situation is no more mystifying than that in which an individual has moral relations with any collective entity, such as a family or a business firm.) This fact, as Alexander Solzhenitzyn has been reminding us lately, makes it very difficult for a State to stick firmly to the principle of mutual non-interference with the internal affairs of others. As an individual, your "internal affairs"—your relations with your appendix or your left knee, for instance—are indeed your affair, in which others may when called upon help out or advise but may not get involved without your consent. But the same grounds certainly cannot be invoked for noninterference with a State which is torturing, bugging, stifling, and otherwise misusing its citizens. Individuals do *not* "belong to" the State as one's stomach belongs to oneself. Individuals do not, as such, "belong to" anyone at all, except as they choose to do so, to identify themselves with other individuals or groups. Individuals are the locus of thought, will, emotion, conscience, and so forth, and all talk of national thought, will, etc., has to be either statistical or metaphorical at best. (There is, indeed, such a thing as "national character"; a modest amount of foreign travel is enough to confirm that. A somewhat less modest amount is enough to confirm that any element of this character you want to mention will be better exemplified by some non-citizens than by most citizens of the country concerned: Some English Canadians out-French the French in rudeness to foreigners, some French people are more open-hearted than most Americans, and so on and so on. "National character" is what most people in that nation are like and what more of them perhaps aspire to be like or hold up as a model for comparison; it is not an irreducible somewhat in virtue of which citizens must hold the State in awe as their parent, guru, or whatever.)

Two conclusions emerge from these reflections, then. The first is that a certain amount of nationalism in international affairs, what we may call "international nationalism," seems justifiable. The second is that the kind of nationalism which a nation can exercise with respect to its citizens is not—at least, not so far as this argument goes.

V

Is there a basically different argument, then? Perhaps the sort of premises from which I have been arguing above are simply one set among many others, no better than they. Perhaps I have been exploring a sort of "individualism" which is simply arbitrary, or even unreal. Thus Charles Taylor, in his interesting and admirable book *The Pattern of Politics*, remarks, "The dialogue within the United States is carried out by what purports to be a reference to values of Lockeian liberalism, the traditional foundation of the American way.

Everybody from the hippy to the Bircher argues his case from the premise of the individual's freedom to pursue happiness in his own way." And he goes on to say, "Faced with this model, it is natural for Canadians to wonder whether we have an identity. For we have not and could never have one of this kind." But is this really so? Professor Taylor presumably does not mean to imply that these ideas are peculiarly and uniquely American—their origin in Locke, an Englishman, not to mention the ideals of the French revolution, would be enough to dispel any such notion. And whoever may have thought of it, do we seriously want to suppose that nations can adopt just any old "ideal" they wish on these matters? Is it perfectly all right for the Russians to throw people in jails, concentration camps, and psychiatric institutions for criticizing the regime, because this is called for by the National Ideals? I not only don't believe this for a minute, but I don't believe that the Russians themselves believe it either. (Notice how, instead of just saying that such behavior is perfectly all right, they take pains to invent justifications, implying that they agree justifications are required.)

Which apparently contrary facts may have been overlooked in our allegedly narrow individualist view? A quick glance at the daily papers suggests some answers. "Twelve wounded in northern Portugal as Communists fire on Catholics." "Crowds throw rocks at British troops in northern Ireland." "Shostakovitch considered his music an expression of the Russian people." "Blacks, whites pelt each other on Boston beach." In each case, individuals are doing things; but they would not or even could not be doing just the things they are if they didn't belong, or see themselves as belonging, to various groups. Some of the groups are voluntary ("Communists," "Catholics"), some not ("Blacks," "Whites," "The Russian people"). In each case the behavior is voluntary enough, at least in the sense that each person decides to do what he or she does, and presumably could have decided to do otherwise. But in each case too, there is plenty of room for doubt about the freedom of each actor to do as he does. Talk about sociological "forces" is not idle. Each stone-throwing Boston white, each Communist and Catholic, if we look into their backgrounds, will be found to have been subjected to an elaborate program of conditioning which eventuates in a high probability that the subject of the program will faithfully shoulder his rifle or heft his rock with probably no thought at all that there is a question of moral right involved that is not automatically settled by the sheer fact of his allegiance to a Cause. The case of Shostakovitch makes an interesting comparison. He doubtless could have, but did not, flee to Western Europe at the height of his creative powers. When the Russian State reprimanded him for bourgeois deviationism, he submissively accepted the criticism and wrote more "acceptable" music. In 1960 he joined the Communist party—not before, despite the advantage for him of belonging. The government paid him well for his music, and bestowed high honours upon him. A Solzhenitsyn, we know, does differently. But Shostakovitch was at least as great a composer as Solzhenitsyn a writer. There is no simple accounting for these things. (But isn't it important that Shostakovitch and Solzhenitsyn faced a clear choice and made it in the light of their considered thought, while the average rock-thrower probably just reached for his rock upon seeing others do so?)

The facts of identification with groups, classes, associations, races, and so on, do not require us to abandon "individualism." Those who claim that classes are the units of social action talk also of "oppression," for example of the working class. Are they worth listening to if they can't point to actual members of that class and say just how and how much they are oppressed? Similarly with any other talk in group terms. Groups consist of individuals, and any morality which is made out on the group level will inevitably borrow, as has our account of international morality above, its terminology and conceptual machinery from the situation of individuals. What matters is this: If people are to be free to do as they please, they must be free to identify with whom they please. Among the classic freedoms of the individual defended by the most ardent individualists are several which are inherently group-related: freedom of assembly, freedom of religion, freedom of expression. Yet what does leaving them free to do this mean? And having done it, how does that affect the situation?

It is absurd to suppose that individualism commits one to the sole defense of freedoms which could have been enjoyed by Robinson Crusoe on his desert island. But it does commit one to recognizing one person's freedom to act as a Buddhist just as much as the next person's freedom to act as a Catholic. It therefore commits one to recognizing that no State as well as no individual or group, may force anyone to be Buddhist or to be Catholic. Does it commit one to recognizing a freedom of each to think the other a wicked and irretrievably damned soul? Perhaps, but not to act on it.

The question which arises is, what constitutes an illegitimate pressure in these matters? To take a still-current example, consider the situation of contemporary Canadian universities. There are no private universities remaining in Canada, for all practical purposes. Those who wanted to go, or to send their daughters and sons, to a private university would continue to pay the same taxes to their provincial and federal governments for support of the public universities as they did before. But the governments do not *forbid* the establishment of private universities: It merely happens that, in the circumstances, their action effectively makes the existence of private universities overwhelmingly unlikely because prohibitively expensive. Now what about foreign students and foreign scholars? Great financial incentives are established to make it difficult—but not impossible—for foreign students to attend, say, graduate schools in Ontario. If a department has a vacancy, it is urged, cajoled, but not absolutely required, to hire a Canadian citizen for the spot. (The threat of requirement in future is not equivalent to requirement right now, after all—right?) It might have been supposed that a university, being an institution dedicated to the spread and improvement of knowledge, would like to get simply the best students and the best scholars it can. (Some enthusiasts have suggested the agreeable hypothesis that simply being a Canadian is in itself a qualification for some posts, so that if the foreign competitor is only *otherwise* better qualified, then the native is really better qualified after all!)

Yet it may seem anomolous if a public university in country X has mostly citizens of Y and Z among its academic personnel. It will seem anomolous, no doubt, to its taxpayers, and it will not be true to form by world standards. This brings up two points. The first concerns the analogy or lack of one between the citizens of a province or nation and "their" university. (If the latter is regarded as a private association, much like a club or business firm, then does its freedom to operate as it wishes extend to excluding persons of different religions? Different races?) Since citizens are involuntary supporters of their universities, at least in the financial respect, should they, in compensation, have even more freedom to enact otherwise arbitrary exclusions and distinctions? It would seem that they should have at least as much. The second is that much nationalism is defended as a sort of retaliation against other countries which do likewise. Retaliatory tariffs are a strong case in point. Tariffs restrict consumer freedom and protect business operations whose level of relative inefficiency makes them unlikely survivors in a free international market. But if other countries adopt them, it is difficult for the first not to retaliate, at the risk of considerable economic distortion. The same arguments are invoked regarding foreign applicants at universities, and in many other areas of life it is possible for those arguments to be deployed with varying degrees of force.

But the lower limit of that force is zero. At their worst, such arguments are sheer me-tooism. "*They* cut people's hands off for theft: Why shouldn't we?" "They have a law against foreign professors being deans; to protect ourselves, so should we." But "protect ourselves" against what? Often the answer is question-begging: Protect ourselves against "foreign take-overs," simply parses out to "excluding foreigners," which is the point at issue and takes us back to square one. If hiring people solely on their merits, or buying the best goods at the lowest prices, leads to "foreign take-over" (which would seem to imply something about the quality of the local product in both cases), though advantageous on all other counts, then the sheer foreignness of the foreign take-over must be what is really wrong, if anything is wrong here.

On basics the first argument is more promising: X-ians, if they like, may run their institutions so as to exclude non-Xians, and no reason need be given other than simple wanting-to on the part of the X-ians. But while more promising, this runs up against the same snag described a few pages back. Where X is a nation-State, what "the X-ians" want is invariably only what most or even only some, and at the limit only what the people who happen to be in power among the X-ians, want. There will always be some who would have wanted it otherwise if they had their say, and to put it briefly, they don't.

Why do people think that nations have peculiar rights to override the wishes of the less numerous or less powerful of their citizens when it comes to operating allegedly "public" services? We are back almost to where we began. In section II, we considered a argument for the legitimacy of the State, which gave credence to a more-than-minimal one despite its apparent overriding of individual choice. But the saving condition was that everyone must come out better or at least as well as he would have if he had had his choice. Yet when it comes to public operations which tend to establish a public's national "identity," and individuals or groups who do not share the national Identity as currently conceived by governments are genuinely thwarted in their aspirations, then it is difficult to see how compensation is possible. People talk of the "right to an identity," but this is ambiguous. Everyone may identify with whom he or she pleases: That is, with whatever group, etc., will have him or her on the terms in question. But just for that reason, nobody has the right to be a member of a nation full of like-minded people. Others have no duty to conform to your image of Nationhood, any more than you do to theirs.

There are two points to consider here. First, a national identity, if it is thought a good thing to have, may be an object of aspiration within certain limits. Ideally, those in the nation would, on reflection, come to see this identity as a desirable thing, not by being forced into it, but by seeing it and liking what they see. A State aspiring after nationhood has, after all, considerable momentum. The power of national symbols to stir hearts is well known; the thirst after a national identity nearly ubiquitous; and the advantages of membership in an efficient nation-State on the international stage all but impossible to resist, while international efficiency is substantially a function of internal solidarity. If it plays its cards right, it will not need to coerce people into sharing the identity in question: They will drink it in with their daily soup, and it will be as palpable as an Indian's curry or a Frenchman's paté. If it plays its cards wrong, it will not deserve the allegiance it won't get.

Second, schemes of compensation for non-joiners can be more thoroughly pursued than they generally tend to be. Couldn't grants roughly equal to the level of public support for public universities be given directly to individuals who preferred "private" ones, if the universal right to a university education is insisted upon? Can't small beaches for nudists be established, as well as big ones for the suited majority? Lawmakers are not as accustomed to searching for such compensating devices as they could be. Numerous considerations of efficiency make such things difficult, of course. And contrary to some, I do not argue that considerations of efficiency are wholly subordinate to antecedent rights, simply because, as with the health insurance schemes considered earlier, if one person's noncooperation is making it impossible or much more expensive for a great many, there will be some point at which he would owe compensation to them for lost opportunity. But even taking this into account, concern for the position of people who do not want to join must be a major concern of any scheme which is likely to disadvantage non-joiners. Needless to say, too, the more intense and rampant the nationalism, the more probable it is that non-joiners will be disadvantaged, and the more serious will their disadvantage be.

VI

The foregoing considerations have been rather abstract. How do they bear on the various problems which we in Canada, as well as most other countries in one way or another, have been facing? It is always dangerous to suppose that philosophical considerations can be applied simply, directly, and unequivocally to complicated social and political phenomena, and when examples are mentioned, they must be understood to be tentative. We have to say, "all else being equal . . ." or "assuming the facts are such-and-such. . . ." For since there is a great deal else to be unequal and a great many facts which might not be as we thought or might change the picture if we knew them, and since, moreover, the collection and analysis of these matters belong to the task of the social scientists and to people engaged in public affairs, it would be folly for theoreticians to make any very flat statements. Indeed, my examples are intended to illustrate this as much as my positive conclusions about nationalism.

23

To take an important example, what about economic nationalism and the fear of foreign control of our industries and resources? Here we need to distinguish between two very different possible interpretations. In the first place, even extreme nationalists, so far as I know, always argue that restrictions on foreign ownership or control would be economically advantageous, in the long run, for Canada as a whole. But as we have seen above, it is not unreasonable for nations to pursue the economic advantage of their citizens vis-a-vis others, within fairly wide limits. (And in the present case, there is hardly call for charitable concern for, say, the welfare of the United States!) Again, if the question is whether the control of these resources ought to be public rather than private, or more public than it is, this too is not a question of nationalism in any very essential sense; it is, rather, a question of socialism. Insofar as these are questions of economic advantage, the problem is whether public versus private controls, or domestic rather than foreign ownership or control, is better for the whole society, and these are issues which turn on complicated economic considerations. On the other hand, suppose that we were all asked to sacrifice our economic welfare, at least to some extent, in order to rid ourselves of foreign ownership or control. Suppose, that is, that the only "advantage" in domestic control and ownership was simply that of control and ownership itself, and that other things were equal or even disadvantageous, not just in the short but also in the long run. We should then have an issue of nationalism in the pure sense. And the considerations adduced in this paper do condemn this sort of nationalism. (Incidentally, it is worth noting that in this respect, I probably mirror the sentiments of the great majority of Canadians. Indeed, it would be plausible to claim that among the elements of Canada's national character, a strong aversion to "nationalism" would rank high on the list. Those who are most insistent on injecting hefty doses of nationalism into the nation's cultural blood-stream in the interests of "asserting our identity" might do well to reflect on this not unlikely possibility. It is, in this writer's opinion, one of the most attractive of our putative national qualities.)

Again, take government promotion of domestic artists, writers, and musicians. Organizations in Ontario interested in promoting musical concerts will discover that the fees of domestic performing musicians are materially reduced by government subvention, while on the other hand foreign artists are required to forfeit a considerable percentage of their fees for income tax, to be refunded in whole or in part the following tax return year at earliest. Canadian symphony audiences will find that the compositions of contemporary Canadian composers are frequent occurrences on programs, while those of even the most

24

renowned foreigners are by comparison rarely heard. Foreign musicians and music are not forbidden, but they are economically discriminated against. Here again, I think, it is important to distinguish quite different underlying justifications for these discriminations. On the one hand, there is the quite general issue whether governments ought to be spending public money on things from which only a tiny fraction of citizens benefit, at least directly. Supposing that this issue, which is not an issue of nationalism as I am understanding that term, is resolved in the affirmative, then a certain amount of what otherwise looks like "nationalism" is well-nigh inevitable. If we are to encourage music in this country, it is only good sense to do so by encouraging home-grown musicians and musical organizations, since these will presumably remain here and continue to benefit us, whereas the evanescent appearances of foreigners will perhaps do less for us. Again, whether those things are really so is arguable, but the point is that to support discriminations of the type I have described on these grounds is not nationalism in the most important sense of that term. And with regard to the funding of musical compositions, it is extremely debatable whether the cause of good music, as distinct from intensity of domestic compositional activity, is materially forwarded by these policies. Well, let us now suppose that they are not. Let us imagine, for instance, that a Beethoven were to arise in some foreign country which for some reason, not only didn't encourage but actively discouraged his musical activities. And imagine that the conductor of the Montreal Symphony Orchestra wants to perform the works of this great composer, but is disenabled from doing so because the relevant governments insist that the works of a local composer, greatly inferior in the estimation of both conductor and audience, be performed instead, on the ground that Canadian audiences ought to hear Canadian music. Clearly, this would be roundly condemned by the principles I have been advocating. (And I am sure that virtually every Canadian music-lover would join in the condemnation, if the case was just as described. Happily, no such extreme case is likely on the policies of present provincial or federal governments, by the way. Any resemblance to real cases is purely coincidental.)

For examples of "nationalism" at its best, we should turn to such groups as the famous "Five" in nineteenth-century Russia. Here a group of composers set out to oppose the music fostered by the conservatories, on the ground that that music was largely German in origin. And in the event, they carried the day: Their music is popular the world over, while that of such composers as Anton Rubinstein is scarcely heard at all. But two interesting points should be observed. The first is that The Five were not asking for exclusive government recognition and subsidy, but only for a fair share of performances and

25

public exposure. They were not insisting that the public continue to listen to their music even if bored to tears by it, on the ground that it was their sacred duty as Russians to do so. The other point is that the greatest of all Russian composers, Tchaikovsky, was not a member of The Five, and did not aim at producing peculiarly Russian music. He simply wrote what he felt in his heart. Yet it is his music above all others that we think of as distinctively Russian; and in any case, we recognize its greatness as transcending nationality. "Nationalism" in the arts is capable of being an interesting aesthetic quality, one (or one set of them) among others. The greatest art may or may not be nationalistic; so may the worst—though if nationalism is foisted on it, one suspects, it is more likely to be in the latter category.

Now, if governments were to choose between promoting good art that was not distinctively national, and promoting mediocre art which was, which ought it to do? Well, isn't it absolutely *obvious*?

Selected Bibliography

Encyclopedia Britannica (Chicago, 1969), vol. 9, p. 671, article on Woodrow Wilson's "Fourteen Points."

Gauthier, David P., editor, *Morality and Rational Self Interest* (Englewood Cliffs, N.J., 1969).

Mill, John Stuart, *An Essay on Liberty* (many editions).

Nozick, Robert, *Anarchy, State, and Utopia* (New York, 1974).

Taylor, Charles, *The Pattern of Politics* (Toronto, 1970).

Aboriginal Rights

MICHAEL McDONALD

How would you respond to the question "What sorts of treatment do the native peoples of Canada deserve?"

Since native people are amongst the most underprivileged Canadians, you might respond on the basis of your attitude to the poor. Thus, if you believe that Canadians should have welfare rights, then you would claim that Indians like other Canadians should not be allowed to fall below some national standard of minimum welfare. You may believe that this is best done through providing a guaranteed annual income or through the provision of various goods (such as food and housing) and various services (such as medical care and job training). You would then find yourself in agreement with Prime Minister Trudeau who in 1969 said that native people

> ... should become Canadians as all other Canadians and if they are prosperous and wealthy they will be treated like the prosperous and wealthy and they will be paying taxes for other Canadians who are not so prosperous and wealthy, whether they be Indians or English Canadians or French or Maritimers, and this is the only basis on which I see our society can develop as equals.

On the other hand, another person might make a libertarian response and deny that anyone has a right to welfare. He might argue that no one deserves "free passage"—that everyone should work his own way. The debate would then be joined over a whole set of familiar issues. What are the relative merits of free enterprise and planned economies? What does "equal opporunity" involve? How much may the government interfere in citizens' lives? And so the argument will wend its way over time-worn paths until one or both of you get tired and change the subject.

A very effective way of changing the subject is changing it so that you both wind up on opposite sides of the original question with you arguing against any special treatment for "the poor Indians" and your libertarian opponent demanding that they receive significant advantages from white society. I think this reversal is likely to happen if you shift the topic from welfare rights to aboriginal rights. Topic shifts of this sort, those which get the attacker and defender of a particular *status quo* to change places, very often provide interesting material for the political philosopher. Such is the case with aboriginal rights.

I. Entitlement Theory

What is the reason for this reversal in positions?

I would suggest that there is something different about the ways in which we ground welfare and aboriginal rights. That is, when we argue for someone's having a welfare right we usually base our arguments on quite different sorts of premises than when we argue for aboriginal rights. The initial problem is then to characterize these sorts of differences.

Fortunately, this task has been made easier by the recent publication of *Anarchy, State, and Utopia* (New York, 1974) by Robert Nozick, who defends Locke's libertarian political philosophy. He argues that neither more nor less than the minimum or night watchman state of *laissez-faire* economics can be justified. In the course of this argument, he has to explain how people may legitimately have the exclusive use of various things, i.e. how they may come to own things. It is this discussion of "justice in holdings" that sheds light on the salient differences between welfare and aboriginal rights.

According to Nozick there are two primary ways in which I can have a just holding. If the object is unowned, I may under certain conditions come to own it; this is called "justice in the original acquisition of holdings." If the object is owned, then its owner may under certain conditions transfer it to me; this is called "justice in the transfer of holdings." Thus, for example, if you want to find out if the Atlantic salmon in my freezer is mine, you would want to know how I came to have the fish in my freezer: If I caught it, stole it, bought it, received it as a gift, etc. In short, you would ask for a history of ownership. The fish is mine if its original acqustion was just, and all subsequent transfers, if any, are also just. Insofar as you can trace this history, you can determine if I have *clear* title. To the extent that you cannot trace this history, it is not clearly mine, e.g. if all you know is that a friend gave it to me but you have no way of knowing how he got it, you can't say for certain that it really is mine.

If you get a clear history and then find that the original acquisition or one of the subsequent transfers was unjust, then you or someone else has the problem of deciding how to rectify this injustice in holdings. The rectification of injustice in holdings is the third part of Nozick's theory of just ownership. Thus, if you find out that my generous friend stole the salmon from a seafood store, you'll have to decide whether or not you should tell me to return it.

Now let us imagine that you decide to settle the question of my ownership of the salmon by using welfare principles solely. Let us assume that whatever welfare criterion you intend to use will only apply to the two of us in this case. First, you appeal to 'need': You say that you are hungry and desperately short of protein, while I am not; since needs should be satisfied, you should have the fish. Say that I ignore that plea, so you try a hedonic appeal: You claim that you will enjoy eating the salmon much more than I will; hence, by the greatest happiness principle, you should have the salmon. It is not difficult in either appeal to imagine how I would have to respond to prove that I have a better title to the fish according to the criterion used. I would argue that I am needier than you or that I would really enjoy it more than you. Further it is not difficult to imagine the two criteria coming into conflict: You need the protein, but I would enjoy the dinner more. Then we would have to sort out which criterion takes precedence, e.g. that needs take precedence over wants. It is also not difficult to foresee some of the problems we might have in applying these considerations: How can I compare my need or enjoyment with yours, how can we properly take into account the effects of giving the fish to you or to me on each of our future needs or enjoyments, how do we know what counts as a "need" as opposed to what counts as a "want"? These are all problems which make up the bulk of philosophical debate about utilitarianism.

In our argument about who has the better welfare claim to the fish we proceed in a quite different way than we did earlier in trying to decide if the fish was a just holding of mine. Then we asked if the salmon had been justly acquired by me or justly transferred to me; in short, we looked backwards in time to see how the fish came into my possession. In the second case, we applied welfare criteria by looking to our present and future conditions to decide the issue according to our relative positions on the scale of need or enjoyment. Two major differences in the determination of ownership stand out in these cases: These are different attitudes to (a) the past and the future, and (b) the characteristics of the affected parties. Both (a) and (b) require some further explanation.

Regarding (a), we have seen that what mattered in determining justice in holdings were the acquisitions and transfers of the object; that is to say, the principle for the determination of ownership was *historical*. In the use of welfare criteria, we looked only at present and future considerations, viz. the relative degrees to which my or your having the fish would meet present and future needs or yield present and future enjoyment. Here we decided who owned the salmon on the basis of *end-results*. Our approach in the second case was *a*historical.

Regarding (b), you will recall that in the application of the welfare criteria we were concerned with the degree to which each of us had or lacked certain characteristics: If you were needier or would enjoy it more, then the fish should be yours. We were concerned in this case with the resulting *patterns* of the alternative distributions. In the first case, however, we proceeded without reference to patterns. There were no characteristics (such as need) which I might or might not have that would be determinative of the question of my ownership. It mattered not why I caught the fish (e.g. that I was trying to satisfy my hunger or pass the time of day) or even what I would do with it (e.g. eat it, throw it back in the stream, or use it for fertilizer). Nor did it matter why someone transferred it to me (e.g. because I paid for it, or because I am his son, or because he simply felt like it). In fact it doesn't even matter if I have a freezer full of Atlantic salmon and you have none or even no food at all. Justice in holdings is *unpatterned* in that there is no natural dimension (what I call a "characteristic") or set of dimensions according to which the distribution of goods should take place.

II. Aboriginal Rights

We can now see how Nozick's approach to justice in holdings, which he calls "entitlement theory," ties in with the topic of aboriginal rights. Aboriginal rights are none other than original acquisition rights which haven't been transferred to anyone else. To defend the aboriginal rights of Canada's native peoples necessarily involves us in presenting a theory of original acquisition. Moreover, we must be willing to defend our theory of original acquisition against not only rival theories of original acquisition, but also against non-entitlement theories of ownership.

At the beginning of this paper, the argument about providing help to native people was carried on between a person who held a non-entitlement theory of the distribution of goods and one who held an entitlement theory. As you recall, one argued that native people should be helped on the basis of need. This, we have just seen, is an argument based on end-results and patterns. The other disputant argued that native people were not entitled to help. This argument is essentially historical and unpatterned.

Introducing aboriginal rights into the argument forced a change in the disputants' positions because it introduced a historical and unpatterned basis for the native peoples' entitlement. Now it was possible for the libertarian defender of property rights to argue that the natives had been dealt a historic injustice which stands in need of rectification. The defender of welfare rights must reject this approach, not because native peoples shouldn't receive significant benefits, but because in his view the only true basis for the reception of benefits is need. That is, he was arguing that benefits should be distributed in a patterned way with a view to the end-results achievable.

Now it is important to realize that we cannot simply let the disputants "agree to disagree." In practical terms, we are talking about claims to at least half of Canada. According to Peter Cumming and Neil Mickenberg in the second edition of *Native Rights in Canada* (Toronto, 1972), aboriginal claims have been superseded by treaties for less than one half of Canada. This would leave standing aboriginal claims to British Columbia, Quebec, the Maritimes, the Yukon, and parts of the Northwest Territories. Think of what this means to established settlements and to plans for Northern development. Remember, too, that "the natives are restless": they have been pressing their claims in the courts (in 1973 the Supreme Court of Canada split four to three against admitting an aboriginal claim), over the bargaining table (in Quebec native people have received a large cash and land settlement for allowing the James Bay Project to proceed in a scaled down form), at the barricades (in British Columbia), and before a royal commission (Mr. Justice Berger is carrying out an investigation of the effect of the proposed Mackenzie Valley Pipeline on native peoples). The question of aboriginal rights is a real, not an ivory-tower, question.

In my examination of this question, I do not intend to say much more about non-entitlement theories except by way of contrast to entitlement theories. I shall instead focus on various problems that I see in the application of Nozickian and Lockean entitlement theories to the question of aboriginal rights in Canada. I will argue that some of the problems anticipated in such an application of entitlement theory can be adequately handled, but that other problems—particularly those at the core—are much more difficult and may well be insurmountable.

I shall proceed by presenting a number of objections to an entitlement defence of aboriginal rights. I shall first state the objection in the broad and general way it occurs in non-philosophical discussion. Here I have tried to draw upon statements made by politicans, lawyers, and native people, as well as from discussions I've had with students and colleagues. Then I shall try to make an entitlement response to the objection. This response will consist, first, in sorting out various objections that have been confused and run together in the non-philosophical context. After that, I shall see what kind of reply can be made within an entitlement theory. I have tried to give each objection a name which suggests the sort of objection made and renders the arguments easier to remember. This mnemonic aid is important because the arguments are often interrelated and used together for or against aboriginal rights.

31

A. The Vandals' Argument

This is the kind of argument that Trudeau has used:

> If we think of restoring aboriginal rights to the Indians well what about the French who were defeated at the Plains of Abraham? Shouldn't we restore rights to them? And what about the Acadians who were deported—shouldn't we compensate for this? And what about the other Canadians, the immigrants? What about the Japanese Canadians who were so badly treated at the end or during the last war?

A similar position was taken by many Americans in response to James Forman's demand that American churches and synagogues pay $500 million as reparations for years of slavery. In his book, *The Case for Black Reparations* (New York, 1973), Yale law professor Boris Bittker cites the *New York Times* response to Forman: "There is neither wealth nor wisdom enough in the world to compensate for all the wrongs in history."

An objector might ask if the descendents of the Roman victims of the Vandals' sack of Rome in 453 A.D. should be able to sue the Vandals' descendents? Here, however, we see the need to distinguish two separate objections. The first is what I shall call "Historical Disentanglement," and the second "Arbitrariness."

A.1. Historical Disentanglement. The first objection rests on practical difficulties in sorting out historical issues. The problem is to find out who is a descendent of the victims of an injustice and who is a descendent of the perpetrators of that injustice. In the Vandals' case the problems seem well-nigh insuperable. Even if some sorting out is possible, there will probably be enough intermarriage to confuse most cases thoroughly. Intermarriage has been alleged a serious barrier to reparations to blacks in the United States.

In the case we are considering, however—that of native Canadians—we can get some powerful assistance from the facts. A quarter of a million Indians are registered under the Indian Act of 1951 as members of recognized bands. While we may have problems with the fairness of some of the provisions of that Act (e.g. Indian women who marry non-Indian males are deregistered and non-Indian females who marry Indian males are automatically registered), the fact remains that we have an accurate, though somewhat incomplete, record of many descendents of the purported victims of injustice. The cases of the unregistered Indians and of the Metis are more difficult, but we have two important facts which will help disentangle matters. First, these people have regarded themselves as native people. And secondly, they have been regarded by white Canadians as natives insofar as they have been objects of the same informal extra-legal distinctions (including racial prejudices) as those under the Indian Act. It should not prove to be too difficult to arrive at a consensus on who is or is not a native person amongst the Metis and other unregistered claimants of this status.

This, of course, leaves the question of tracing the descendents of those purported to have violated aboriginal title. Here again the facts help us—in this case it is the legal fact that only the Crown could seize land. In the case of New France, we can regard the Crown as the inheritor of whatever title France had to aboriginal lands.

It is also possible that we might in hard cases make use of a test Nozick suggests for determining the descendents of victims and perpetrators on the grounds that *persistent* inequalities are most likely a result of historical injustice. (While Nozick does not suggest 'persistency' as a criterion here, I think it might make his suggestion more plausible.)

A.2. Arbitrariness. The second distinct element in the Vandals' Argument is the suggestion that the defender of aboriginal rights wants to make an arbitrary and invidious distinction between rectifying the injustices done to aboriginal peoples and the injustices done to non-aboriginal Canadians. This is, I think, what Trudeau was asking, namely, how could we defend rectifying the injustices done to the Indians and ignore the injustices done by our nation to the French, the Acadians, and Japanese?

Trudeau goes on to say that we cannot "redeem the past"; we can only be "just in our time." This seems to let us argue that if we can't wholly rectify all the injustices we have ever done, then we needn't rectify any. The most favourable interpretation I can put on Trudeau's conclusion is that we may have to face a multiplicity of competing claims of all sorts including a number of competing claims for the rectification of past injustices. We may then not be able to do everything that we ought ideally to do; in an imperfect world we may have to pay our most morally pressing debts in full and make only token payments on the remainder. There need be no arbitrariness in the recognition of aboriginal rights, for we can still recognise other past and present injustices. We may not be able to fully satisfy all the claims for rectification, but that isn't arbitrary either—there is no obligation to do more than one can.

B. The Forefathers Argument

There is another way of taking Trudeau's conclusion that we cannot redeem the past, and that is to say that we are only responsible for our sins and not for the sins of our fathers. How can I be blamed for what my French-Canadian ancestors did to the Indians of New France? How can anyone do more than be just in his own time?

Let's sort out this argument.

B.1. Backwards Causation. The first thing to clarify is whether saying that I ought to rectify injustice *X* involves saying that I am one of *X*'s causes. If my children ruin my neighbour's prize roses, may I not have an obligation to make reparations? If I do, it needn't be the case that in so doing I am admitting that it was I who tramped through the roses. I may not even have to admit that it was somehow my fault that my children were in the garden. I may have told my children to stay out of the garden. Moreover, I may have done the best I can to instill in them a sense of respect for others' property. Then there is nothing more that I should have done. (After all, there are outward bounds like child abuse for determining how far a parent can go in instructing his children.) Indeed my children may not have acted deliberately, purposely, or even intentionally; it was an accident pure and simple, for which even they are not to blame. But there it is: The roses are ruined, and I am the one who should set it right.

The point is that "responsibility" can be used in a variety of ways. Sometimes it is used to indicate causality, in which case contemporaneousness or precedence in time is essential. But in the rose garden case, it was used to indicate who was *liable* for damages. The concept of liability is most highly developed within the law, but we do use it outside the law in our ordinary attributions of moral responsibility. The question then is whether anyone today has liability for the past violations (if any) of aboriginal rights.

There is a further confusion in this argument. This is to claim that backwards causation must be involved because I can only have obligations of my own making. Thus, I could have an obligation to contemporary Native peoples respecting aboriginal rights only if I had undertaken to respect these rights, i.e. if I made a promise to or contract with their ancestors. It will take only a moments reflexion, however, to see that many obligations we have are not entered into voluntarily (or involuntarily either), e.g. not to kill, to express gratitude for favours received, to be kind, and to be honest.

B.2. Benefits Received. In (B.1.) I didn't really so much respond to the Forefather's Argument as clear the way for a response to it. That liability-responsibility is different from causal-responsibility is important; nevertheless, it does not tell us if Canadians today have liability-responsibility for violations of aboriginal title. Neither does knowing that all obligations are not of our own making tell us if the rectification of this putative injustice is our responsibility.

A much more telling response is an analogy with the receipt of stolen goods. If person *A* steals person *B*'s watch and then makes a present of it to *C*, do we think that *C* has an obligation to return it to *B* even though he had no idea that he was in receipt of stolen goods when he accepted the watch? Surely, the answer is "Yes!" We might go on to say that *A* owes *C* something (an apology at minimum) for inconveniencing and embarrassing him. We would, I think, give the same answer even if the thief *A* can't recompense *C* (say that *A* is now dead). It is worth noting here that no one is blaming *C* for *A*'s stealing *B*'s watch or even for unwittingly accepting stolen property. *C* needn't feel any guilt about either of these matters. He should, however, feel guilt if he doesn't return the watch to *B*. I see no reason to change our views about returning the watch if instead of talking about *B* and *C* we talk about their heirs. I would not extend this to *A*'s heirs, however, who presumably have not benefitted either from *A*'s theft, itself, or the gift of the watch to *C*.

The parallels with the case of aboriginal rights should be fairly obvious. Non-Indians have in Canada benefitted (albeit in very unequal degrees) from the non-compensated supercession of aboriginal title. This is not to say that non-Indians *today* refused to compensate native people for the loss of aboriginal rights *during* the last and preceeding centuries. These non-Indians certainly can't be held responsible for being born into this society or for immigrating to it. In this respect, breast-beating over what has been done to the 'poor native' is neither due nor appropriate. Guilt is appropriate only if nothing is done to remedy injustices in the treatment of native people including, in particular, the rectification of past injustices.

Of course, the case for reparations becomes more difficult if we change the analogy somewhat. For example, what, if anything, does *C* owe *B* if after *C* receives the watch he loses it? It would be different if *C* were keeping *B*'s watch in trust for *B*, for then he could well be responsible for not losing it. This problem posed by lost or ruined articles seems quite likely to occur with the passage of significant periods of time. If we are talking about *C*'s and *B*'s great-grandchildren, the odds are that by this time the watch has been lost or no longer works.

This is, I think, the kind of thing that Bittker has in mind when he says that there would be no case for reparations to blacks if in the period since the Civil War there had been an unbroken ascent up to a present state of genuine equality. That is, the argument here is that reparations are not due if the relative advantage seized by the act of injustice gets lost or equalised in the course of history, so that it no longer makes any difference. It is *not* crucial to this argument that *both* the benefits accruing to the oppressors and their heirs and the evils suffered by the victims and their heirs no longer remain. It is enough to have the first without the second.

B.3. Inheritance. There is a way of taking the Forefather's Argument that avoids the reply just advanced (B.2.). There I argued that if you can inherit benefits, you can inherit burdens chargeable against those benefits. This is like having to pay estate taxes and creditors before receiving an inheritance. As we have just seen, if you inherit nothing, you do not have any obligation (save, perhaps, "a debt of honour") to pay any debts chargeable against the estate. This suggests that there would be no aboriginal rights if there were no rights to make bequests; that is, aboriginal rights disappear if no one may rightfully inherit anything.

Native people could use this as an effective *ad hominem* argument in pressing their case. They could say to the rich and powerful in our society that Indians and Innuit will give up their claims to aboriginal rights if the rich and powerful will surrender all the property that they have inherited. This would not mean the end of private property but only the aspect of it—which I call "bequeathability." Other aspects of private property would remain (*viz.* rights of alienability, exclusive use, security, management, income, and so forth) but these "standard incidents" of property would be limited to the life of the holder. (To make this suggestion effective, we would have to set a limit to the life of corporations, for under our laws these "artificial persons" can be immortal.)

C. *The Double Wrong Argument*

The objection here is that to rectify one injustice another will have to be done, so that in rectifying the injustice done to the native peoples an injustice will have to be done to non-native Canadians by taking away from them land or the profits therefrom which they have in good faith purchased and improved. Moreover, the settlement of aboriginal claims will impose an enormous burden on those who in some cases are already disadvantaged.

The main response to this has already been made in the Fore-fathers Argument (B.2.). No one has a right to receive and retain what is not another's to give. "Good faith" here excuses one from complicity in the original theft; one is not to blame for the theft, so one needn't feel guilty about it. It does not excuse one from returning the stolen goods or the equivalent. Remember that we are working within the context of entitlement theory; justice in holdings demands justice in acquisition and transfers. To give weight to the claims of those who have unjust holdings is just the sort of thing end-result theorists would do.

Nevertheless, the entitlement theorist can reduce the practical force of this objection by pointing out that third party beneficiaries (here, non-Indian and non-Innuit property owners) must return what remains of that which was wrongfully transferred to them. Given the ravages of time, one may not have to surrender any of one's own goods in making this reparation because nothing of value remains. I say "may not" because among the benefits received from the stolen property is that there is less drain on one's own resources. Thus, in the watch analogy, *C* or his heirs may benefit from not having to purchase watches of their own because they have the use of the watch stolen from *B*. So if the watch breaks after a few years while in *C*'s possession, *B* might ask for rent for the use of his watch over the years before it broke. If *C* is now bankrupt, there may be little *B* can get (unless it is the case that entitlement theory would demand that *C* work the rent off). If it is the case that in addition to bankruptcy *C* also dies, then *B* cannot demand that *C*'s would-be heirs pay for it out of their own justly acquired resources (including working the debt off). Death without the transmission of a benefice would seem on the entitlement theory to end the case for repayment simply because the unjust holding no longer exists. Presumably, in this wealthy nation, most of the benefit has been transmitted to us.

A final remark on the plight of the small property holder. According to the principles of rectification of injustice in holdings, it surely must be the case that those who have benefitted most from unjust holdings owe more than those who have benefitted least. Keeping in mind the complications about inheritance discussed earlier, it should be the case that in a society like ours, in which most wealth—especially capital—remains concentrated in a few families, the wealthiest would have the most to lose by the recognition of aboriginal rights. Here I would think especially of those who have benefitted most from the exploitation of natural resources (like gas, oil, and minerals) in the areas in question, particularly Alberta, the North, and B.C. Of course, it has already been argued (B.3.) that these same people have the most to lose by denying aboriginal claims for they would thereby undermine their own claims to inherited wealth.

D. The Sovereignty Argument

In an article in *The Globe and Mail* (21 February 1973), Cumming has suggested that one possible reason for the Government's reluctance to recognise aboriginal rights is the fear that in so doing there would be a recognition of aboriginal sovereignty over the lands in question, to wit, Trudeau's reference to the Plains of Abraham. This is evident, too, in the same speech when Trudeau says, "It's inconceivable, I think, that in a given society one section of society have a treaty with another section of society." Trudeau is not the only politician in Canada's history to express concern about holding the country together; this is a country which has been plagued by threats of separatism—from Quebec, the West, and the Maritimes.

If it is the case that the recognition of aboriginal rights would necessarily involve a recognition of a separate aboriginal nation or nations then it is not clear what an entitlement theorist like Nozick would say. Nozick's invisible hand explanation of the emergence of a dominant protection agency as the (minimal) state never comes to grips with the fact that there is more than one nation in this complicated world. The fact of nationalism should also have some effect on Nozick's proposal for utopia—allowing diverse experiments in types of communities *within* a single nation. Are nationalists entirely wrong when they think that they must have control over the state and not just over the community? Another interesting way of putting this question is to ask what sorts of self-determination (determination particularly of a group's identity) are not possible in a libertarian society? Leaving aside these complex and difficult questions, it is possible to argue that if sovereignty is an issue here, then surely we must talk about more than justice in holdings.

The simplest way of dealing with this objection is to deny, as Cumming does, that sovereignty and property rights are connected except in an indirect way. In ordinary disputes over land ownership, neither claimant is trying to set up an independent nation. The adjudication usually follows the laws of the nation in which the property is situated. Although in a few difficult cases there can be arguments about which of two nations' laws are applicable, the dispute is primarily about ownership and only secondarily about sovereignty. It should be pointed out that no less an entitlement theorist than Locke claimed that rights to property are quite independent of rights to rule, for he maintained that property rights should survive changes in government including violent changes brought about by war.

E. The Litigation Argument

The general argument here is that claims to aboriginal title are unlike ordinary property claims. They are not amenable to the usual sorts of tests used by the courts to decide property rights. In particular many aboriginal claims are such as to deny courts the use of a most effective procedure for deciding between rival claims in cases where due to the passage of time both records are missing and memories are uncertain, namely, "prescription" which is "the operation of time as a vestitive fact." If this is correct, then how can anyone maintain that aboriginal claims can be settled in the same way as ordinary disputes about ownership? Indeed, how can anyone maintain that they are property rights at all?

This argument can be taken in part as a necessary corrective to the oversimplified reply that I just advanced against the Sovereignty Argument. There I argued that sovereignty and property were different kinds of rights. This may have left the impression that all property rights are alike and that aboriginal rights are like other property rights. Neither of these contentions are true.

I agree with A.M. Honore that "property" is probably best thought of in terms of a list of "the standard incidents of ownership." This would be a list of the rights which a property owner has in the standard, full-blown case. It would include rights of physical possession, use, derivation of profit and capital, security, management, and so forth. One would probably also have to say something about the duties of ownership as well, in particular the prohibition of harmful use. If some of these incidents are missing in a particular case, we could still talk about "property-rights." In fact all the Indian treaties deny Indians the liberty of converting their reserves into capital, i.e. they may not alienate their lands, only the Crown may. In this sense, reserves could be seen as belonging to a particular people in perpetuity, not just to its present day occupants; thus, future generations would have patrimonial rights. Aboriginal land claims involve the same kind of arrangement. (I should add here that if a whole people, conceived as a group extending across time into the future, can have property rights, then such a right might well play havoc with many of the positions that Nozick defends on the basis of actions in a free market.)

So part of my reply to this argument is that while aboriginal titles may lack some of the standard incidents of property it may well be possible to still think of them as property-rights. To properly establish this reply would require a great deal more space than I presently have. I think more needs to be said, however, about this argument along somewhat different lines.

First, there is the issue of "prescription." In the law it is the case that the passage of time can extinguish or establish ownership. This is determined by time limits established by custom or statute. For example, in some jurisdictions if you have made use of part of someone else's land as a right-of-way for twenty years, then the courts will uphold your right to continue to do so and thus bar the landowner from preventing your passage. Thus, time has given you a right you formerly did not have and extinguished a property-right that the landowner had. The point of prescription is quite straightforward: The passage of time is used as conclusive evidence because it simplifies the work of the courts in determining ownership. Thus, the jurist Savigny said, "All property is founded in adverse possession ripened by prescription."

The problem for aboriginal claims is that in many cases the land claimed is not now and has not been occupied by the claimants at all or on an exclusive basis for many years more than the limits set by law for the extinguishment of title. Yet it seems unfair therefore to deny title even though it is fair to do so in ordinary cases. In ordinary cases the law protects the property-owner's exercise of his property-rights before the period of prescription has elapsed. That is, if he wants to prevent his title from lapsing, he need only take action. Thus, in the right-of-way case, the property owner can put up a "no trespassing" sign before the twenty years are out; this completely extinguishes your claim to a legally guaranteed right-of-way. If it is illegal to post the sign, then using the passage of time to effect a transfer of title would be unfair. The parallel here is that native peoples have not been given an opportunity to present their aboriginal claims, either through the courts or directly to government.

Secondly, the Litigation Argument does raise important doubts about the appropriate *forum* for the determination of the value and extent of various aboriginal claims. Cumming says that "the court is by far the least appropriate forum for dealing with aboriginal rights" because "litigation is expensive, time-consuming, and abounds with technical difficulties." He proposes instead that there be direct negotiations between the government and native peoples. Thus, this is essentially a practical, not an in-principle concern.

Thirdly, the Litigation Argument hints at a problem which will concern us in the next and final section. The problem, as seen from the perspective of this Argument, concerns the relationship between particular property-rights and the existing legal system. One way of finding the general area of difficulty is to ask if there can be property without laws? If there cannot be property without laws (as has been argued by generations of contractarians, Kant among them), then is property merely a creature of law? If property-rights can only be created and destroyed by law, what must be said about the entitlement theorists' claim that we have a natural right to "estate" in addition to "life and liberty"? In the next section I will consider some of these questions.

F. The Acquisition Arguments.

Thus far, in all the objections and replies, I have tried to apply entitlement theory to the question of aboriginal rights. If I am right, then a number of interesting and plausible objections to entitlement theory and its application can be answered. In neither the objections nor the replies have I asked if native people actually have a claim to these lands on the basis of just original acquisition; for the sake of argument I have assumed that they do, and then gone on to ask whether such claims should be recognised. Obviously, if native people in general or in particular did *not* make a just original acquisition of the land, the whole case for aboriginal rights fails. This would not show that all the native peoples' claims to land ownership are null and void, but it would remove the most important and the largest claims.

There is more than this practical issue at stake here. The whole entitlement theory rests on original acquisition. If the justice of an original acquisition is called into question then so also, Nozick says, are all subsequent transfers. If *all* original acquisitions can be called into question, then, perhaps, all claims to property rights are challengeable. One way of calling all original acquisitions into question is to deny that sense can be made of the concept of "original acquisition." Another way would be to deny that original acquisition as imagined by entitlement theorists can be a basis for rightful ownership.

So now I will turn to the "keystone" issue. I should say that some of the sharpest criticisms of the original acquisition doctrine come from Nozick himself. He writes in an almost ironic, or shall I say, "contra-puntal" way that involves the reader and enlivens debate. I will present four objections and responses. The responses, I should indicate, are partial and do not, I think, save entitlement theory (though, curiously enough, they save aboriginal rights).

F.1. The Jus Tertii Argument. One way of challenging aboriginal rights *within* the framework of entitlement theory is to deny that the Indians and Innuit had made original and just acquisition. This could be denied on the grounds that Indians and Innuit weren't the first human beings in Canada and that Indians and Innuit acquired the Northern half of this continent by force. In any event, given the lack of records of property acquisition, it could be claimed that no one can know for certain if the native peoples' ancestors acquired the lands justly as either first possessors or as a result of just transfer. This would at the very least make aboriginal claims suspect.

The argument presented here rests on a claim like the following: If Bill's acquisition of Blackacres from Alice is unjust, then Chuck's acquisition of the land from Bill need not follow the rules of just transfer in order to get as good, or better, title than Bill has to Blackacres. The underlying contention is that if title is, so to speak, 'spoiled' at any point the property is simply up for grabs. Here I am assuming, that the just owner Alice in not laying claim to Blackacres and that Chuck is in no way acting on behalf of Alice. The question is not, then, one of Chuck's rectifying an injustice done to Alice by Bill. The objection rests on the contention that given Alice's not laying or transferring her claim to another, Bill's act of injustice returns Blackacres to an ownerless situation from which Chuck may claim it.

Before questioning this contention, I would note that even accepting this reasoning there still is a difference between showing that Bill's title is spoiled and raising a suspicion that it may not be clear. In some cases, it simply is impossible for a possessor to prove that he has clear title; however, this does not mean that others can prove that he does not. Surely the burden of proof rests on those who charge wrongful possession.

Now as to the argument itself, it is worth noting that the practice under common law is not to establish ownership *absolutely* but *only relatively*, i.e. to decide who has a *better* right to possess. It would, I believe, be the case that a court would hold that Bill has a better title to Blackacres than Chuck and that Alice has a better title than Bill. Regardless of the court's decision, it is certainly more convenient for a court to decide matters in this relative way (adjudicating only between the rival claims presented to it) rather than trying to do this once and for all (which would involve ruling on every conceivable claim.) In this case, the court would settle the dispute between Bill and Chuck leaving it to others such as Alice to bring suit separately.

Which approach should an entitlement theorist adopt—that unjust acquisition or transfer returns the object to an ownerless condition or that it simply 'weakens' the possessor's title? I wonder if in answering this question we will have to fall back on utilitarian considerations, e.g. about which procedure would be the most orderly and least disruptive for a given society. I am not sure how this question would be decided on purely entitlement grounds. That is, I don't know what *natural* rights to the ownership of Blackacres are held by Bill as opposed to Chuck. I would suspect that this cannot be determined without a *policy* decision about the rules governing property. Entitlement theory does not say which is the appropriate way of deciding ownership in this case. If this is right then it indicates an important gap in entitlement theory, for it means that the theory of justice in holdings has to be patched up by resorting to utilitarianism.

Apropos the question of aboriginal rights, it would seem that if we proceed on the basis of who has better title rather than on the basis of who has absolute title, then native peoples' claims would seem to be stronger than those of successive possessors.

F.2. The Spoilage Argument. In *The Second Treatise of Government*, Locke presents an objection to his view of justice in original acquisition:

> That if gathering the Acorns, or other Fruits of the Earth, &c. makes a right to them, then any one may *ingross* as much as he will.

Locke says that this is not so; one may take "as much as one can make use of to any advantage of life before it spoils . . . Whatever is

42

beyond this, is more than his share and belongs to others." Locke grounds this limitation of original acquisition on God's will: "Nothing was made by God for Man to spoil or destroy." Yet it is clear that God's will is not capricious, for as Locke says earlier:

> God, who hath given the World to Men in common, hath also given them reason to make use of it to the best advantage of Life and convenience.

Men then have a right of self-preservation which entitles them to take the means thereto, viz. by acquiring the necessaries of life. Self-preservation grounds appropriation and sets limits to it.

Now it could be argued that the spoilage provision sets the limits too widely in that it allows me to refuse to share my bounty with my starving neighbours so long as I can use that bounty for "the best advantage of (*my*) Life and convenience." Matters are weighted heavily in favour of the propertied and against those without property. But let us for the sake of argument accept spoilage as an outward limit of just original acquisition. We can then ask whether native peoples violated the spoilage principle in acquiring these lands? If they did and if the Europeans who came here could make use of the wasted portions, then aboriginal claims may be defensible on the grounds of wastage.

If this question is answerable, it would have to be on the basis of historical evidence; however, it is fair for the philosopher to ask about the determination of the criteria for wastage and spoilage: By what marks do we identify something as waste? Here it is tempting to ask if the thing in question is used for anyone's benefit. But will any minute amount of incremental benefit suffice to justify ownership or must there be some standard margin of benefit for this use to count here for title? Must there also be standards of efficient use? Would there be a combined standard, e.g. "Makes the best use of X for the greatest benefit"? Any benefit or efficiency standard would seem to be hopelessly utilitarian and redistributivist. On the other hand, having no standards at all would effectively deny a right of self-preservation to those without property and the correlative duty to share for the propertied.

If we try to fix on some mid-point, (i.e. having a spoilage provision which is compatible with entitlement theory) then the question is how to justify our selection of standards on an entitlement basis. This is a particularly troublesome question in the case of aboriginal rights. In many cases an advanced agricultural and industrialised economy came into contact with a hunting, fishing, and gathering economy. The patterns of resource use were bound to be different. What would appear as under utilisation in one economy might appear as over utilisation in the other. Clearly Canada's native peoples made ingenious use of the often harsh environment, but their uses could not support the numbers of people that present-day uses can. (In this paper I am being deliberately silent about how much longer we can continue our use-patterns.) However, if we move in the direction of giving title to the Europeans rather than the native peoples, then we would have to surrender our ownership claims to any society which could support more people here more efficiently. This seems quite obviously in direct opposition to the whole thrust of an *entitlement* theory: If I am entitled to something, if it's *mine*, then I should within the limit of non-harmfulness be able to use it as efficiently or as inefficiently as I wish for whosoever's advantage I choose. This would accord with Nozick's slogan: "From each as they choose, to each as they are chosen."

Tentatively, then, if we are willing to deny the right of self-preservation and more especially the correlative duty of sharing when necessary to provide it, then we can still hold the entitlement theory and so avoid the conceptual difficulties posed by the spoilage principle.

F.3. The 'Proviso' Argument. Spoilage is not the only limit Locke sets to original acquisition; he also suggests what Nozick calls "the Lockean Proviso," namely that there be "enough and as good left in common for others." This, Nozick says, "is meant to ensure that the position of others is not worsened." Thus, we can imagine a parallel argument to the Spoilage Argument being advanced against aboriginal rights on the grounds that aboriginal possession violated the enough-and-as-good proviso.

Factually, this is going to be a tricky argument to work out for not only must it be shown that the native people did not leave enough and as good to the immigrants, but also that the immigrants have taken just enough to rectify this violation of the proviso. This will be very hard to prove, given the relative wealth of natives and immigrants. At present, indeed, native people could justifiably argue that the immigrants haven't left enough and as good to them.

Here, as in the Spoilage Argument, there are serious conceptual problems in determining the appropriate criteria. Nozick advances two interpretations of the Proviso:

> Someone may be made worse off by another's appropriation in two ways: first, by losing the opportunity to improve his situation by a particular appropriation or any one; and second, by no longer being able to use freely (without appropriation) what he previously could.

Nozick accepts the second or "weaker requirement" and not the first or "the stringent requirement." The difference between the two seems to be between characterising the proviso as applying to appropriation (ownership) or to use. But then it must be remembered that earlier Nozick says that "the central core of the notion of a property right in

X" is "the right to determine what shall be done with *X*." If I have a right to *use X*, then would I not have a property right in *X*?

Be that as it may, Nozick argues that those who are unable to appropriate (because everything is now owned) are likely to be compensated for this restriction on their liberty by having their prospects increased by a system which allows (virtually unlimited) private acquisition. Nozick says the free market will make up for their loss of acquisition and/or use rights. The point is to compensate these people enough for not being able to appropriate or use what they could have had they been born earlier. Nozick suggests that the level of compensation can be determined by getting "an estimate of the general economic importance of appropriation."

But this, I suggest, won't do for several reasons. First, if this isn't forcing on someone a kind of compensation that he doesn't want, then in the case of those who really want to make acquisitions the state will have to take something away from various property-owners. Secondly, as my colleague Jan Narveson has argued, the level of compensation will probably have to be set high enough to amount to a tidy guaranteed annual income. Thirdly, it isn't clear how much compensation is to be given to any particular propertyless person. Does he get as much as he would have been likely to get if he were in the position of the last person who acquired property or as much as if he were the first person to acquire property? In either case, the primary basis for distribution (his acquisitiveness) seems suspiciously patterned. Fourth, if the benefits of a free market economy really do provide enough compensation, then why does it seem so unlikely that anyone who has more than a little property, e.g. E.P. Taylor, would want to change places with one of these people who can't acquire any property because everything is owned?.

All of which suggests that on a *pure* entitlement theory—one which is based on historical entitlement—there would be no room for the Proviso. On a pure entitlement theory if you are born after all the accessible and useful unowned objects have been taken up by your predecessors, you are simply out of luck. This denial of the Proviso would also seem to be in agreement with Nozick's criticisms of Rawls' contention that a system of natural liberties allows distribution on morally arbitrary grounds—that the distribution of natural talents is not on the basis of desert leads Rawls to design the social system to compensate for this "arbitrariness" by favouring (other things being equal) the least talented in the distribution of goods. Nozick criticises this as a "manna-from-heaven" model that totally ignores who has made these goods, i.e. Rawls ignores the crucial fact of historical entitlement. Similarly, the Proviso seems to ignore the crucial fact of appropriation.

Finally, as in the Spoilage Argument, we can ask what it is to leave "enough and as good"? If the standard is *usability*, then do we adopt the native peoples' idea of what is usable or the non-native immigrants'? If we defend the latter, then in effect we are denying native peoples their ways of life. According to the Proviso this would seem to demand that we compensate the native peoples for that loss. Yet is that something for which adequate compensation is possible other than allowing them to maintain their standards of use and so their way of life? Would not "the base line for comparison" be very high indeed then?

F.4. The Invalid Acquisition Arguments. In both the Spoilage and Proviso Arguments, aboriginal title was challenged on the grounds that Indians and Innuit had acquired too much, i.e. more than they were entitled to acquire. It is possible to raise a different objection by claiming that they failed to acquire anything or scarcely anything at all. The heart of this contention is that native peoples did not perform the appropriate acquisitive acts. We get a variety of objections of this kind based on different views of what is an appropriate act of acquisition, that is depending on what sorts of human actions bring things out of a state of ownerlessness into a state of property. Before trying to get this argument off the ground, it is worth noting that both Nozick and Locke start with the assumption that before individual acquisition things are in an ownerless condition (the *res nullius* doctrine); there is another school of thought that assumes that before private acquisition takes place, things are held in common by all men (the *res communae* doctrine).

The major problem in raising this objection is fixing on some kind(s) of action that can be plausibly regarded as acts of original acquisition, i.e. upon the *rites* that generate property *rights*. Nozick raises very serious problems about Locke's criterion for ownership, namely that one owns that with which one has mixed one's labour. He asks about the boundaries of such acquisition:

> If a private astronaut clears a place on Mars, has he mixed his labour with (so that he comes to own) the whole planet, the whole uninhabited universe, or just a particular plot?

Nozick also asks why mixing one's labour with something isn't simply throwing one's labour away, and if it isn't, then why should one have title to more than the value (if any) added by one's labour? If 'mixing labour' is the acquisitive act, then surely these and related questions must be convincingly answered if entitlement theory is to proceed.

We have already seen that if usage is made the standard there are serious problems in determining whose standards of use should prevail. In fact, it would seem that an entitlement theorist should shy away from recognising usage as the acquisitive action, for anyone could take your title to X away from you by finding a better use for X (if you are already using it) or putting it to use for the first time (if you haven't

46

used it yet). I would think that an entitlement theorist should say that it is solely up to X's owner whether and to what use X shall be put. Yet it is Locke who denies that the Indians of America have any ownership rights beyond what they use for food and clothing; English settlers have rights to the land itself because they till it. In short Locke denies aboriginal rights because the Indians don't use the land in the same way as the English immigrants.

Perhaps, then, it will be suggested that acquisitive actions are *conventional*—literally consisting in the conventions (customs or laws) of a particular people. Thus in some society you own only what you actually have in hand or on your person at the moment, while in another you own whatever bears your mark, and in still another society you own only those things entered in the central ownership registry. Of course, there will be problems when societies with different ownership conventions each want to make exclusive use of the same objects. Each society (assuming no overlap in conventions) can say that the other society's people haven't really acquired the goods in question because of a failure to follow the appropriate conventions. I do not see how an entitlement theorist can say which set of conventions (in part, presumably, adopted for non-arbitrary reasons having to do with different patterns of usage) should prevail on the basis of entitlement theory; it seems to me that he must resort to patterned and, in the end, possibly redistributivist considerations. I think it is on the basis of these considerations that our society will have to deal with the contention (if it can be proven) that the Indian treaties are invalid because the whites and the Indians had totally different conceptions of ownership.

Conclusions

First, I hope to have shown in my consideration of entitlement theory that a number of plausible objections to it, (A) through (E), can be answered. These are essentially peripheral objections. Once we get to the core of the theory, however, serious and, I would maintain, insurmountable problems arise. The entitlement theory of original acquisition cannot be maintained without resort to non-entitlement considerations—patterns, end-results, and pure conventions. To cleanse entitlement theory of these additions will make it so unattractive that it cannot be accepted as a theory of justice in holdings.

Secondly, and somewhat surprisingly, I think that I have made out the case for aboriginal rights. I claim that this country ought to recognise aboriginal rights *on the basis of original acquisition*. Of course, this conclusion depends on the validity of my claim that the only rationale that is advanced and is plausible for the present system of holdings in Canada is entitlement theory. I contend that it is on basis of entitlement theory alone, that we could ever hope to justify the way in which most holdings are distributed in Canada. Just because entitlement theory won't work does not mean that our society won't proceed as if it does. The argument for aboriginal rights is provisional. But it ought to obtain until we are willing to redistribute holdings in this country on a truly just basis.

The Rights of Women:
The Theory and Practice of the Ideology
Of Male Supremacy

LORENNE M.G. CLARK

The test of strength of any ideology is the extent to which its basic presuppositions remain not merely unquestioned but literally unrecognized. The more such assumptions appear to be simply a part of the fabric of fact, the stronger the intellectual hold of the ideology they support and the greater the difficulty of changing the practices arising out of it. Despite the varying strands within it, the empirical claims made about virtually every aspect of it at some time, by someone or other, the tradition of western political theory is deeply ideological. Over time, many of its unmentioned original assumptions have been brought to light, questioned, criticized, and either rejected or accepted in the light of other "facts" accepted as empirically verifiable, even if not verified, or other values held to be important enough to justify the retention of such assumptions despite their divergence with other accepted or acceptable beliefs. It is my belief, however, and that of other feminist scholars in this and related fields, that one such assumption that has not yet reached the light of day is that of sexual inequality and the superiority of the male sex. It now seems to me certain that politics, the theory on which it is based, and the practice and practices arising out of it, including of course law and legal theory, articulates an ideology of male supremacy. Politics is the ideology of male supremacy, or, one might say, the ideology of male supremacy is the conceptual meta- or super-structure which is assumed at the foundations of political theory.

Doubtless the first response of many who are hearing this for the first time will be, so what is new about that? which is, of course, merely a polite way of saying that what I am asserting is not significant. It certainly is news to no one that virtually all the major political and legal theorists, and indeed politicians and lawyers (frequently an identical class), have been male and have been sexist. This has been treated as equivalent to asserting merely that, as *individuals*, they have assumed the superiority of the male sex. Many female, as well as male, scholars and theorists following in their tradition have treated such ideas as the idiosyncratic quirks of these particular men, who, after all, belonged to a benighted age, and have simply read these remarks out of their works, and read in "human" for "man" and assumed what we almost came to accept as true—that "mankind" is a generic term and not a gendered one, and that it is to be read as referring to "mankind" i.e., "humankind," both male and female. Feminists have always found it mildly irritating to confront sexist remarks again and again, but it was not until we began to question the assumption about the rightness of attributing such a denotation for the actual terms used that we began to feel deeply outraged. What I and others are now claiming is that it is not just an unusual coincidence that virtually all male theorists have been sexists and that it is not possible to expunge the sexism from their works and leave the human significance of their contribution unchanged. What we are claiming is that they are necessarily sexist and that most of their theories are unworkable once non-sexist principles are assumed. They are sexist in so far as they are political and legal theorists and not merely in so far as they are the particular individuals they are. Indeed, it could be the case that they were personally non-sexist while remaining sexist theorists. In so far as my claim is that sexism is one of the unquestioned assumptions of the tradition, then it follows that they must be sexist so far as their theory and political practice is concerned, whatever their personal beliefs on the matter may be. The claim that virtually all political theory and theorists are sexist is trivial if it is assumed to mean only that it just so happens that because of their own particular political, social, histori- cal, economic, and so on, background each of these men, and the theories they propounded, "naturally" reflect the prevalent biases of their own day, but that, like most "mere prejudices," these can be discounted without serious consequences. But this is not what the claim means, and it is reasoning such as this which has been used to buy off feminists who began to comment on the sexism so prevalent in the works to which they were required to give serious study. Underly- ing this gloriously liberal and generous reasoning is of course the view that the false and the true are incompatible, that the true can survive without the false, and that since most of what they said, or at least those parts of it which "we" (i.e., other men) in the tradition dignify as "significant," is true, then it must be able to survive without benefit of the false. But that is exactly the assumption that is now being questioned. When the false is removed, when the theories are stripped of their sexist assumptions, nothing is left of any significance whatso- ever, except, of course, as an ideology of male dominance. Thus, the claim is not trivial because it insists that the sexism is systematic and structural, that it is a necessary presupposition of everything else, and that without it, the theory is something quite different from what it is with it, and not one which is compatible with non-sexist assumptions. What Marx claimed for the proletariat, feminists are now claiming for women. Political theory up to the time of Marx was the ideology of the

50

bourgeoisie, serving the interests of the dominant class, whose dominance was assumed, or asserted to be "natural" as, for example, in Locke where it is said to be the dominance of those men who are naturally more rational and industrious. Political theory up to our own time (including Marx) is the ideology of the male, serving the interest of the dominant sex, whose dominance is likewise assumed and asserted to be "natural"—the dominance of those who are naturally stronger, freer from the grinding necessities of biological reality, more aggressive, more contemplative, and rational.

The fundamental problem with which traditional political theory has failed to come to grips, indeed the fundamental reality politics was devised as an escape from, is reproduction. It is precisely because of this fact that politics represents a flight from reality, and why, stripped of its sexist assumptions, it is, as we know it, incapable of providing us with a set of workable social institutions guaranteeing equality to all regardless of sex. At its very heart politics assumes that reproduction is demeaning, that fundamental meaning and importance for man, and here I mean the term literally, cannot derive from the genesis and nurturance of children. The idea of politics, and the theory to support it, was born from a sense of the futility of the reproductive function. It was designed exclusively by men, exclusively for men, as an escape from the world of the household, the realm of the "merely" biological, of pure necessity. As Hannah Arendt points out in *The Human Condition* when discussing the Greek *polis:*

> The distinctive trait of the household sphere was that in it men [sic] lived together because they were driven by their wants and needs. . . . Natural community in the household therefore was born of necessity, and necessity ruled over all activities performed in it. The realm of the *polis*, on the contrary, was the sphere of freedom. . . . What all Greek philosophers . . . took for granted is that freedom is exclusively located in the political realm, that necessity is primarily a prepolitical phenomenon, characteristic of the private household organization, and that force and violence are justified in this sphere because they are the only means to master necessity. . . .

One might like to know what else besides wants and needs would determine one to live anywhere, and to note that the force and violence believed necessary to confront the natural has continued to be a fact of life in the family. But the main point to be taken from this is that political theory begins from the conclusion that satisfying forms of social organization cannot arise out of, and be for the sake of, the mode of reproduction. It represents an attempt to find new methods of creating social bonds and the institutions necessary to foster and

51

support them. The central fact to be grasped is that it is based on a rejection of the process of reproduction as a meaningful principle of social organization. It is this assumption, that reproduction as such is of no importance in the creation of a significant life for man, that is *the* sexist assumption at the very basis of political theory, out of which everything else flows and without which there is no need for politics as we have known it.

But since reproduction is necessary if there is to be any continuing social unit at all, the rejection of it as a meaningful human activity, and as the primary organizing principle of social life, necessarily condemned women to carry on an indisputably necessary social function without any recognition whatsoever and without any power to shape other social institutions in ways which were compatible with this central process in individual and social life.

The reproductive process took place outside the political sphere, not merely in the sense that it just happened to be a non-political activity, but in the strong sense that it was declared by *fiat* not to be a political activity and not to have any significance within the political sphere. It was by *definition*, by arbitrary and deliberate convention, and not by mere historical accident, set apart from the political realm and declared to be of no political importance. It was a merely private matter, to be contained within the household walls well out of the public eye. The family was not, and is not, an acknowledged political institution so far as political theory has been concerned, and reproduction is not, and has not been, an activity of acknowledged political significance. And if women are assumed to be capable of being fitted into the ontology of politics—if "mankind" really is taken to be generic and to refer to both males and females—one central question remains glaringly obvious: Who, then, is doing the reproductive work?

While the household was for men a place of refuge from the storms of public life, which is, of course, why privacy ultimately became a value men sought to protect, the family became for women and children a prison from which they could not escape, and within which they had no rights, for rights after all, exist only within a political and legal framework. Women and children remain in an eternal state of nature while the state, civil society, develops for adult males. Private and public literally were not conceived to be distinctions which women could make, much less diverse realms they might enjoy. Theirs was the eternal world of the natural and the private.

This is a point of no small importance when one considers the immense value the public had for men. That they created this value for themselves is of course of no small importance either, but the point is that they had the power to enforce their values, and it was their value structure which shaped their political thinking. Participation in politics became the means whereby men gained value and status. It is here that the idea that value comes from the recognition of other men first arises. The Greek view, expressed so well by Arendt, was that:

> Every activity performed in public can attain an excellence never matched in privacy; for excellence, by definition, the presence of others is always required, and this presence needs the formality of the public, constituted by one's peers, it cannot be the casual, familiar presence of one's equals or inferiors.

The *polis* was, for the Greeks, ". . . the only place where men could show who they really and inexchangeably were." As they conceived it, and as it has been conceived ever since, the only truly human life was that which was achieved in the public as opposed to the private sphere. The merely private was an object of contempt. It was literally a state of deprivation, a condition of being cut off from the realization of one's highest capacities and from the possibility of achieving real value. It meant being doomed to a mere animal life because one was incapable of achieving excellence in the eyes of one's peers.

But what did this mean for women, doomed as they were to the eternal private, for it was to the realm of the exclusively private that women, and (other) slaves were relegated? As Arendt points out:

> The distinction between the private and public realms, seen from the viewpoint of privacy rather than of the body politic, equals the distinction between things that should be shown and things that should be hidden. . . . Women and slaves belonged to the same category [as laborers] and were hidden away . . . because their life was "laborious," devoted to bodily functions. . . . To live an entirely private life means above all to be deprived of things essential to a truly human life.

Women could have no excellence, no value, could not, by definition, achieve a significant and truly human life. This is the sexism that lies at the heart of our politics, and which must now, finally, be contended with.

But I am not asserting in what I have developed so far that reproduction is women's only, or even their primary, function, or that men have no reproductive function. That view is, indeed, a consequence of the ideology I am now attempting to explicate. It takes two human beings, a male and a female, to create new human life, and it ought, though it has not, at least as a general phenomenon, for some time been the case that men shared the reproductive function beyond the initial procreative stage. For the reproductive function is not simply the creation and birth of a new human individual. Creation and birth are but the first steps in the process. It is the whole process from conception through birth and subsequent development to a state of more or less independence that constitutes the reproductive process. The fact that women carry and give birth to the child is merely a differentiation of function, but does not make the whole process their single-handed function or responsibility. The view that it does, or that it should, is itself a product of the ideology of male supremacy and has no basis in fact or justification in logic. I am not merely making an impassioned plea on the part of motherhood, asking only for "true" recognition of the real value women had, and continue to have, as reproducers. What I am saying is that women have been construed to be nothing but reproducers because men have abdicated their share of this responsibility. It has fallen to the lot of women to bear the full weight of the burden because men refused to acknowledge their joint responsibility for the process of reproduction. The biological facts made it easy to do this. Women have the child and they get stuck with it. And the disvalue attached to it by men allowed them to feel righteous for rejecting it.

But that does not change the facts. Reproduction is a necessary social fact; it is the central fact around which all theory about social organization ought to rotate. And until there is mutual acknowledgement that it is a responsibility that ought and must be shared between the sexes, there can be no sexual equality. The only non-sexist political theory is one that begins from recognizing that reproduction is not simply inevitable, but is, in fact, necessary, and that it is a process that must be shared, fully. In so far as politics, and political theory as we know it, assumes that reproduction is not a political activity, that it has no political and human value, and that it must lie outside the public realm, that politics and that theory must be rejected. As it stands, it reflects a rejection of the male role in reproduction and substitutes for that reality an image of man the *producer*, a creator of things rather than of persons.

In its early phases, as for example, in Greek society, the appropriate products of creation were thought to be not the crass commodities of the marketplace but enduring ideas, and entities such as the *polis* itself, which can survive the vicissitudes of time and mutability, and serve as lasting monuments to man's higher capacities. To free themselves for these "higher tasks," men relegated the reproductive function to women alone, and refused to take any account of it whatsoever as a political fact. They, and the theories they produced, then proceeded to deny to women any functions other than reproduction, and went on to devise institutions which, while they assume the family and the reproductive function as the substructure necessary to produce the ontological components of the political world, neither women, children, nor the assumed "natural" structure, the family, in which they are confined, figure as a part of that ontology. Women, children, and the family are relegated to the ontological basement, outside, underneath, the political structure, invisible within it, gaining nothing from it, and serving only to provide the means for its sustenance. Within terms of this framework, women, children, and the family are apolitical and ahistorical, unassimilated to the political and historical processes which change and develop over time. It is remarkable that even so thoroughly process-oriented a philosopher as Hegel assumed the unchanging, doubtless because unchangeable, irreducibly and recalcitrantly "natural," character of the family. But the family, as we know and have known it, is no more natural than anything else based on the false assumption of the fixed nature of the sexual roles and the inequality which rests on it.

As political theory developed, however, the paradoxes inherent in it because of its fundamental misconception about the role and value of reproduction, and its assumed but frequently unstated premise as to the inequality of the sexes, only became more apparent, though that did not, of course, mean that they were noticed. But starting as it did from the assumption that reproduction had no political value, it followed that it had no economic value either. This aspect of the paradox only shows up fully when we get to Marx, for of course Marxism is no less a part of this tradition than any other political theory. I would like to interject at this point, however, that the critique of political theory that I and others are now engaged in does not necessarily falsify Marxist theory, but that it does show it to be incomplete. It is incomplete in the sense that the complete realization of the Marxist dialectic would not necessarily abolish sexual inequality. I accept Marxism, however, as providing a basically true description of society in so far as the relations of production and the development of inequality through the class structure is concerned.

But the Marxist assumption that the fundamental determinant of any political system is the economic factor, and that the economic factor is the product of the relation between individuals and the modes of production, posits an ontology of producers and an epistemology which cannot make truth claims of important sorts about women. Women are *not* determined by their relation to the modes of production, but by their relation to the modes of reproduction, and men can be said to be determined by their relation to the modes of production only on the assumption that they are not, and will not be, determined by their relation to the modes of reproduction. Thus, reproducers have no ontological status within the theory, and the only truth claims which the theory can make about women are restricted to assertions that can be made about them in terms of their relation to production.

In so far as women can be freed of the reproductive function, then of course they too can become "free" to become producers, and hence to be determined by their relation to the modes of production. The difficulty is, if they do become producers, what happens to reproductive work? As it stands, the analysis Marx puts forward appears to presuppose the role of women as reproducers. Certainly it assumes that men are, in fact, producers, at least within the framework of capitalist society. But the question then is, *ought* men to remain determined by their relation to production? If so, then how can women be freed from reproductive work in order to become producers, since the reproductive work must still be done? And if not, what changes must occur in order to permit men to be determined, at least partially, by their relation to reproduction? Within a Marxist analysis, the ideal of sexual equality can be realized if and only if men *and* women are able to be determined by both, or by either, their relation to production and/ or their relation to reproduction since both forms of labour are necessary. Within the theory we have, however, there is certainly a strong bias in favour of seeing freedom in terms of members of both sexes being able to be determined by means of their relation to production.

As the theory stands, it simply assumes that with the overthrow of bourgeois capitalism women will be fully integrated into the productive labour force. Indeed, it appears to hold that pressure for such integration is necessary in order to bring about the proletarian revolution. But who, then, is doing the reproductive work? And why does the theory have such a marked tendency to extoll the virtues of production at the expense of reproduction? Marxist theory is, among other things, a theory about how persons are determined by their relations to the mode of production. Thus persons who are not determined by this relation simply cannot be talked about within the theory; individual women can be said to be members of a particular class if and only if they can be accommodated to the role of producers because then, and only then, are they determined by their relation to the mode of production. Their role as reproducers thus puts them outside the framework of analysis, so that they cannot be assigned a class position, and reproductive labour cannot be analyzed as a form of labour.

Now while this may be unobjectionable in so far as Marxist theory is meant to be only an accurate description of capitalist society, it clearly is objectionable if it is being assumed that even after the revolution, productive labour will still be the fundamental determinant of political life, and that reproductive labour, and those who do it, will remain valueless and unidentifiable within the theory. The basic question is, does Marxist theory hold that determination by means of one's relation to the modes of production holds for *any* political society or only for capitalist society? And that is really to ask whether or not Marx assumed that men (but men only) *ought* to be determined by their relation to the modes of production? It would appear that Marx assumes either that the proper mode of determination for *all* persons is production, with, of course, collective ownership of the means of production, in which case one wants to know why production is so much more valued than reproduction, or that the proper determination for *men* is production, in which case one wants to know why men should not be determined at least partially by their relation to reproduction, and why women should not be allowed to determine themselves in terms of their relation to production if they choose.

As it stands, however, woman's visibility within a Marxist analysis entails that she become a producer. Full visibility within the analysis requires that her identity be totally separated from her reproductive abilities and function. Unless reproduction is treated as a form of, or indeed as identical with, production, a woman cannot be identified in class terms. Unless reproduction is treated as a form of labour (all puns intended), women cannot be shown to be economically determined to their particular class positions.

Their class position is held to be determined by the class positions of their fathers or husbands. But this shows clearly that reproduction is not being treated as a form or mode of production, because if it were, their class position would be determinable independently of that of their fathers or husbands. Why, if reproduction is production, should their class be determined by anyone other than themselves? Of course, once women become producers, as opposed to reproducers, they do become visible in the analysis, and their class position can be determined independently of that of their fathers or husbands. But this just shows that, *qua* reproducers, they have no class position and their labour is not a form of production. And they are classless *because* their labour is not a form of production.

This latter follows because reproduction as such is not considered labour in the sense required within Marxist theory. The labour of reproduction has no determinable market value within the structure of analysis. It is not remunerated and is presupposed by the theory of surplus value rather than being treated as itself productive of surplus value. The role, and by that I mean the economic role, of reproduction is nowhere worked out clearly in Marx. At best it is assumed to be a form of production, as it is for example, in this passage from *The German Ideology*:

The production of life, both of one's own in labour and of fresh life in procreation, now appears as a double relationship; on the one hand as a natural, on the other as a social relationship.

57

Notice here the explicit separation of the notions of 'labour' and 'procreation.' Yet both are treated as forms of production. Notice also the distinction between the alleged *natural* relation of reproduction and the alleged *social* nature of labour. What "social" can be taken to mean here, in so far as the relation of reproduction can be said to be non-social, certainly escapes me. If that isn't social what on earth is? And this is a point to which I shall return. Thus, while reproduction is asserted to be a form of production, this is just as obviously not consistently adhered to or assimilated within the theory or it would be possible to determine a woman's class position independently of that of her father or husband. The assumption of a functional inequality between productive and reproductive labour and of natural, if not fixed, sexual roles in terms of labour function which underlies the class structure creates a conflict between production and reproduction, but this does not show up within the theory. As reproducers, women have no class position and their labour is not 'labour' in a sense that is determinable within the theory. (This surely is something of an ultimate irony, where labour is not labour.)

The disvalue, or theoretical non-value, of reproduction also shows up clearly in discussions of what the future for women would be like once the ideal Marxist state has been achieved. The following quotation is from August Bebel, *Women Under Socialism*:

> ... the moment all the means of production become the property of society; when collective labour, by the application of all technical and scientific advantages and aids in the process of production, reaches the highest degree of fertility. . . . Woman shall be like man, a productive and useful member of society. . . .

Why, one might well ask, will women only truly come into their own when they can become *like men*? Why should the only useful and valued labour be the labour of production? Doesn't reproduction make one a useful member of society? Apparently not. But so far as I am concerned, it is only to the extent that men are prepared to become like women, and to share in their rightful responsibility for reproduction, that women and men can both truly come into their own as equal members of society.

But the issue of the relation between production and reproduction raises other, deeper issues to which I now wish to turn. One of the questions which has long puzzled feminists who are Marxists is why should capitalism, or the development of the class structure necessary for the development of capitalism, require the subjugation of women? As is well known, Engels says in the *Origin of the Family, Private Property, and the State* that the oppression of women and the emergence of private property came about at roughly the same time.

But it remains a question, indeed a controversy, as to the direction of causality. It is, of course, possible that there is no causal relation between these states of affairs, merely a correlation, but some—Magas, for example, in *Sex Politics: Class Politics*—have held that,

> ... the development of productive forces gave rise to private property, resulting in the subjugation of women as well as the subjugation of most men. . . .

But this still leaves unclear why private property developed, and why its emergence should have resulted in the oppression of women. Others, such as Kate Millett in *Sexual Politics*, have argued that it was the subjugation of women that gave rise to private property: The ownership of women was the first form of private ownership, and women the first form of private property. But this fails to explain why the oppression of women began at all, and why this should have led to the development of the concept of private ownership of the objects of production. According to Guettel in *Marxism and Feminism*, Engels was basing his analysis on the relations of production. She interprets him as arguing that,

> ... one of society's first important cultural adaptions was assigning to the woman tasks compatible with childbearing and childrearing, and to the man (for the most part) all others. . . . As long as the division of labour was reciprocal there was no exploitation and hence no domination in the sense of *propertied* advantage. . . . The basis of male supremacy was the development of *property*. . . . It is not just a matter of the kind of work but who *owns* the means of the kind of work, which yields the productive surplus. . . . Engels concentrated on the transition from society before private property to society based on private property and exploitation, and tried to show in general how family forms and the position of women depended upon what people owned and how they made a living.

She offers some plausible suggestions how private property might have emerged and then transformed a mere division of labour into an exploitive relationship, but her account still leaves some rather basic matters unresolved. If reproduction is a form of production, then ownership of the means of reproduction is as necessary for the maintenance and development of class society as is the ownership of any of the other modes of production. The assimilation of reproduction to production *necessitates* ownership of the means of reproduction, and, hence, to the extent that this is the Marxist thesis, then private property must have preceded and been the precondition of the oppression of women. But how did control of the means of reproduction pass from the female to the male? A simple division of labour could only have become exploitive if women ceased to have control

59

over the means of reproduction and men took over such control. This, surely, is what is meant in talking about women as objects of private ownership and as forms of private property. From a Marxist point of view, the difficulty with this interpretation is who owns the means of reproduction? Since *all* men own their wives and children, this is not a notion of dominant *class* ownership but of dominant *sex* ownership, and this does not fit into the Marxist framework of analysis. This indicates to me, yet again, that neither Marx nor Engels really worked out the relation between reproduction and production. Western political and legal theory has assumed the private ownership of *both* the means and products of reproduction *and* the means and products of production, and it has not assumed the former to be a mode of the latter, though there may in fact be a connection between them which has so far been neglected. The belief that there is not merely a division of labour but a justified exploitive division of labour because of the "natural" dominance of the male is already assumed at the point where political theory begins.

This thesis is compatible with arguing either that private property is conceptually prior to male supremacy or that male supremacy is conceptually prior to private property.

Why are social arrangements governing such things as marriage and legitimacy necessary? I contend that structures of enforceable rules are necessary only if there is the assumption of a fundamental inequality between sets of persons. Marx, of course, utilizes this principle in arguing that the acquisition of property has to be limited only if the social system is to operate to the advantage of the dominant class. Similarly, marital relations must be regulated only if the social system is to operate to the advantage of the dominant sex. The forms might differ, depending on which sex is dominant. But the point is that the forms are necessary only because one sex or other is concerned to preserve its dominant position. (I would like to argue that sexual equality entails social structures which do not depend on artificial relations created through normative rules, but that is not particularly germane to the present discussion, so I shall save it for another time.) Both of the approaches mentioned are compatible with saying that male supremacy, motivated either by the desire for certainty of paternity, or by the simple desire for power, is the precondition of private ownership, at least of the means and products of reproduction. Only if there is the desire to ensure certainty of paternity, or simply to enforce a felt superiority, is it necessary to treat women and children as owned objects and hence to preserve them as the exclusive property of particular males. But the maintenance of male power requires the appropriation of the means of reproduction in just the same way that the maintenance of class power requires appropriation of the means of production. In order to maintain male superiority, women must be converted from natural counterparts and companions in reproduction to forms of private property, either collectively or individually.

This last point, coupled with the opacity surrounding the relation between production and reproduction in Marxist theory, creates another difficulty for Marxist predictions with respect to the future. If communism requires the collective ownership of the means of production, and reproduction is a form of production, what is meant by collective ownership of the means of reproduction? Even if this entails that no one particular man, woman, or set of individuals any longer "owns" particular children, who does the reproductive work? Further, collective ownership of the means of reproduction could mean the ownership by all men of all women. It is in just this sense that the destruction of capitalism by means of a proletarian revolution does not ensure the emancipation of women. Since any person, male or female, has the capacity to be a producer, one can understand the concept of collective ownership of the means of production without difficulty. But since gestation and birth make it clear that at least this part of the reproductive process is the exclusive ability of women, it is not at all certain what the collective ownership of the means of reproduction amounts to. If it means that women, and women alone, will have control over both the timing and products of reproduction, that is, or might be, all to the good, but it still does not settle the question as to who does the rest of the reproductive work, both in terms of expenditure of labour and its labour value. Who works, who pays, and who sets the value on what is paid? This is simply not a problem which is even mentioned, much less discussed, in Marx and Engels. All that is assumed is that women will be able to be producers. It is nowhere asserted that men will be able to be reproducers, much less be *required* to share this function in order to ensure that all persons, regardless of sex, will be able to be producers without requiring sacrifice of their productive labour and economic value in society in order to fulfill a reproductive role.

On the Marxist model as it stands, either women's ability to become producers will still somehow have to be fitted around their still-assumed-to-be-natural reproductive function, or the reproductive function will have to be eliminated. That the latter is now a distinct possibility is what I find extremely frightening. To the extent that women become producers, they are de-sexed, at least in the sense that their reproductive abilities must be totally denied. This is to return to a point made earlier, that woman's visibility within a Marxist analysis requires the severance of her identity from her reproductive abilities. While no feminist wants her sexuality totally identified with her

61

reproductivity, it seems too much to assume that her equality necessitates the abolition of her reproductive ability as *any* part of her identity. And this is a point of no small importance: With advances in technology, more and more of the reproductive function can in fact be transformed into a form of production. But to the extent that this is true, its logical outcome is the artificial production of children. Indeed, Shulamith Firestone, in *The Dialectic of Sex*, has already suggested that the complete equality of women can only be achieved once all babies are produced artificially. Only then will that part of the reproductive function which is irreducibly the ability of woman, as opposed to men, become totally obsolete and the source of even the periodic invisibility of them and of their unique labour. But why should the reproductive function have to be totally abolished in order to allow women to assume their equal place within society? Surely this represents the complete victory of the dominant sex and of the values they have enforced, namely, the utter redundancy of the female in so far as she has a unique role in the reproductive process and the utter obliteration of the reproductive function as such. Production no longer presupposes reproduction and women no longer have a reproductive identity and, just as importantly, neither do men. Thus, full visibility within society, at least in so far as a Marxist analysis is genuinely descriptive of society, entails the destruction of our sexual difference and of at least that much of our sexual identity as rests on our differentiated reproductive abilities.

And what, one may ask, about children? Isn't this too, the complete victory of the view that the social bonds between individuals are not, or ought not to be, the product of our relation to the mode of reproduction? What on earth is wrong with seeing the social bonds, the ties of natural love, trust, and affection, which are produced through our relation, first as children, and then as adults, to the process of reproduction, as the primary bonds of social organization? In the final analysis, what good are contracts when these other ties are missing? And what kinds of individuals would we create if we were to transform reproduction purely into forms of production thereby destroying the ties of love, trust, and mutual affection which are the natural result of reproductive genesis and nurturance? As I see it now, the maintenance of sexual difference, not inequality, but difference, and of those ties which are the result of the reproductive as opposed to the productive process, necessitates a new, or an alternative to, politics in which the basic forms of social organization revolve around, and arise out of, the relations of reproduction, in which reproduction and production are conceived to be at least equal and parallel forms of labour, and from which no sex-role structuring arises. Leaving the alternative to politics for future discussion, I would like now to return to the issue of the relation between private property and the oppression of women.

While the desire for certainty of paternity or simply for power can be seen as necessitating the subjugation of women, I am not entirely happy with this explanation, though this may reflect nothing more than my own bias in favour of political and economic, rather than psychological or sociological, explanatory models. But it does seem to me that the idea that men wished to create a sense of felt continuity and to ensure certainty of paternity are interesting and plausible accounts of what gave rise to the development of political, social, and legal theory. Certainly, the issue of certainty of paternity is one which is adverted to frequently by many political theorists. While Rousseau is perhaps the most striking in this respect, he is by no means unique. In talking about women as wives and mothers, and of the necessity of their being nothing other than wives and mothers, and educated strictly with these objectives in mind, Rousseau says, in *Emile*,

> . . . a child would have no father if any man usurp a father's rights . . . she alone can win the father's love for his children and convince him that they are indeed his own.

Frankly, it doesn't seem to me to say much for men if they can only love children once they are firmly convinced that they are their own, but be that as it may, it seems to me that there may be a good reason why the certainty of paternity became such an issue: the ability to inherit property. Part of a felt sense of continuity, at least following the emergence of private property, is the ability to pass on what is one's own to what one knows to be one's own progeny. Thus, it seems likely that it was the emergence of private property which gave rise to the need to ensure certainty of paternity in order to ensure certainty of inheritance. It is, then, the emergence of private property which necessitated the subjugation of women. Why private property emerged is another question, and not one which I intend to pursue here, but it seems clear that, at least since the emergence of private property, and I mean here the ownership of the means and products of production, political theory has functioned to justify individual ownership and to ensure certainty of paternity. Thus the concept of male supremacy is a result of the emergence of private property and is a function of the desire to retain control of both the property arising from reproduction and that arising from production, since both are needed to ensure individual continuity through time. If, and only if, men have the ability to control the property of their productive labour and of their generative role in the reproductive process can they be assured of immortality.

63

It is interesting and important to note here, too, that other (alleged) "sciences" also supported the ideology of male supremacy at the time political theory was emerging. Aristotle's biology is almost as obvious a case of ideological self-serving as are the racial theories endorsed by Hitler. You will recall that Aristotle held that the woman's role in reproduction was merely to provide what he called the "material," whereas the male contributed the "form," to the embryo. In *De Generatione Animalium*, he states:

> The male contributes the principle of movement and the female the material. This is why the female does not produce offspring by herself, for she needs a principle; i.e. something to begin the movement in the embryo and to define the form it is to assume.

Thus, women are the mere raw materials of reproduction. The whole identity of the child was contained in the male seed, the woman providing, as it were, only the fertile ground required for its development. Woman's role in reproduction was denigrated as far as possible. The point to be taken from this is that it is meant to establish that the child is somehow much more the man's than the woman's, something, hence, over which he ought to have control, and about which he has a right to insist that certainty of paternity be guaranteed. While the reproductive function was being denigrated, it was nonetheless true that men wished to retain control over it, indeed to establish more control over it than they likely had had previously, and more than they had a right to. On the one hand, while ownership of the means and products of reproduction will not be enough to satisfy the desire for individual continuity if no value is attached to reproductive labour, on the other, no satisfaction can be derived from passing on the valued objects of one's productive labour unless one can ensure that they pass to those who will also value them and perceive them as tangible evidence of the continued existence of their creator. Man is embodied in his objects. Thus, however valueless reproduction is, the means and products of it must be strictly controlled in order to ensure certainty of paternity for the purposes of appropriate, valued, i.e., legitimate, inheritance. Why a preoccupation with individual as opposed to species, or societal, continuity should have arisen also remains an interesting question, and, again, not one I intend to pursue further here, though it seems obvious to me that the emergence of private property must have been its precondition.

But given that both did emerge, control of the means and products of both forms of labour can be seen to be necessary. It is a chicken and egg question as to which came first: the desire to control the means and products of production or of reproduction. What seems clear to me is that ownership of both forms became necessary and that it was at this point that political theory began. Politics and its derivative structures are the formalized attempt by men to retain exclusive control over the means and products of both production and reproduction. Thus, it became necessary to justify individual ownership of both the products and means of production and the products and means of reproduction. The first laid the basis for a class society and the latter for a sexist society.

For the future, it would seem to follow that if the destruction of the class system necessitates the grasping of the means of production by the proletariat, then the destruction of the sexist system necessitates the grasping of the means of reproduction by women. Technology has now provided women with the means whereby this can be accomplished. But what this might entail, I shall also, for the moment, leave to your imagination.

Selected Bibliography

Arendt, Hannah. *The Human Condition.* University of Chicago Press, 1958.

Engels, F. *The Origins of the Family, Private Property, and the State.* (introduction by Eleanor Burke Leacock).

Firestone, Shulamith. *The Dialectic of Sex*, Bantam Books, 1970.

Guettel, Charnie. *Marxism and Feminism.* Toronto: Canadian Women's Educational Press, 1974.

Magas, Branka. "Sex politics: Class Politics," *New Left Review*, No. 66, March–April 1971.

Rebel, August. *Women under Socialism.* (trans. Daniel De Leon), Schocken Books, N.Y., 1971.

The Rights of the Press:
A Publisher Hits Back

CONRAD M. BLACK

Freedom of the press is endangered whenever the interference or negligence of a particular group reduces the press's ability or inclination to report events accurately, record facts, or express opinions. This should not be confused with the right of everyone to take issue with the media. Any group capable of asserting pressure on the media poses a threat to impartiality of information and liberty of expression. The media are most vulnerable to this form of pressure in their own newsrooms, where the uniform biases of the so-called working press have canalized the flow of public information with tendentious ideological rigidity for more than ten years.

The balance of power within media enterprises has shifted toward the journalists, away from management, in the last twenty years. The rise of electronic journalism has added a new dimension to the power of the media as well as to public comprehension. This includes not only television but less astounding developments, such as photo-typesetting, computers adapted to news wires, and the growth of vast car-radio audiences. Journalists have acquired a more vivid public personality than was possible in the days of the hot-metal newspaper and network radio. Thus enhanced, and by technology rather than by higher professional standards, the journalist has become a more formidable employee and a greater influence in society.

There has been a simultaneous decline in the editorial role of the media proprietor, especially the publisher. With the rise of the newspaper chain, the publisher has become a local coordinator and functionary, answerable to his absentee employer on economic matters, with a mandate to ensure that the journalistic content is sufficiently anodyne to avoid disputes with advertisers, sufficiently formless to avoid strikes in the newsrooms. The media are now, in administrative techniques, an industry like the others; more profitable than most, perhaps more strategic than any. The proprietors take relatively little interest in the journalistic aspects of the business. Lord Thomson of Fleet may be the greatest businessman in the history of the media; he is, on balance, an indifferent publisher. The successors to Joseph E. Atkinson, J.W. McConnell, Jacob Nicol, Pamphille Du Tremblay, Max Bell, Victor Sifton, Michael Wardell and both John Bassetts are comparatively pallid and equivocal. (Brigadier R.S. Malone, now publisher of the Globe & Mail, is a conspicuous exception.)

To further entrench themselves, the journalists have taken on both the airs of a learned profession and the more militant tactics of organized labour. Journalistic faculties have sprung up offering curricula which all agree are less valuable in the formation of reporters and technicians than six months work in subordinate positions. Most graduates of these faculties have difficulty composing English or French sentences, haven't the remotest idea of how to construct a good news story, and have no notion of the technology or administration of the industry. In no other field has the education boom of the sixties been a greater disappointment.

In a rather feeble gesture toward professional organization, a few press councils have been established, embracing all the media and established along provincial boundaries. Though headed by worthy individuals, the councils have limited competence and authority, are inherently incapable of really policing, let alone upgrading, the industry, and are more frequently used by the journalists' unions to harass and pillory the patronal side at the approach of collective negotiations than for any other purpose. The pretensions of journalists to professional status are, in a word, preposterous. Of irregular formation, with no regulatory or admissions body and only the sketchiest insistence on avocational norms and standards, journalism constitutes a sort of craft. Almost nothing is required; skill is a non-essential asset; unusual intelligence can generally find an outlet, and professional integrity, though exotic, if not rare, is more or less appreciated.

Coexisting serenely with agitation for professional recognition is a stridency borrowed from organized labour. Strikes are not infrequent. Many journalists belong to such unions as the Typographers', and the Newspaper Guild has been known to certify clericals, circulation drivers, and other improbable comrades. Journalists' demands are similar to those of other types of employees in other types of enterprise: higher pay, greater job security, more control over the quantity and quality of their own work. Recently, there have been growing demands for "co-management," complete functional autonomy for themselves, within only the most general budgetary guidelines. Management, the employers, who under this scheme would cease to be anything more than impotent paymasters, pursers of no non-economic consequence, to date have successfully resisted this great leap forward for the journalists, though not without a number of temporary and permanent cessations of publication. There have been a few ostentatious capitulations, including several departments of the C.B.C.

The journalists have skillfully advanced their professional aspirations by recourse to syndicalist pressure and their more mundane collective demands by invocation of professional dignity and prerogatives. By these means, they have, over fifteen or twenty years, added much more than a cubit to their social, professional, and economic stature. They were underpaid in the fifties. They are overpaid in the seventies.

The partial emasculation of the individual publisher, accomplished by his employers and his employees, has overturned the balance of power within individual newspapers, within the media generally, and in society. As the syndical activities of the journalists have become more determined, a collective sameness has imposed itself on the traditional individuality of the working press. In this as in other fields, the inflationary era has led to a great deal of job-creation. The proliferating ranks of journalists have a lower average age and briefer professional formation, as well as a more academic one, than their predecessors. There tends to be a greater uniformity than previously in their social and political views. Less and less do newspapers and broadcasting outlets and networks present an internal variety of opinions and interpretations. It has become virtually impossible to counteract the partisan or ideological influence of one newspaper or station with that of another, partly because of the decline of competition between newspapers. It is ultimately in the interests of the advertisers, source of three quarters of newspaper revenue, to cover a metropolitan market with just one paper. As a result, Montreal, Toronto, and Ottawa are the only Canadian cities with any real daily newspaper competition.

More important for the decline of interpretative balance within the media is that their opinions and constructions of events are controlled, even in the measure that they ever were, not by the publishers, but by the memberships of newspaper craft unions. There is an industry-wide, or profession-wide, opinion on most issues, and a uniform slant to public and social questions. It is not a question of one newspaper against another, much less of liberal against conservative reporters, but of the liberal or in some cases radical-liberal press against the other elements of society, the considerable majority, in fact.

This phenomenon has created a serious schism between the media and the public. In these circumstances it is unusually easy for politicians to exploit public hostility toward the media. This was the principal lesson to be learned from former U.S. Vice President Agnew's much-publicized outbursts in 1969 and 1970 against "the effete corps of impudent snobs" responsible for television news coverage. Agnew was not a particularly renowned or esteemed figure even then, yet his remarks were received with general jubilation. Those who witnessed the spectacle of the almost uniquely distinguished Walter Cronkite, anchor of CBS News, wanly explaining to his forty million nightly viewers that such attacks were a menace to a free press, will retain also an appreciation of how much better the press has become at dispensing than receiving criticism.

A Canadian Gallop Poll in February, 1969, revealed that two thirds of Canadians believe that their news is sometimes deliberately slanted. Public irritation would surely not be as great if the synthesization of press opinion had not been accompanied by an informal redefinition in rather virulent terms of the role of the contemporary journalist. I reported to the Senate Committee on the Mass Media chaired by Keith Davey, in our company's brief of November 7, 1969:

> The traditional concept of the journalist as a dutiful raker of muck has, in the minds of some, yielded to a more pedagogical role. . . . We believe that this concept is elitist, abusive, unjustified by journalistic experience, and more likely to serve as an excuse for quixotic excesses on the part of ill-qualified and self-important journalists than as an elevating dialogue with the readership.

The ideological and interpretative conformity that prevails in the media and the decline of the editorial influence of management would not in themselves lead to controversy if the media were not so zealously disposed to contradict public opinion. I reported in 1969:

> Whether as customer or pupil, the public supports the media, and the power of the media, dependent on credibility, will not survive abuse. There are presently inadequate safeguards to ensure that those vested with the influence and heady individual exposure of almost the least important by-lined journalist are intellectually and psychologically qualified for their positions.

My experience with journalists authorizes me to record that a very large number of them are ignorant, lazy, opinionated, intellectually dishonest, and inadequately supervised. The "profession" is heavily cluttered with abrasive youngsters who substitute "commitment" for insight, and, to a lesser extent, with aged hacks toiling through a miasma of mounting decrepitude. Alcoholism is endemic in both groups.

The nature of these jobs and of the people who hold them encourages a leftward bias. The journalistic function is in considerable measure an investigative one, an aspect that has been given increased emphasis by the recent indiscretions of public men. This role breeds an oppositionist attitude, particularly when the press, and the public, are brazenly lied to by office-holders. This is certainly a legitimate, even a primordial role of the free press, but it becomes a contagion that individual journalists have great difficulty resisting. The attitude of Canadian correspondents returned in the last year from the long and debilitating coverage of the Watergate affair in Washington reflects this

69

condition to an exaggerated degree. The former Washington correspondents of the CBC and the Toronto Star, in particular, spend half their time conjuring Canada's own scandal, and the other half bemoaning its absence.

Many public and business leaders have not conducted themselves in such a way as to disabuse the left-wing journalist of his suspicions. That does not relieve the journalist of his obligation to simple justice. The press, admittedly, is in a difficult position: To practice self-discipline is never easy, especially when the individuals involved have virtually no experience at it, but that is the traditional responsibility that power comports. The working press is close to the centres of authority in a democratic society. Familiarity breeds contempt, and, in the absence of familiarity, simplistic cynicism often arises. In either case, the temptation would be great for the press to be hostile or sceptical about the central functioning of society even if newsworthy people behaved irreproachably.

Add to natural oppositionist tendencies the frustration the press collectively feels at having great power but often indistinct responsibilities. This situation was apostrophized by Stanley Baldwin as harlotry. This was perhaps rather uncharitable, but for so potent and egocentric a group as the media to be consigned to a role of reporting on the sayings and doings of others, of those whom it is conditioned to disrespect and oppose, creates inevitable tensions. And for every Franklin D. Roosevelt or John F. Kennedy who can beguile the media, there is a Lyndon Johnson or Richard Nixon to evoke a visceral antipathy. Trudeau and Stanfield, Lévesque and Bourassa—we are tentatively approaching the day when the media will have an unofficial power of advice and consent over the nomination of political candidates. Paradoxically, the greater the indirect power of the media becomes, the greater also will be their collective sense of frustration.

Another aspect of the media's situation which tends to confirm their oppositionist stance is the youth and resulting inexperience of most journalists. The formless structure of the craft, the lack of academic or other formal requirements for admission to its practice, the comparative absence of any seniority system, and the adversary nature of the work itself all put a considerable premium on the youthful properties of zeal, dogmatism, and belligerency. The moral and social climate of the nineteen-sixties, with its emphasis on the fashions, attitudes, mores, political contrariety, alleged creative energy, and simple numerical strength of the young, especially those born between 1945 and 1950, lent weight, if not prestige and legitimacy, to them and to their contentions. In the unique atmosphere of the late sixties and early seventies, when economic prosperity coupled with serious political and social contestation, the craft of journalism expanded its ranks to embrace the young. For many publishers and editors, this was an earnest effort to comprehend the discordant phenomenon of youth and harness its energy to the ancient and rather dowdy, not to say hidebound, occupation of the scribe. For many others, it was appeasement and opportunism, unreasoning, and unprincipled. In none of the learned professions and in no other skilled occupation was there such deference to the fact of youth, such a swift and sure passage from the novitiate to sufficiency and even eminence. This truckling to the vanity and self-importance of youth by and among journalists could have had no other effect than the encouragement of destructive, glib, and righteous reporting. That consequence has been remarkable to all in the last ten years.

The syndical position and activities of what calls itself the working press add to its predilection for oppositionist interpretations of events. Publishers, like other employers, are usually identified by their organized employees with the establishment and the status quo. Generally, this is not an inaccurate appreciation of the publishers' attitudes. Reaction to the employer naturally promotes a left-wing bias in the reporter's renditions of events. It is accordingly not surprising that until very recently there was almost universal press sympathy for strikers, protesters, fugitives from justice, separatists, disaffected students, and other visible elements in the broad spectrum of the discontented. It pleased the journalist, as it pleases most people, to think of himself as an underdog, a person with a cause, if not a mission. To the antagonistic mind of the freshman journalist, in the uproarious atmosphere of the late sixties, with every hot paragraph bringing dozens of letters or calls from students or housewives or simple media buffs, doted on by the public, almost autonomous of the employer, and only a couple of years out of university, if not high school, all incentive was toward quixotry, cynicism, and the dialectic.

There was nothing evil or conspiratorial about this. Few journalists had any real concept of ideology. A very small proportion of them had any intellectual attainments at all. Journalism tends to attract the sort of person who settles whimsically on it as a calling, or comes to it after disappointments elsewhere, because of the relative ease of entry to the field. These people, discouraged and purposeless, are easily influenced by their angrier colleagues. It is by inadvertence, inexperience, the investigative nature of the press, the antithetical role of the employee, and the negligence of the employer, and not by any organized subversion, that the press veered away from being a mirror to society, and became a perverse sort of irregular and often disloyal opposition.

The individual journalist, if he has any panache or talent, soon becomes something of a celebrity. He develops a following and soon tastes the toadying of all manner of people within his beat: municipal officials, athletes, dramatists, or whomever. He often rubs shoulders with other and older celebrities. Much of his social life is built up on the press-circuit: bars, hangers-on, media groupies, the stifling and depraved gossip of the degenerate little media community, and the fawning of unfulfilled women, boys, and hucksters. It is a corrosive and a corrupting environment, which makes a particular mockery of the sanctimonious pretentions of many journalists. The relationship between power and corruption is well-known. In the case of the press of North America, neither is absolute but both are excessive.

There has been a good deal of attention in the last few years to concentration of ownership in the media. The social attitudes of the media proprietors are not significantly more conformist than those held by what passes for the elite of Canada's journalistic commentators. This group gravitates between the *Toronto Star*, *Saturday Night*, *Macleans*, and the CBC. And the ideological sameness which prevails among the working press is quite as drearily predictable, and much more evident to the public, than that found among the communications proprietors.

The most comprehensive and durable subject of this journalistic slant is anti-Americanism, the most pristine of Canadian left-wing causes, allowing as it does for escape into the proverbial last refuge of patriotism. Admittedly, in the years between the assassination of President Kennedy and the fall of President Nixon this sport was in open season. The lack of restraint shown by the nimrods of Canada's press was great. It is useful for our purposes to reexamine this doleful episode. The 1968–1969 period is selected as the practical height of the international opprobrium that enshrouded America's external personality, and for comparative purposes, as it was at this time that Canada's media leaders were at their most declarative in appearances before the Senate Committee on the Mass Media.

The political editor of the late *Toronto Telegram*, Fraser Kelly, informed that committee that the great majority of Canadian working journalists were ideological liberals. Mr. Kelly's lead story on the U.S. presidential election, November 6, 1968, pronounced the election as having been between two men who had "failed miserably" to attract thinking voters. Mr. Nixon had won almost by default over "Hubie baby . . . a puppet of Johnson," whom Mr. Kelly "can't stand." The sole redeeming feature of the election was that "Americans have at least been made to face the brutal truth," namely that "the ugliness and injustice is now in the open." For a news story, the principal story about an important event, on page one of one of Canada's best newspapers by a journalist of relative distinction, this is really not very good, or even professional.

The night before, the Washington correspondent of the CBC, Campbell MacDonald, who by virtue of his position might have been expected to show some insight into American affairs, spent the evening dismally predicting to his viewers a hung election with the next President of the United States to be named, in effect, by George Wallace. Even his guests in the studio, and all the other commentators on other networks were unanimous in the view that a Nixon victory was indicated. The CBC went to rather ingenious lengths in this period to give almost all major occasions a particular anti-American twist. The first American moon-landing, which most people considered a significant American achievement, the CBC observed with Dr. Ralph Lapp, an obscure, renegade American scientist, sadly recounting the dangers of the military-industrial complex, and exposing, surely to the mystification of viewers who sat up much of the night watching it, the evident hollowness of the occasion. The implications of the death of North Vietnamese President Ho Chi Minh were discussed by the CBC's blowhards-in-residence on the subject of East Asian affairs, Chester Ronning and Rabbi Abraham Feinberg. The Rabbi remarked that he had never seen any evidence that Ho was an autocrat. Even the moderator was moved to ask if the Rabbi would have said this if the million-and-a-half refugees who fled the North after the 1954 Geneva accords had been Jews. This was the only pin-prick in a long and uninformative hagiography that featured many gratuitous acerbities toward the United States.

In the randomly selected week of February 15 to 19, 1969 CBC's 6 P.M. News: 1) falsely alleged that the Canadian Council for Fair Taxation, an organization of Canadian small businessmen, was an American-dominated front for U.S. (inevitably) "multinational" corporate opposition to the White Paper on Taxation; (February 15): 2) specifically blamed all economic problems of Canada and the Western world on American participation in the Vietnam war; (February 16); 3) accused unnamed American interests of plotting to fill Canada's Arctic waters with oil tankers, heavy-laden and leaky-hulled, without consulting any Canadian authorities; (February 17–20); 4) blamed the U.S. for the North Vietnamese invasion of Laos; (February 18–19); 5) declared that rioters who attacked the U.S. embassy in Manila were protesting "legitimate" grievances; (February 19). Correspondingly, the "National" failed entirely to cover the Japanese general elections of December 27, 1968, in which the government was returned with a heavy majority on a pro-American platform, having given two campaign reports in preceding days forecasting the rejection of the Japan-U.S. alliance.

Neither the CBC nor the Montreal Star gave any introduction

beyond some innocuous attribution of expertise to Wilfrid Burchitt, one of the former leaders of the Australian Communist Party, when he was called upon to give his wildly partisan explanations of world events, with particular emphasis on praise of the Kim Il Sung regime in North Korea. (October 25, 1968, and January 10, 1969, in the Star). In January, 1969, the publisher of the Montreal Star, Derek Price, told the Senate media committee that there was no cause for alarm in Quebec, that the province was in fine shape, and that any contrary impression had been dishonestly left by the Toronto press. The following Saturday, January 31, the *Star* devoted the entire break page of its "News and Review" section to the Black Panther movement of militant American blacks, with perhaps 3,000 members. There were dark hints that this group was about to produce the long-awaited and definitive immolation of America.

The record of the *Star* in this area was an astonishing one. The Washington correspondent, Raymond Heard, represented the Anti-Ballistic Missile debate in the U.S. Senate as a question of "whether Canadians get fried alive to protect Americans" (March 26, 1969). In the same and sequential news stories, Heard routinely reported that Mr. Nixon would spend 300 billion dollars on the program, would indefinitely escalate the Vietnam War, and so on. The *Star*'s pièce de résistance was by the angry left-wing columnist, James Eayrs, who wrote of the Amchitka nuclear test, October 6, 1968, that the Nixon administration had been "insouciant to the point of brutality" and "careless to the point of criminality." The "troglodytes" of the Atomic Energy Commission had hazarded "sending a million pairs of ragged claws scuttling across the floors of silent seas, making the green ones red." Eayrs also wrote that the Amchitka test "undermines inhibitions against resorting to nuclear weapons in war."

This catalogue could be almost endless. No responsible newsman in the world thought that the American scene in the late 'sixties was very edifying, and most thoughtful people had serious reservations about some aspects of the Vietnam War. Nor is there anything wrong if someone is not an admirer of the U.S.A. None of that is at issue here. The press of Canada, with few exceptions in metropolitan or national roles, deliberately and almost hysterically embellished upon the American situation, larded the news with sizzling strips of Americophobia, and placed the frustrations and prejudices of the Canadian journalistic establishment in vivid relief. No small part of this was the stifled adolescent rage accumulated by years of obscurity, inferiority, and amateurishness in comparison to the U.S. media. It need hardly be emphasized that the shortcomings of American society were most fully and accurately reported by the free press of the United States. In addition to their own petulance, the Canadian media revealed and expressed a profound social bias. The fraternity of professional writers, from which the working press drew their principal inspiration, became inordinately nationalistic in this era. Moderates such as Robert Fulford regretted "Johnsonian imperialism" (Vietnam), and Arnold Edinborough, Hugh Garner, Peter Newman, Mordecai Richler and others wrote in sorrow rather than anger. Writers who were younger, or better attuned to the spirit of the day, however, addressed themselves to the subject with amazing incivility. Thus, Farley Mowat wrote: ". . . demonstrably the United States is currently engaged in almost every form of domestic and external brutality, aggrandizement, degradation of the individual, and destruction of freedom." Margaret Atwood contributed this stanza to what purported to be a poem:

Star-spangled cowboy sauntering out of the almost-
silly West, on your face a porcelain grin,
tugging a papier-mâché cactus
on wheels behind you with a string,
you are innocent as a bathtub full of bullets.

With this sort of drivel being produced by the people the Academic-Journalistic Complex was touting as evidence of the nascent and different Canadian culture, it is little wonder that anti-Americanism became such an irresistible fad. This coverage of American affairs had its domestic parallels, and is only cited as the most egregious aspect of the general media predilection for left-wing causes.

The nature of these liberal or radical-liberal trends was in general conformity with international movements in the same direction. It was a rather odd combination of nihilistic rhetoric and reverence for aged people and things. Mao Tse-Tung, Bertrand Russell, Herbert Marcuse, the nostalgia campaign of Eugene McCarthy, and almost any recourse to strike, were all venerated by the authors or sympathizers of the Battle of Grant Park and the "Days of Rage." There was still great faith in the redistributive welfare programs and egalitarianism was popular, provided it did not impinge upon the tutorial prerogatives of the Academic-Journalistic Complex. Civil rights were a little fuzzy. They were laudable if being exercised by disadvantaged ethnic or economic groups or even students. They were a bourgeois relic if defined to mean one should not occupy offices of executives or university presidents, should not close down all roads into Washington, D.C. on May Day, 1970, should not hurl excrement at policemen, should not fly the Vietcong flag on U.S. federal government flagpoles. As always, the Canadian media were obsessed with American events, perhaps even more so in dissent than they had been in earlier times of emulation.

There were many expressions of concern in the late sixties that the leftward bias of the media in Canada would permanently endanger the society, most of whose members were alienated from the media's singular presentation of events. This has proved not to be the case. As was stated earlier, there was never anything conspiratorial about the evolution of press attitudes. Fadism asserted itself in the usual manner, with an assist from demographic, syndical, and industry trends, and in regrettable coincidence with an unbidden series of disruptive international events. Anti-Americanism has subsided somewhat, with the failure of the American Vietnam effort and the fall of Richard Nixon. Enthusiasm for old liberal programs has abated considerably. The welfare programs don't work very well and are very costly, feeding inflation and high tax-deductions at source. The media aren't in favour of a high income tax anymore, because their collective demands have been so successful that they are now among its victims.

In the wake of fervent commitment has come disillusionment and cynical posturings. What is left of the old egalitarian spirit now concentrates on anti-establishment disgruntlement. The media would endorse higher corporation taxes or succession taxes, or a tax on capital, but not personal incomes or luxury sales or any discomfort close to home. Trudeau is no more popular with the press corps in Ottawa than Diefenbaker was. The economic situation has deteriorated in the last five years; the communications industry is not doing much hiring. Great causes are few; exaltation of soul is in short supply; and strikes, protests, and students in general, are no longer romantic and have reverted to being a bore.

The leftward bias of the media now, unlike five or ten years ago, is fatigued and passive, and even shows early signs of self-criticism. Balance may prove to be self-restoring. No improvement in professional standards is likely. No leadership should be expected to arise suddenly from the press or its employers. The public reaction to the alarms and excursions of the communications industry has been both inspiring and reassuring. Neither stampeded nor enraged, the public has sharpened its skill at resisting the telephone subscription-solicitor and at turning off the set. Some members of the public have been conscripted to media causes. Some have become irascible in their objections to those causes. But the vast mass of the public has retained, in regard to the media, a glacial serenity. The silent majority lives on, not untouched by economic factors but almost indifferent to the press. The communications industry's profits continue at a high level. The biases of the media remain almost unanswered, but, as was predicted in 1969, the power of the media has declined, along with their credibility and that of other institutions.

Even the journalistic community itself, recuperating from the exertions of having run amok in the past decade, between riveting fads, is growing collectively older, paunchier, and, incidentally, wiser. It would be symmetrical and unsurprising if the next crusade on which the Academic-Journalistic Complex embarked was a conservative orientation. Those who have revelled in the iconoclasm of the last decade would be as lonesome as the middle-of-the-road veterans of the fifties were when the press became perplexed in the extreme in the sixties. Liberalism will not vanish in the media; it is a normal attitude for a unionized employee paid to investigate and conditioned to suspect people and institutions. Radicalism, however, is abnormal for a highly-paid quasi-celebrity with claims to professionalism. The process is essentially somewhat reactionary and if it perceives that the greatest danger to liberal society comes from the left rather than the right, it will adjust accordingly. Any expectation of originality, however, of heightened integrity or creativity, or representativeness is likely to be disappointed.

The Proclamation of Human Rights

LOUISE MARCIL-LACOSTE

As a member of the Civil Liberties Union, I participated during recent years in different stages of the deliberations which led to the proclaiming of a Bill of Rights in the Province of Quebec. I shall offer here some reflexions on the philosophical significance of certain issues that were raised in the evolution of the Bill of Rights through these stages. I shall write with no pretence of being a specialist in political philosophy. Rather, I shall discuss these matters as a more worldly philosopher who holds that in these episodes we find questions raised of a kind which challenge all professional philosophers and all conscientious citizens to take counsel together.

I Historical Background

The chronology of Quebec's coming to declare a Bill of Rights might be said rather pragmatically to culminate in the passing of Quebec's Bill 50 which has its first Reading in the Assembly on November 29th, 1974 and was finally passed through a third Reading on June 27th, 1975. At least two years of protracted consultations by members of the Civil Liberties Union had preceded the latter date. But the final implementation of that Bill, through the creation of a Human Rights Commission *and* the appointment of its President and members, should be counted as still more recent. Such chronology may be unexciting in itself, yet important for what it indicates: The time taken to reach a third Reading is especially interesting, because Quebec was one of the two Canadian provinces that did *not* have a Bill of Rights by 1974; that *opposed* the ratification by the Canadian Government of the International Declaration of Human Rights of 1948; that *refused* to support the 1966 International Pacts concerning civil, political, economic, social, and cultural rights.

There were many considerations which made Quebeckers so reluctant for so long to endorse such proclamations. The most publicized problem which delayed the passing of Quebec's Bill of Rights were not always the most fundamental, let alone the most interesting from a philosophical point of view. It is the latter kind on which I shall concentrate here. It is useful to begin by noting that the Canadian Government offers as its Bill of Rights a short list of rather vague sounding principles. By comparison, the *kind* of legislation sought by the Quebec Government for its own Bill of Rights was very different: It wanted to translate into laws a complex set of specific principles, to be realized concretely through a particular new legal instrument for the promotion and protection of well-defined rights and freedoms.

The Dialectic of Criticism and Commitment

As I see it, Quebec's slowness to endorse any proclamation about Universal Rights derived from scepticism about what many Quebeckers took, rightly or wrongly, to be mere expressions of pious good will. I take this scepticism to be worthy of philosophers' scrutiny, since it valuably illuminates the difficulty for a rational individual of moving from critical appraisals to some act of commitment. In the last three decades, philosophers have devoted themselves to what they would call *critical analysis.* This has profoundly restricted their willingness to speak positively of human *knowledge* in matters of ethics and of political or social debate. What was most often claimed in the past about these matters is that we do know, or can easily come to know many statements of value to be sound and true or monstrous and false. Modern critical analysis has proved a salutary antidote to dogmatism by making us cautious about claims to know for certain what is politically right, morally wrong, and the like. Indeed, the analytical movement has mainly made us think more profitably about matters of *metaethics* ('moral semantics'), so that we are much more sensitive about the meanings and uses of evaluative terms, as well as the structures of moral, political, and social arguments. In matters of *normative ethics,* however, analysis has not taken us far. The questions of normative ethics are the substantial questions about what we ought to pursue as beings with reason, about how we should treat one another, about which things we need to regard as the inalienable rights and duties of persons sharing a common world.

Not a few now believe that this apparent failure of critical analysis to help us significantly in making wise decisions must reveal the futility, the necessary irrelevance of critical thinking. I take this belief to be sadly confused. Consider, for example, the following statement: "*Critical people are negative people and they are unable to commit themselves to any constructive position.*" This now rather popular saying is false, but it shows the timeliness of the issue which I wish to discuss: the relationship between a critical attitude and a moral commitment. I shall try to illustrate this question in reflecting upon the recent Declaration of a Bill of Rights in Quebec by selecting a few issues and arguments as they have been discussed, and by examining the problems which they generate. First, my focus will be on objections

79

raised against the Declaration. Next, a perspective will be offered which allows us to formulate conditions for a positive conclusion. My main position is rather simple: For the complex kind of moral and political commitment which a *wise* Declaration of Human Rights requires, a critical attitude is essential. This position involves at least two different corollaries: (1) The mere raising of objections is not the whole function of the critical attitude; (2) no whole-hearted passion to adopt a moral, political or social position constitutes a sufficient condition for arriving at a commitment worthy of a human being.

As I said, the event which I want to discuss did not occur without taxing antecedents. In fact, my remarks on chronology were but prolegomena to a topic which merits philosophers' attention. When a government decides to proclaim a Bill of Human Rights in a solemn manner, one has the feeling that the *State* is acting like a person who tries to play the role of a moral philosopher. Of course, our ordinary political life does frequently involve appeals to such virtues as justice, respect for human dignity, love of peace, concern for equality, and so on. Usually, however, such appeals form an ordinary part of our political give and take: It is seldom that a public issue will reach a level of debate that resembles philosophical discussion on solemn, abstract matters like the essence of justice. In the historical context of the Declaration of Rights, however, the public debate was driven to a philosophical level. Citizens of Quebec found themselves eventually led to truly philosophical discussion of what should be called *just in social life*. In such a case, a whole society is expected to assess nothing less than what constitutes the foundation of a social contract.

But when the state itself comes to resemble a person who is a moral philosopher, it also becomes all too like an ordinary person who finds that each philosophical issue raises a host of others. Indeed, the everyday political instruments of pressure, bargaining, and propaganda look rather misplaced when it is time to determine honestly and assert what constitutes the essence of human dignity. Yet here it seems to many that the philosophical tools of critical analysis do not make clear anything but negative conclusions as to what we are NOT entitled to believe about civil liberties. The 'academic' and the 'non-academic' issues correspond: *More* than pragmatic or rhetorical means to forge a consensus must be at stake; yet *more* than such negative statements about freedom are required from critical thinkers.

At this precise point, however, when we all try to break the impasse, I am struck by the following paradox: It seems that *because* the attempt was made to offer more meatily positive ideas than those of typically pious rhetoric, much more has been said *against* the Declaration than *for* it. On the one hand, one may have expected that the practical aspect of the aim would make the matter easier. For Quebec was not attempting to settle all philosophical discussions and present the results in a perfect treatise. But Quebec was seeking to assert in an effective way the philosophical doctrine that a human being has a right (or many rights) which must *transcend* the level of ordinary conditions or even the level of ordinary laws. Surely, this is a doctrine which has long puzzled politicians and philosophers. If the matter has always been so difficult, it should have come as no surprise that so many problems and objections were mentioned.

II The Quicksands of Scepticism

Adhering to a general kind of scepticism—although perhaps unhappy with its limitations—some intellectuals have argued that we should not indulge in the setting of pointless and painfully sophisticated traps for naive people. I often suspect that this view results from an unfortunate sort of perfectionism, from the view that only perfection would be worthy of pursuit. This very *general* mixture of pessimism and scepticism is philosophically boring, as well as devoid of any redeeming practical value. When all the momentous layers of wrapping are stripped away, its message is little more than this: Whatever one thinks or does, there will always be objections to it. This is safe enough. It is the gospel of someone who can neither put a foot wrong nor a foot right!

It is worth noting, however, that when such pessimistic scepticism was invoked in discussions concerning Quebec's Bill of Rights, it was used in a context where its bearing seemed important. I shall just mention two of the numerous examples. (I) Some argued that freedom of speech *is* clearly a fundamental right, but that *there will always be objections to any definition* which may be given to "freedom of speech." (II) Some argued that self-determination *cannot be* a fundamental right, since the recognition of such a right would entail that *there will always be objections* to the inclusion of collective rights in a code.

From this it can be seen that the sceptical stance had a very understandable basis. That more precise stance could, therefore, be discussed in connection with quite specific arguments and issues. In thus giving more point to the argument that *there will always be objections* by making an attempt to examine the arguments actually used against identifiable positions, the sceptics came to seem quite enlightening, if seriously unsettling.

One appeared to be talking of what is presented as *transcending* the level of ordinary life and laws. One faced a haunting question in debate after debate: How transcendent, how far *above* what is particular in ordinary life and laws must a Bill of Rights be? And some argued that the answer was: "Very far! So far above ordinary human life and laws that it defies human formulation. Thus we simply cannot have a legal account of basic human rights."

Scepticism and 'The Ineffable Stand'

At first glance, this argument may appear irresponsible, but that it need not be irresponsibly offered may be seen from its main conclusion—that we should not seek to spell out legally the fundamental rights of human beings. Indeed, it is urged in this connexion that every intelligent and ethical being knows by intuition, by some moral instinct, what the fundamental rights are. There is a natural illumination to be found in each person's conscience—the proponent continues—and, by itself, this illumination is much stronger and clearer than any written law could be. According to such reason, we should avoid corrupting the purity of natural conscience by indulging in sterile debates over words, definitions, principles, or juristic techniques.

One may call this position *The Ineffable Stand*. It is the position that what cannot be said is much more relevant and morally certain than what can be said. In more technical terms, this position implies a belief in the innate character of virtue, by which I mean the view that the notion and the rules of justice are a natural endowment from birth of all normal human beings which remains within each person's conscience. This view takes any law enacted by humans, even one concerned with fundamental rights, as offering us at best an undesirable burden.

Again, *The Ineffable Stand* implies a belief in the existence and the authority of a natural (moral) law. In this context, "natural" connotes what unites all moral beings in their pursuit of virtue. So it is often argued that, because the natural voice of conscience is itself the *ground* of all codes and conventions, therefore the writing of a code in a particular language implies a reduction, if not a degradation, of pure moral sentiments into cultural idiosyncrasies.

I think that this stand or view is wrong in at least three important ways. (1) In the first place, it is not realistic. It is more concerned with what would be perfect social conditions for ideally reasonable and lucid human beings than with the necessity of improving actual situations. As we know, it is not at all clear that the appeal to naturalness can be upheld either by the kind of 'inner self-evidence' or by the kind of consistent moral wisdom which *The Ineffable Stand* suggests to be forthcoming. It may be remembered that Aristotle,

82

whose doctrines about man's natural capacities for mastering morality encourage this stand, asserted that some men are slaves by nature. (2) In the second place, I think that *The Ineffable Stand* is doomed to lead us to incompatible results. It is held that by virtue of their immanent knowledge of fundamental rights, all human beings agree on fundamental moral issues, while they can disagree over words. But one cannot help asking how it happens that human beings have so much difficulty in agreeing on mere words, if they already agree on the more important questions about virtue and vice? I take this position to be incoherent because it postulates an universal agreement upon the real substance of moral issues in order further to postulate the impossibility of humans' articulating what they agree upon. (3) In the third place, I think that *The Ineffable Stand* despite its appearance of generosity and idealism actually offers an odour of sanctity to various forms of discrimination and injustice. The doctrine that *at the bottom* we all know what is right leads too many to believe that what we observe *at the surface* is unimportant. It encourages us in moments of despair to conclude that we simply have to accept human nature as it is: Deep in our hearts we know that evils are all inevitable. Such a conclusion (which many would call 'gut reaction') makes the easy way seem the best. It seems so easy and so practical *not* to take the steps which would lead to a more just situation.

Scepticism and 'The Unstatable Stand'

Thus, I do not think that what some hold to be naturally felt "or intimately perceived" about moral issues must be sounder than anything which can be articulated in words. If the terms of a Bill of Rights must transcend the particular, such transcendence could not lie in the depths of the ineffable. But if we hold that we should attempt to *speak* and *say enough* we face new troubles. To put it bluntly, there are plenty of arguments against the *very possibility of stating* a clearly defined and finite list of human rights. The conclusion of such arguments I shall dub *The Unstatable Stand*. It is perhaps a more frequently accepted conclusion than what I called *The Ineffable Stand*. Notice that this new position differs from *The Ineffable Stand* in not claiming that what cannot be clearly articulated in words is better than what can.

There are many possible lines of arguments for *The Unstatable Stand*. I have selected four examples which have more in common than the mere claim that it is impossible to spell out in full what rights we have as human beings. They also share the view that a worthwhile declaration must not fail to touch upon ordinary life and ordinary laws. In other words, for the proponents of *The Unstatable Stand*, a declaration must be close enough to ordinary life with its ordinary values and laws to be significant. It must also have the special status, however, of transcending ordinary life and laws for its importance to be recognized.

First Example. It is argued that it is morally impossible to arrive at a significant statement of human rights which would include more than pious and general principles. It is further argued, that the assertion of the primary principles of justice for mankind would be meaningful if these principles were articulated enough to be useful for identifying many forms of injustice. Thus any meaningful declaration of rights would have to include statements which are precise enough to entail, for example, that we should condemn all cases of discrimination which are found in different countries. The arguer sighs and shrugs his shoulders. He adds with a look of despair that, as the declaration is supposed to be the assertion of fundamental human rights, any such precision in a code would violate or jeopardize the universality of the project. Indeed, the arguer continues, for such a declaration to be meaningful, it must nowhere forfeit its universalizability. Otherwise it can only express a personal or cultural taste. If hypocrisy and hollow propaganda are to be avoided, it may well be better to settle for no code at all, rather than one which is either meaningless or too viciously restricted.

Second Example. Another line of argument used against the possibility of stating basic human rights suggests a more logical outlook. We are warned to avoid such statements on further grounds of inevitable inconsistency. Consider the following claims. *A.* "It is inconsistent to say that all human beings have a right to freedom *and* to admit that some should possibly be imprisoned." Here the alleged inconsistency is thought to arise from combining the notions both of a universal right and of a quite possible exception. *B.* "It is inconsistent to say that all human beings are equal *and* to state special rules for women, non-whites, old people, handicapped persons, etc." Here the supposed inconsistency is thought to arise from combining both the idea of absolute equality for all persons and the idea that some classes of persons require different treatment and special rights. *C.* "It is inconsistent *both* to assert the right to speak one's own mother tongue *and* to allow countries the right to proclaim an official language." Here the supposed inconsistency is thought to arise from the notion of a right. Either the allegedly universal human rights apply just to situations in which the persons act as free individuals. Or we acknowledge collective rights as well as individual rights, with a resulting commitment to merely pragmatic politics. *D.* "It is inconsistent to say that all persons have a right to education *and* to say that instruction should be compulsory." Here the supposed inconsistency is thought to arise from giving primacy to a *means* incompatible with the goal of education (freedom, instructions, self-development). *E.* "It is inconsistent to argue that the declaration of rights should prevail over all legislation *and* to make the ways of applying the declaration a matter of further laws or regulations." Here the supposed inconsistency is thought to arise from the notion of the political process of declaring a bill of rights, and then from the notion of the universal status of a bill.

Such reasoning is used to make us wish to conclude that principles of right are too complex to be expressed without gross inconsistency. Inconsistency, we infer, is Original Sin. Silence is the key to an intellectual Paradise or at least the way to avoid an intellectual Hell.

Third Example. The possibility of stating a set of human rights is also denied by those who argue that ideally we should—but that practically we cannot—assert the hierarchy of basic and secondary rights. Some argue that a wise declaration must give one right absolute priority over all others, for the root of much evil, according to their view, lies in not giving special status to any single right. For example, some think that unless the freedom of association is clearly subordinated to a right to enforce civil order, the bill will only serve to promote a state of chaos. Others maintain that grandiose talk of the basic right to private property is used by legislators to enforce socio-economic inequalities; that a declaration which does not begin by the priority collective ownership is a mere bourgeois game. Again, some argue that the Question of Women is the crux of the matter, others the right to fair trial, etc. In their view, having *no* Bill of Rights in infinitely better than having one which does not effectively subordinate quite secondary claims to rights whose primacy must be acknowledged.

Fourth Example. Finally, some people who insist that it is impossible to state what our human rights are to any good purpose will argue on the basis of utility. The argument runs as follows: The declaration involves an attempt to be virtuous which focusses on the bandying about of words and definitions. But this very focus on verbal performances makes a Bill of Rights at best useless and at worst harmful. It is useless because even what is a precise, accurate declaration from a conceptual point of view is likely from a practical point of view to have no impact at all. It is harmful because a declaration gives too many right-thinking persons the feeling that everything has been done already once we have proclaimed how virtuously all human beings ought to treat one another. Such reasoners urge that here it is clearly better to have *not* achieved the ideal, rather than generate the possibly dangerous illusion of having achieved it.

We have now considered four lines of argument. *The first* invokes a supposed incompatibility between expressing precise, meaningful statements and expressing the universality which fundamental rights must have; according to *the second*, it is impossible for a complex declaration to be consistent; if we accept *the third*, then any recourse to a hierarchy contradicts the intended reference to all fundamental rights; *the fourth* expresses a strong scepticism about the effects of such a declaration.

III   The Need for Bills of Rights:
A Reply to Scepticism

Such arguments have often troubled me. But before trying to evaluate them I hope to put matters in a better perspective. I realize that these arguments show the complexity of issues involved in formulating a worthwhile Bill of Rights, but such signs of complexity show that we are on the right sort of track: If everything looked as simple as users of such arguments desire them to be, then *we could be sure that we had turned into daydreaming Mandarins.* In this particular case I infer that a good critical sense is a necessary condition for rational commitment.

Rational commitment to principles requires good reason to believe that we can *tell* when those principles are being violated. In the case of discrimination against women seeking jobs that correspond to their qualifications; in the case of old people forced out of work and denied shelter at rents they can afford; and in so many other cases, we are able to discern or verify that human rights are being violated here and now. The sight of such injustice leads me to a pair of conclusions that sceptics will not wish to stomach. *First*, however difficult it may be to formulate such a Bill, there are persons whose means of getting justice are close to nonexistent in the absence of a declaration. Of course, I am not saying that the mere creation of a solemn document will miraculously uphold all human rights. But in considering *The Unstatable Stand*, I find myself in a position where I must take my own stand and reply that very concrete facts about human suffering and real, at least, negatively, possibilities of reducing it establish humans' right to some chance of greater protection under such a Bill. Perhaps we cannot draft a Bill of Rights perfectly. But, as Kant would put it: "'OUGHT' implies 'CAN.'" We can produce imperfect Bills and improve them, for we ought to do so if we allow that indeed there must be some such guiding code. Admitting this first point but still worried by the difficulties of *The Unstatable Stand*, some have proposed to begin with a limited Bill of Rights and restrict its content to certain rights which are quite clearly violated. Such a Bill is mainly an assertion of human rights against a spectrum of discriminatory abuses. I do not think, however, and this is my second point, that we can (or should) formulate a Bill of Rights which attacks all forms of discrimination and *only* forms of discrimination.

I have two main objections to this view. First, the idea of finding and identifying perfectly clear cases of discrimination is not as easy as it appears. Indeed, since the point is to limit the field of disagreement, the suggestion does not work. Some consider that starvation, torture, execution without trial are the *only* clear cases of discrimination; others that the latter must be defined by distinguishing a *minimal* and an *optimal* level of just conditions; others again argue that the only clear cases of discrimination are those which apply to individuals *only*; some also argue that *only* "universal" cases of discrimination (cases to be found in all countries or cases to be condemned by all countries) may be included in a code against discrimination, etc. Thus, far from restricting the field of disagreement, this suggestion actually carries along too many old and new problems.

My second objection to any restriction of a Bill of Rights to a code against discrimination is probably more important. For not only is it very difficult to draw the line between a punitive option and a preventive one, but it is not desirable in questions such as human rights to limit the attempt to the former. Efforts at correction, prevention, and promotion are often interdependent, at least when the goal is to improve the quality of social life. My *model* here for upholding rights is not that of a punishing judge, but that of an *educational community*.

I shall now turn to the earlier difficulties that were raised about drafting a Bill. The first thing to notice is their focus on the *text* of the code. This is natural enough, since the vital questions largely pertain to our deciding whether or not we should say something and what we can say. Accordingly, that there are problems about words, definitions, consistency, or priority should not surprise us. On the other hand, we should reflect on the possibilities and the limits of the text itself. My argument here is that, while such a focus on the text is unavoidable and important, it should not be allowed to stultify us. We must not look upon the drafting of the text as the sole condition or as the model for solving all problems of human rights.

Notice certain features of the *act* of drafting a text concerning human rights. Here we have an act whose essence is to lead to another act: the making of a statement. If we compare this act, for example, to the act of building a school or of funding a firm, the act of declaring human rights is not very concrete. Of course, one may say that the official and solemn status given to this statement—together with its democratic genesis—makes it much more than the head-line in a newspaper or even more than the content of any other more specific bills voted by a parliament. Now I cannot but agree that the declaration of human rights remains a *verbal* act. But it is not just any verbal act. It has what the late John Austin would at one time have called a *performatory* character: Such uses of words are deeds. As Alexander Sesonke has put it in a useful commentary on Austin: Performatory uses of language alter the *formal relations* between human beings who share common beliefs and rules. Such is the verbal act of making a promise; such is also the verbal and civil act of commitment to marriage which is done by the mutual utterance of "I do." When I promise to lend you my car by saying "That's a promise," I now stand in a new, formal relation of commitment to you. When the couple says "I do" before some figure in authority, they assume the formal relation of being married to each other.

The second thing to notice is that the declaring of a bill of rights is a paradigm of a *political* kind of performatory act. In effect, when the society's authorized statesmen declare certain human rights to be inviolable, this act is the making of a social promise. This is why the declaration of rights has been called the making of a social contract. Clearly, this act is political. The declaration concerns each citizen who stands in varied formal relations to other persons and other citizens. As the Quebec Charter states in its Preamble: It concerns "the foundation of justice and peace," and it is "guaranteed by the collective will." The kind of society to which we belong links formal relations between individuals very closely with political rights and collective rules.

There is one consequence of the political nature of a Bill of Rights, which needs consideration. The collective will to which we refer is not a Platonic Idea in a timeless treasure-house of abstractions. Nor is it Rousseau's abstract General Will. It is the will of a very concrete sort of collectivity which is firmly located in space and time. It is located in our case in Quebec during 1975. The particular stands which *this* collectivity adopts on matters such as justice, peace, dignity, and rights constitute *this* collective will. As M.L.A. Hart has very helpfully written: It is a mistake to ask for a definition of right in the line of metaphysical notions of duty, or outside the socio-political conditions under which the statements have their characteristic uses. In this sense, the question is not so much what ought all human beings do, but what a law ought to enforce.

The General and the Particular in Bills of Rights

As we dwell on this politically performatory character of a society's declaration of basic rights, we are led to a third and crucial factor: the unavoidably paradox-laden nature of a meaningful bill of rights. By "paradox," I do not only mean "a statement contrary to a generally received opinion." I shall use the term "paradox" to express the conflicting relation between *opposed* propositions to which we are led by using sound arguments. Consider again the problems of universality and of consistency discussed in connexion with *The Unstatable Stand*. Some say: "A declaration must be universal. That is, none of its statements must be true of particular countries or particular persons only." Others say: "No declaration can ever be universal—however universal its terminology sounds—because any given declaration is pronounced by a particular state at a particular time." Still others argue that any claim to universality is merely the expression of an "intellectual stiff neck": We cannot make universal claims with good sense, all our knowledge comes from limited experience.

I must ask the reader to bear with me if I reply that here a certain way of accepting paradoxes is healthy and that we must learn to live with them. The recognition of the paradoxical nature of any Bill of Rights worth enacting is quite fruitful. For the paradoxes only arise when we have the courage to try here and now to interpret and apply to particular cases certain moral and political doctrines which are *fundamental* or, if you prefer, *most crucial*. This, I am sure, cannot be done without admitting the limited scope of any experience. All the same, no talk about eternal values can have meaning unless it can be seen to bear on some objects of our present experience.

As may be imagined, the discussions among Quebeckers which I attended were not meant to emulate Hegel's dialectical treatment of the universal and the particular. The main question which kept arising was whether it was rational to try enacting a Bill of Rights which includes *both* 1. universal statements that express as many principles concerning basic human rights as possible *and*, 2. more specific statements that establish the concrete means for upholding these rights in particular situations. In more technical terms, the question was whether a Bill of Rights should refer not only to *first-order relations* (claims and duties), but also to *second-order relations* (conditions under which actions are legally significant). If it included reference only to first order relations, such a Bill would be called prescriptive and permissive: Anything that is neither prescribed nor proscribed would be, in principle, permitted. If it were to include reference to second order relations, it would then be said to offer *regulative law*.

My verdict on such frequent debates remains the same: Both universal and particular statements, with reference to second-order as well as first-order relations, are required for such a Bill to have any *point*. Admittedly, the means for upholding rights vary from culture to culture; they change with constitutions and times. But such facts merely *seem* to conflict with the claimed universality of human rights. The explicit recognition of such varied and mutable means is a precondition of such a Bill's having any real point.

One must be able to infer from the general propositions of the Bill that certain rights have to be upheld among us by those particular means which are here and now historically relevant to ourselves. Against this position, however, there is a puzzling objection: Why should we *pretend* to offer a bill of fundamental rights if actually what we do is to take an arbitrary decision on what justice means for us? Why do we not merely endorse the *Universal Declaration* (or, for that matter, the *Canadian Declaration*)? Should we not leave the question of means to political programs or to further laws?

This objection is as puzzling as it is both sensible and confusing. The *Canadian Declaration* is quite short and vague; at least, it is much shorter and more vague than the *Universal Declaration* itself. Besides, there is a great variety of Bills of Rights arising from different national and historical perspectives. The diversity involved does not simply pose questions about translating the *Universal Declaration* from one language to another. Indeed, there are many *types* of declarations of human rights: charter, code, declaration, fundamental law, constitution, convention, pacts, etc. There are also many sorts of *contents* for the principles included in such texts: The number, the extension, the precision and the meaning of principles vary. Further, there are many *levels* of precision in such statements about means of upholding fundamental rights, the diversity in the nature of such means being plain. Why should the society of 20th-Century Quebeckers be any less arbitrary in its moral principles or political formulations than the peoples of other countries and times?

Such a concern about arbitrariness amounts to much more than a fear of regionalism. There is the question of consistency which has been mentioned earlier, and which is now raised again in the context of intellectual honesty. Why should we wish to *pretend* to offer as universal what is clearly too arbitrary and is possibly inconsistent? This objection rests on confusions which I shall now examine.

If by using the words "universal right," one means to lay claim to a right of an absolute kind, which obtains without condition and without restriction, then there is a first class chance that one merits the censuring charge of holding arbitrary opinions. If "universal" must be used in such an 'absolute' manner in the framing of all such Bills, then we should waste no time on Quebeckers, Canadians, Americans, North Americans who issue the Bills. On the same ground we would have to conclude that even the *Universal Declaration* of 1948 is worthless, not to mention the *International Pacts* of 1966.

It will not be difficult to agree on the non-universality of many assertions in the *Universal Declaration*. Indeed, its preamble tells us that all its statements express a "common ideal to achieve," implying that different countries have different paths to travel and different priorities to establish.

Even the *International Declaration* is not an array of unconditional generalizations. Its principles are not affirmed without any qualifications. For example, it offers a sort of second-order principle to the effect that all of its provisions must be interpreted synoptically in relationship one with another (See Article 30). The most conspicuous example of the resulting qualifications is one to the effect that the right to personal freedom is restricted by the right to take recourse against acts which violate the laws. We find another important qualification when it is admitted that human rights should be recognized, but that their character should be interpreted according to the constitutions of member-countries.

The Dialectical Unity of Meaningful Bills of Rights

When we realize that the *Universal Declaration* itself involves qualifications and invites being relativized to particular forms of life, then we can begin to think afresh about the crucial concept of *consistency*. In framing and in analyzing such Bills and Declarations we are not dealing with questions of purely formal consistency. We need to concentrate on the question whether such a written statement has what I shall call a *quasi-dialectical unity*. We should ask whether the statement acknowledges that its very subject matter must eventually generate a sense in the citizen of CONFLICTING obligations. (Much talk of "dialectical contradictions in reality" can be understood in terms of "conflict" and its most natural senses.) We should next ask whether the total statement offers reasonably clear means of resolving most conflicts between moral obligations, between political obligations, between a political and a moral obligation, and so on. Such a statement should also be *inspirational:* It should inspire human creativity to foresee fresh moral problems, new tensions, additional ways to deal with these conflicts.

We enlarge our notion of consistency, and make it more relevant to human needs, when we allow that the kind of consistency required in framing a Bill of Rights is mainly this characteristic which I call *quasi-dialectical unity*. Settling for this kind of consistency is required in many contexts of those who wish to make philosophy relevant not just to the deriving of logical theorems but also to the morally intelligent performance of political acts. Deductive formal systems have one price. Statesmanship has another. To admit that even the often cited *International Declaration* does not offer 'perfectly' universal or unconditioned sets of principles is not to deny its importance. On the contrary, it is to realize that this Declaration offers common standards to be pursued in differing ways by all people. Only because it is not 'perfectly universal' can it both offer canons by which policies may be judged and also provide grounds for protests and reforms. In the *International Declaration* therefore, one finds an adumbration of standards below which the United Nations had *decided* that it would be undesirable or intolerable for any human being to be allowed to fall. Some may call this arbitrary. But could such a Declaration have any substance, any backbone, any significance, or point without being made relevant to what is particular here and now?

As can be expected, what I say of the *International Declaration*— that it is not given as an unconditioned statement of principles— applies even more clearly to the *International Pacts* of 1966. The latter, let us recall, cover civil and political rights, economical, social, and cultural rights. With their focus on collective rights, these Pacts represent an improvement of the *International Declaration.*

At this point something must be said about heated debates in Quebec over the question of *collective* rights. The debates were notably stimulated by concerns over the notions of *self-determination* and of an *official language.* Indeed, one reason why the Quebec Declaration took so long to evolve—as the Provincial Government argued—was the desire of many Quebeckers to have the issue of an official language settled first. (No one should be surprised if I do not here attempt to settle it.)

There is a general question pertaining to debates over collective rights which needs to be examined. As was mentioned, some have argued that a Quebec Declaration would be a hoax on the ground that there *cannot be* collective rights. They have insisted that the notion of rights applies only to individuals. From this they concluded that what pertains to collective principles or conditions is of a political nature; that it must therefore be discussed and implemented by means *other* than a Declaration of Rights.

The very statements of the *International Pacts, all* concerning collective rights, constitute strong counter-examples to this view. Again, even in the case of rights which usually apply to individuals *qua* individuals—such rights as many that are mentioned in the *International Declaration*—there does not seem to be much sense in denying that they have to be understood partly in terms of collective obligations. After all, what is the point of a society's authorized leaders' solemnly declaring a bill of rights? Besides, there are many fundamental rights which are of a collective nature: The individual's right to education is meaningless outside an actual educational system; the right to free association and to free opinion are plainly inconceivable outside a community. If we look at the *International Pacts*, this point becomes still more obvious.

As the above examples suggest, faith in a rigid distinction between an individual and a collective right is not upheld in ordinary life nor in international documents. Of course, I am not denying that Declarations of Human Rights apply to individuals. Nor would I deny that for a long time it has been a legitimate *priority* in many countries to protect individuals. But the traditional liberal view on private and individual rights seems to me incomplete. The affirmation of such a priority can only make sense against the background of a collectively organized human group. The affirmation of such a priority against the background of some hypothetical State of Nature (or of some apolitical Paradise) is a self-defeating exercise: Every performatory use of language requires a context in which certain social *conditions* are satisfied. Otherwise we babble. One should not rule out the right to self-determination in a Bill of Rights on the 'ground' that such a right does not apply to individuals *qua* individuals. Recourse to this spurious distinction is generally due to clouds of confusion like those we find drooping over such words as "universal," "absolute," and "collective."

The kind of consistency to be expected of a statement of broadly human rights, I have argued, is best brought out by a term like "quasi-dialectical unity." The felicity of a human society's issuing such a pronouncement depends largely on whether that type of unity is realized. To meet this crucial condition is *not* to exclude the creation in human minds of a sense of *tension*, of *competing obligations*, of *conflicts* in many contexts. Rather, we should say that in meeting this condition the declarer is likely to create *fruitful* tension in human minds. We have already explored some forms of fruitful tension. Let me mention another which is particularly taxing today.

The recognition that members of a long oppressed sex, race, or nation have had their right to many benefits systematically denied, presents many puzzles about what may be owed to such persons by way of compensation. The puzzles lead to talk, for example, of compensating women for such oppression by instituting programs of 'reverse discrimination' in matters of admission to professional schools, or posts of leadership. Some celebrated and similar phenomena surround the demands for 'positive discrimination' in favour of blacks as mayors or managers, of the aged as tenants in low rental housing developments, of the handicapped as recipients of grants for special training. Some quite unnecessary tension is created by the public tendency to use the evaluatively loaded ('negative') expression "discrimination." But there is also some inevitable tension here between at least three principles. There is the principle of giving all persons an equal right to compete on the basis of their qualifications. There is the principle that members of groups long denied such basic rights should receive some compensation. There is the principle that societies should seek to distribute and balance positions of power in such a way as to permit justice among its diverse groups. One can easily think of other competing principles closely related to, or constitutive of basic human rights.

For example, we can examine the problem of equality and the alleged inconsistency of stating principles concerning certain categories of persons, such as women, blacks, old, handicapped persons, etc. As we know, proceeding to a categorization has led to the popular (but, I think, misleading) expression "positive discrimination." Its implications are not always clear. Some may argue that "discimination" is here used as a "neutral" word to designate the weighing of differences or the judicative activity of making distinctions. It seems to me, however, that the popularity of the expression "positive discrimination" lies elsewhere—in its ambiguous *moral* connotation. It is in this context that I find it misguided.

Plainly, "positive discrimination" suggests that what we do in taking certain steps concerning some categories of persons is the *same sort* of action (discrimination) which *these* categories of persons have claimed should *not* be done. My first remark on this point is that we are confronted with a very interesting example of my former claim: A bill of rights is unavoidably a paradoxical text. Indeed, as the universal statements have a concrete meaning within the limits of a given social experience, there will always be something apparently incompatible in saying "all" while we are talking about, and for *some* people, here and now. When, for example, we refer to a human being *as a person*, we actually talk about a man or a woman. We may pretend to put masculinity or femininity into brackets—whatever that means—but, indeed, these brackets will rest on a cloudy, if pure, foundation.

My second remark is a corollary. When we state human rights in a meaningful manner, that is, principles of right *and* conditions for the using of rights, the standard of meaningfulness is contextual. To use a shortcut, we can say that the *situation* concerning men and women is not *logical*. Accordingly, the formal opposition between such expressions as "a person" and "a woman" is of no use in the ascertainment of moral principles and conditions.

My third remark is more positive. What we do, in fact, when we

94

consider real problems of inequality is weigh social differences in the light of principles of justice: In order for citizens to be equal, more must be given to those who have less. The last statement is more than the computing of more or less. The principles of distributive justice require a permanent evaluation of social differences, including their positive and negative features. In any case, as we are not all similar and as the situations in which we live are not identical, either we take the very complexity of this situation seriously in which case there is hope for more just conditions—or we are condemned to the emptiness of pious good will.

Conclusion

The business of political philosophy is not to mask such principles and the tensions they create, but to reveal them and to suggest options for at least an imperfect reconciliation. Further work by philosophers on elucidating and improving our intuitions about *Justice, A Person, Equality* and other relevant concepts may well enable us to keep improving the quality of the most attractive options offered. Similar tensions will be felt when we try to establish some shifting context-relevant hierarchies for ranking principles which come into conflict at a particular time and place. Again I expect that the tensions, if accepted intelligently and constructively, will inspire political philosophers to provide stronger analyses and better recommendations. The notion of utility, as was recognized before, is also going to make tensions arise when we try to establish priorities in matters of rights and obligations. I say: Let those tensions become far more clear in our political and philosophical consciousness—for only then can human reason do its best work for society and its individuals.

I have focused primarily on certain debates concerning a particular Bill of Rights, debates which arose and continued for much of the last two decades in Quebec. But the issues raised are plainly those that philosophers will have to reckon with in every age and society. The kinds of conflict and tension that I have emphasized will appear in new guises in different lands and epochs. A quasi-dialectical unity is often uncomfortable to live with, but it is after all both a binding and a liberating force. Those who try to remove the discomfort once and for all are those who do not understand human nature, or human rights, or the value of conflict for human reason. If ever politicians largely succeed in persuading us that they have found the Final Solution for removing tensions between what is universal and what is particular, or for ending tensions between universal principles, then we should begin to suspect that we are being charmed to sleep.

95

The Right of Nations to Self-Determination

DAN GOLDSTICK

The Algerian War of Independence dragged on from 1954 to 1962. In the end, France had to admit its inability to put the rebels down by force and agreed to the holding of a referendum in which the Algerian people voted overwhelmingly for independence. Like all modern wars, this one had been fought not just with guns and ammunition but also with words and ideas, and not just on the territories of the belligerents but all over the world. The Algerians vehemently had demanded the right of their nation to self-determination. Successive governments of France had replied that there was only the French nation, that Algeria was as much a part of France as Normandie or Picardie, and that the separation of such a province from the French nation as a whole was equally unthinkable in every case.

By 1962, though, it had proved to be thinkable. By that point world public opinion, especially in Africa and in Asia, had been thinking of Algeria as an oppressed nation for some time. It is certainly no accident that the principle of the self-determination of nations has been a very prominent battle-cry throughout large parts of the world in the course of this century. It is no accident that the self-determination principle figures so prominently in those repetitious but important U.N. debates that go on each year as the shifting tide of battle between world imperialism and its victims—fought out economically, militarily, politically, and ideologically—tends more and more, as the century wears on, to turn decisively against the forces of imperialism. That so very little is heard of the principle of national self-determination in those English-speaking lands which to a greater or lesser degree have materially benefited from imperialism is also not surprising from the standpoint of Marxist analysis.

In Canada, a country, as Lord Durham wrote in 1839, of "two nations warring in the bosom of a single state," it should not be surprising that the national right of self-determination is a very live issue in one of those two nations (the weaker one), among separatists and anti-separatists alike, while very little is ever heard of it in the political life and theorizing of the other nation, even by way of philosophical rebuttal. Certainly, however, more is heard of it in English-speaking Canada than in the U.S.A., for instance, and as the realization grows among English-speaking Canadians that their nation occupies a two-sided position, experiencing the brunt of imperialism as well as some of its benefits, interest in the topic of self-determination is very likely to increase.

96

This is not the place to develop and justify the Marxist position on the nature of contemporary imperialism. For lack of space, the sketchy hints below must necessarily omit some rather essential qualifications and complications, as well as the wealth of substantiating evidence both available and necessary to make the case sociologically.

In Marxist analysis, every modern capitalist country is dominated by a handful of super-rich monopoly corporations who run the show on all decisive issues by their economically predominant power over the press, television, the arts, the universities, churches, political parties, and all the other means of controlling public opinion, as well as (partly by means of) the state. Under such a system, the great majority of the nation works for the capitalist class to produce the goods and services which comprise the national product, and, for the sake of corporate profits, they are collectively paid less for their labours than the sum of the prices for which this total product is sold. But the same workers who are thus *exploited* are also, together with their families, the nation's principal consumers. Since the total product which they manufacture in the capitalists' employ must sell on the market for more than they get paid for collectively producing it, there is bound to be a shortage of consumer purchasing power in the economy relative to the quantity of goods and services produced. There are a number of ways of staving off the tendency to a crisis of "overproduction" and resultant depression which is inherent in this whole setup.

But at any rate this sort of background does make clear, it is argued, why every capitalist nation has a basic *need to export* built into its very economic system. Both goods and capital must be exported. As the capitalist states cannot each export their domestically generated surpluses to one another, there is a need for countries held permanently in a sufficient condition of industrial underdevelopment to provide continuing markets for the manufactured goods of the dominant capitalist nations, rather than becoming themselves manufacturing competitors, and to provide cheap raw materials and agricultural products in exchange for the manufactured goods which they buy. In order to keep their underdeveloped trading "partners" poor, it is generally essential for the manufacturing nations to exercise political control—either through overt colonialism, or more subtly—over the lands they dominate economically. Thus, a local chieftain can be installed in office in a country, and can even, on occasion, be allowed a handsome "royalty" on the raw materials extracted from his land, provided he deposits the great bulk of his resultant nominal wealth in the big banks of the imperialist nation—as is the case with Middle Eastern oil, for instance (though the example has been somewhat oversimplified here).

97

The rest of this paper will be concerned with arguing the Marxist-Leninist case for the right of nations to self-determination considered as a moral issue in *applied philosophy*. This will necessitate 1. some remarks on political philosophy in general, as traditionally understood, and as it ought rather to be understood according to a Marxist view; 2. some discussion of the role and authority of international law, inasmuch as published objections to the principle of national self-determination have sometimes stressed the point that in fact it is not a right encoded formally in international law; 3. a consideration of the *democratic* basis of the right of nations to self-determination, and of exceptions to it, as well as the extent of formal recognition which now has been granted to the self-determination principle internationally; 4. the rebuttal of objections to the national self-determination principle based on radical anti-national considerations or on imaginable electoral complexities; 5. the justification of a definition of nationhood for these purposes, in the light of the democratic end which the principle of national self-determination must serve. Throughout, the object will be to justify, by example as well as by generalized argumentation, an approach to political philosophy which proceeds from an appreciation of the real facts of the contemporary world in which we live.

I. General Remarks on Political Philosophy as a Branch of Ethics

Classical political philosophy is largely balderdash: The central theoretical claims by which the great writers in the field such as Plato, Locke, Rousseau, and Hegel developed their various conflicting systems are propositions with next to no chance of being anywhere near the truth, objectively considered. This does not prevent these systems from being monuments to their creators' genius. It most certainly does not stop them from being impressive human documents of their times. Some can still be highly instructive reading for the perceptive, and even profound, observations they are capable of making about society. But they always made the systematic claim of being far more than that. These classical social philosophers all claimed—even Hegel, in the end—to be establishing a rational political system that possessed universal validity, independent of the changing pattern of human history. It is as such that they ask us to judge their work. And, so considered, their various systems are theoretical castles in the air which the thoughtful modern reader, without "standing on his head," honestly cannot take seriously.

Some of these philosophers were great progressive influences in their time. Historians are well aware of the way in which Locke inspired the ideology of the American Revolution and Rousseau that of the French Revolution. By contrast, Marx and Engels aimed to substantiate their scientific, social theories by reference to verifiable empirical facts. It was, perhaps, traditional political philosophy almost as much as the philosophy of history which they had in mind in their early joint work, *The German Ideology*, where they wrote:

> When reality is depicted, philosophy as an independent branch of knowledge loses its medium of existence. At the best its place can only be taken by a summing-up of the most general results, abstractions which arise from the observation of the historical development of men.

From this point of view the role of political philosophy is a dependent and subordinate one. But that is still not the same as no role at all. Politics is nothing if it is not a sphere of conflict, including the conflict of ideas. The conflicting ideas often concern such things as human rights, liberties, "lesser evils," nations' priorities, nations' "welfare," social justice and injustice. All the topics just listed are ethical topics, and that is no accident, for political debates are frequently debates over what *ought* to be done. Much of the confusion that generally reigns in these debates involves a failure to distinguish clearly the different concepts which are employed. Now, if philosophers have been good at anything, it is the drawing of distinctions— indeed, they often carry it far beyond what is useful or necessary. At any rate, it does look as if there should still be some role for philosophy in drawing important distinctions and clarifying some of the concepts that figure prominently in political debates.

According to this conception of political philosophy, its main contribution is in that branch of applied ethics concerned with the political application of fundamental moral principles in the light of sociological knowledge. Instead of trying to be an independent branch of thought, political philosophy will have to subordinate itself consciously to scientific sociology in order to understand the social world with which it is trying to deal. Accordingly, the *principal* basis of Marxist political theory is to be sought, not in the realm of philosophy at all, but rather in Marxist sociology, the science of "historical materialism."

To assume, however, that there is any role, even a subordinate one, for political philosophy to play in its own right is to assume that there exist specifically political principles of right and wrong, whether possessing universal validity or, as the Marxists claim, valid only for specific societies at specific points in their history. It assumes that not all political questions of right and wrong can always be answered by reference *directly* to general ethical principles which are not concerned specifically with politics. There are philosophers who deny this. They are so attached to their preferred ethical First Principles that they cannot see the place for any Second Principles, as it were, except as rules of thumb indicating how best to carry out the First Principles in various circumstances. Some philosophers, for instance, propound a morality which advocates promoting the greatest happiness for the greatest number of people, no matter what. And many have objected that this is unrealistic. It precludes, for example, any moral principle of *veracity*, as ordinarily conceived.

A Non-political Example:
The Moral Obligation to Tell the Truth

According to the proposed theory of morality, one should tell the truth whenever it will produce more human happiness than lying would; one should lie whenever that will produce more human happiness, even if only slightly more, than telling the truth. But most people have a moral aversion to lying; it hurts them to practice deceit. Not that they never lie; they do, but only after some conflict with their conscience, and it takes more than a *slight* apparent advantage to induce them to tell lies. A person who feels this way about lying will not be induced to lie by the thought that *slightly* more human happiness will be produced (in the long run) if he lies than if he does not. If he has in his conscience a moral aversion to lying, as well as a moral concern for people's happiness, there will be cases, according to the magnitude of the lie or the amount of human happiness at stake, where he sacrifices human happiness for the sake of veracity, as well as cases where he sacrifices veracity for the sake of human happiness. That is the way most people are, psychologically. Nor is this a bad thing. For, if one were really to dispense with any independent aversion for deceit, and set oneself to decide each moral question by reference directly to the "greatest happiness for the greatest number" principle, the odds are strongly— human nature being what it is—that he would *miscalculate* the actual amounts of potential happiness and unhappiness for other people which were involved in many cases where he could, in fact, take the line of least resistance or greatest advantage for himself by telling a lie. People are only too prone to equate the general interest with whatever is to their own selfish advantage. This is why a *certain amount* of psychological rigidity on moral questions can sometimes be to the general advantage. For, owing to the fact that, *in general*, deceit does produce more unhappiness than happiness, the greatest possible happiness of the greatest number is apt to be promoted best when people feel some moral aversion for deceit, in addition to whatever general moral concern they may have for human happiness. On the other hand, too much rigidity would not be in the general interest either. From the standpoint of promoting the greatest happiness for the greatest number of people it is desirable that society's members should feel an emotional attachment not only for this "greatest happiness" principle itself, but for another principle, such as veracity. The idea of adjusting a person's psychology so that as far as his moral conscience were concerned he cared only for the maximization of human happiness has the defect, it is argued, of not actually being in the interests of maximizing human happiness.

A parallel point can be made in connection with socialist ethics. The Marxist, for example, takes the goal of replacing capitalism with socialism as his *fundamental* political principle. Does that mean he cannot have any *other* principles as a socialist? Certainly not. In the interests of socialist revolution, Marxists are in favour of the class struggle of the working class and of the organized labour movement as a highly important part of that struggle. Now, a basic moral principle of trade unionism is the taboo on crossing strikers' picket lines. A "good trade unionist" has an aversion to crossing picket lines and can only be induced to do so for the most weighty of reasons. It is obviously much to the advantage of the cause of unionism that such psychological attitudes should be prevalent. And indeed, committed Marxists are to be found among the staunchest of unionists in this respect. As they see it, it is in the interests of *socialism* that they should have *also* a psychologically independent commitment to the cause of unionism as well; for, without that, the chances are that their overall behaviour would be less serviceable to the cause of socialism. Hence, Marxist ethics can favour the attaching of psychologically independent moral concern to derivative principles, in the area of politics, for instance, as well as to more fundamental principles. It also explains why Marxists are so insistent that no concrete rule of behaviour whatsoever should ever be ascribed absolute moral validity, irrespective of social conditions as they change historically.

For Marxist political philosophy, therefore, the pertinent question will always be: What political principles do *existing* social conditions make desirable. It might be thought after all this that the particular principles which Marxist morality contains ought to be distinctively Marxist, and not such as non-Marxists could also accept. But, in fact, most, if not all, are like the precept against picket-line crossing, accepted by many non-Marxists as well as by Marxists. The principle of national self-determination is another. Indeed, it is not even a specifically working-class precept, although, and not just coincidentally, probably its most prominent champions in this century have been Marxists, who are generally the staunchest democrats around. To defend such a claim country by country through the twentieth century is beyond the scope of this philosophical paper, and in raising the issue of democracy here we are, moreover, getting a little ahead of ourselves.

Before discussing the application of the principle of democracy to world politics, we ought to consider the position of those who object to political philosophy, not on the grounds that nothing is needed to deal with political issues beyond general basic morality, but because that morality has no place in political issues. The objector does not deny that *moral appeals* are common in politics, and even an indispensable part of the politician's trade. He only denies that *sincere* attention to moral considerations has any place in politics as far as the unduped are concerned. He professes to be unduped himself, of course, and prides himself on his own political ruthlessness and lack of principle; or, alternatively, rejecting politics moralistically as being irremediably wicked, he prides himself on how pure and non-political he is; he concentrates on doing good to those around him, and is prepared to let the rest of the world go to blazes. In both cases the individual in question denies the applicability of morality to politics and in both cases the objection to him is a moral one. How can he be so callous? Has he no conscience? How can he face himself if such issues as war and peace, slavery and freedom, mass starvation and prosperity, are entirely matters of indifference to him, morally speaking? Can human actions motivated by moral considerations have any real effect? It is not necessary to suppose that such an effect is a *primary* determinant of what happens politically to answer this question in the affirmative. If moral considerations could have no effect whatever, why are moral appeals in politics so rife? It must be because moral arguments do have some effect. If so, is it not preferable in general that good arguments should prevail over bad ones? If that is the case, then political philosophy does have a role to play.

II. On International Law in General

People who deny the applicability of morality to politics often deny the validity of international law. After all, international law does differ radically in enforcement from the laws of individual countries. In the case of international law, what chiefly secures its observance by the parties affected (governments) is simply their own mutual advantage and convenience. Beyond that, there is nothing but the force of public opinion. But to withhold the weight of one's own opinion from this force, by denying the legal validity of international law, would be justifiable only if promoting the general observance by sovereign states of the rules of behaviour in question were not a morally desirable thing. In claiming that promotion of such observance really is a morally desirable thing, the Marxist need not, of course, maintain that any violation of international law will always be morally wrong.

There are those, however, who oppose the promotion of international law upon moral grounds, in the name of what they call "world law." They object to the fact that the first principle of international law is the principle of national sovereignty. They favour a world government, instead, and to which they want the existing states to surrender their sovereignty and their military force. In the days when the U.S.A. and its allies enjoyed an automatic majority in the United Nations Organization (roughly 1945–1955), and the days when they at least had a predominant influence (roughly 1955–1965), the tendency to look upon the U.N.O. as the beginning of a supra-national authority was much more popular in the NATO countries than it is today. In any case, Marxists would always reject as utopian any dream that sovereign states defending radically conflicting interests from one another would ever agree, without being forced, to surrender a crucial portion of their sovereignty to any authority which they did not have reason to believe would uphold interests substantially compatible to theirs. A state may sometimes voluntarily subordinate itself in certain respects to another, like Canada to the U.S.A., or to an alliance of states, like Italy to the European Economic Community (the "Common Market"), but only when its ruling class calculates that its interests will be best served by taking such a step; in Canada's case for a peaceful share in the economic exploitation of Latin America (among other reasons), in Italy's for a share in the exploitation of Africa and more effective competition against the U.S.A. But where fundamental cleavages of interest exist, no state will ever surrender its sovereignty to an authority *not on its side* unless compelled by the superior force. Thus, promotion of the ideal of a supra-national authority could actually operate to endanger peace in the world.

It may, presumably, be taken for granted that all states and all persons have a very great interest (even if not, in all cases, an overriding interest) in the preservation of world peace insofar as this means the avoidance of thermonuclear war which would almost certainly terminate the lives, either speedily or agonizingly slowly, of the great majority of the readers of these lines as well as their author. Post-1945 history, however, which has seen a number of instances where nuclear war has more or less narrowly been averted, proves that the existence of such a common interest in avoiding it is no *guarantee* at all, in itself, that World War III will continue to be avoided. The co-existence on our planet of socialist and capitalist states, and of capitalist states with fundamentally conflicting interests from each other, is likely to continue for some time. Under these conditions, the existence of international law prescribing the respect by states of one another's sovereignty is one fortunate circumstance for which we can be thankful.

Another good reason for regarding international law as a positive thing under existing conditions is the world fight against imperialism. Since 1945 overt colonialism has been replaced in most cases by "neo-colonialism." Most pre-1945 colonies have now been granted legal independence and sovereignty by the ruling imperial power which often has managed to continue its domination and exploitation, alone or in conjunction with other imperialist powers, principally through reliance upon a local élite which exerts the coercive force of the state. This change is certainly not symptomatic of imperialism's strength, for the new mode of rule is definitely less secure than the old. It sometimes happens that a puppet government may be overthrown, or its rulers may have second thoughts about their foreign subservience. It may be necessary for the imperial powers involved to have recourse to severe economic pressures (directly, or through such institutions as the World Bank and the International Monetary Fund); and, failing that, they may turn to armed action, preferably through a foreign-organized coup d'état from within but, if necessary, as a last resort, by means of a direct military invasion, such as the U.S. attack upon Cuba in 1961, or the more successful French action against Gabon in 1964. Here is where international law enters the picture, for it expressly forbids direct or indirect armed action by one state against another state's sovereignty. The promotion of international law in the world community accordingly makes such actions that much more difficult for their perpetrators. Though certainly not developed historically for any anti-imperialist purposes, the actual thrust of international law under today's conditions is by and large anti-imperialist in operation. Under today's conditions, international law tends to operate in favour of the principle of national self-determination. Therefore, Marxists should be in favour of it.

III. Self-Determination as a Democratic Requirement

To justify international law morally by reference to the principle of national self-determination illustrates the political priority accorded here to the self-determination principle. Its justification in turn, as suggested above, is democratic. How could anyone be a genuine democrat without acknowledging the right of a nation to determine for itself its own form of government, including its governmental relationships with other nations? But to call this a right is not to call it an absolute right. As Lenin wrote in 1916, in the context of arguing *for* the recognition of such a right, against the views of other Marxist theorists, like Rosa Luxemburg, who were inclined to oppose it:

> The several demands of democracy, including self-determination, are not an absolute, but only a *small part* of the general-democratic (now: general-socialist) *world* movement. In individual concrete cases, the part may contradict the whole; if so, it must be rejected.

A relatively non-controversial example of this may be found in the way Germany's right to national self-determination was quite properly set aside in May, 1945 in the higher interests of world peace, anti-fascism, and the national rights of Germany's neighbours.

Some readers may find it strange to see Lenin speaking here of the world socialist movement as a continuation of the world democratic movement. In this, however, he just follows in the footsteps of Marx and Engels, who wrote in the *Communist Manifesto*:

> ... the first step in the revolution by the working class, is to raise the proletariat to the position of ruling class, to win the battle of democracy.

If "democracy" means *rule by the people*, how can there be democracy in the economic sphere unless the people rule it; and how can the people rule it without owning it? And if economics is as sociologically basic as historical materialism claims, how can there be anything more than *formal* democracy in society at all without the social ownership of the materials and equipment used in production? That, at any rate, is how Marxists reason on the subject.

This is not the place to argue at length for the principle of *democracy*. Like other moral-political principles, it, too, is not eternal in the Marxist view, and only modern conditions have made it feasible. The existing productive technology and consequent social order in the European Middle Ages, for instance, clearly made a functioning democracy out of the question. But where it is practicable, government by the will of the governed seems obviously more likely to meet the governed people's needs than any alternative. In this connection, Marxists will readily endorse the words of Thomas Jefferson: "Sometimes it is said that man cannot be trusted with the government of himself. Can he, then, be trusted with the government of others?"

Though from a Marxist perspective the principle of national self-determination is certainly more fundamental than the principle of respect for international law, it is worth noting that for its part the self-determination principle, while not enshrined in international law in any binding way, has been accorded legal recognition to the extent of an explicit mention in the United Nations Charter (included, it is said, as a sop to the Soviet Union). The second of the four stated purposes of the United Nations is "to develop friendly relations among nations based on respect for the equal rights and self-determination of peoples."

IV. Objections to Self-Determination on Anti-National or Electoral Grounds

When talking about *self-determination* we are, of course, talking above all about the democratic right of secession from a country or from an empire. The parallel right of separate nations to band together in an alliance, a confederacy, a federation, or even a unitary state, will scarcely be contested. But the exercise of a right of secession is bound to "rock the boat." There are bound to be loud voices (if not guns) of protest.

In Canada the most prominent theoretical critic of the self-determination concept has long been Pierre Elliott Trudeau. A very vocal democrat, he has never expressly denied the right of national self-determination, but he has stubbornly rejected any explicit recognition of it on the grounds that anything promoting the concept of the nation in the sphere of politics and government is dangerous and reactionary. As a private citizen in 1965, for example, he wrote:

> From a philosophical point of view, the aim of a political society is not the glorification of a 'national fact' (in its ethnic sense). A state that defined its function essentially in terms of ethnic attributes would inevitably become chauvinistic and intolerant.

The main reason why national chauvinism is objectionable is that nations exhibiting it oppress and exploit other nations. To recognize the right of all nations to self-determination is therefore to strike a blow against imperialist oppression and exploitation. But to oppose such recognition on the grounds that it would encourage chauvinism is clearly to turn the whole question on its head. In today's world it is not the anti-imperialist side that stands to benefit from such an attitude.

Some of the theoretical argumentation which has been published against the principle of national self-determination revolves around such questions as: How would a nation's will be expressed? In a referendum? In the election to office in the territory occupied by the nation in question of a new government pledged to a policy of secession? In the election of a secessionist government by the majority vote of the citizenry? By a mere plurality? These difficulties lose their interest as serious *objections* to the self-determination of nations when it is noticed that, if they really were, they would be objections also to

106

democracy itself. In practice many nations—and the United States was not the first of these—have had to exercise their right of self-determination by means of armed insurrection. It is unlikely that a break-away movement in a subject nation could ever without *at least* majority support succeed in winning an armed revolt against the ruling state, which always starts out in such wars clearly possessing the preponderant advantage in military strength, in economics, and in control of the police, the government bureaucracy, the communications network, and the media of propaganda. Where it is possible for a nation to exercise its right of self-determination in a peaceful way through a voting procedure, the particular conditions of the case will determine what exact method of testing the nation's will is going to be employed. In general, it is hard to fault the plebiscitary method by which Newfoundland and Labrador, after two successive ballotings among three different initial alternatives, opted to join the Canadian Confederation in 1949.

V. What is a Nation?

Perhaps the most persistent line of theoretical criticism of the right of nations to self-determination has centred on the problem of defining what a *nation* is. Since what is at issue here is the right of a part of a state to secede from its rule, there is no point in using the word "nation" in that sense which is relevant in the context of discussions on "international" law, for instance, where the word "nation" is simply another synonym for "state." We must use "nation," in this context, to stand for a sociological unit whose existence as a separate state would not be out of the question as a practical proposition if it were to choose such a separate existence and other nations did not interfere with its independence. We must use "nation" for a group of people whose political self-determination it would be reasonable to call undemocratic to deny.

Doubtless the standard definition of the concept of a *nation* current in Marxist circles is still that of Stalin:

> A nation is a historically evolved, stable community of language, territory, economic life, and psychological make-up manifested in a community of culture.

How original his writings on the national question really were we need not inquire here. His famous definition of a *nation* has been attacked on a number of grounds by Marxist as well as non-Marxist writers, but if we are careful not to take it too rigidly (a fault which it could be argued he himself did not avoid), the stated definition will still stand up fairly well for the most part.

There are, indeed, points on which the definition apparently could benefit from some elaboration or amendment. For instance, a good case can be made for interpreting the "community of culture" criterion for nationhood as including the requirement of a *national consciousness*, that is, some active sense on the part of a population that they jointly constitute a nation. Such a stipulation might seem unnecessary, since only populations which do possess such a sense of nationhood are going to demand the right of self-determination in any event, but the proviso will be of actual use in some cases in delimiting the boundaries between nations—that is, it is not always going to be clear-cut what nation a population belongs to; and what nation it *thinks* it belongs to may sometimes be the deciding factor. It may seem that such a proviso must needs make the definition objectionably circular—and, certainly, someone who did not know what the word "nation" meant would hardly be enlightened sufficiently by being told it meant a group of people who, among other things, considered themselves to be a nation. We can avoid this difficulty here, however, by understanding "national consciousness" as a population's sense of possessing jointly a *right* to exist together as a separate country should they so choose.

A noteworthy feature of Stalin's definition is that in addition to ethnographic factors it expressly mentions two further criteria of nationhood: The necessity of a common territory and economic life. As far as territory is concerned, the point of including it is obvious. A population, such as Europe's gypsies, however cohesive otherwise, plainly cannot even be considered a candidate for existence as a separate country if it does not possess a common territory. It could not demand the right of self-determination in the name of democracy unless there were a territory which it occupied and in which it constituted the majority of the population. The same would clearly apply to the Jewish people living outside of Israel if they were more ethnographically homogeneous than they are. The requirement of a common economic life, however, is more debatable. Are North and South Korea two different nations just because (thanks to the U.S. military occupation of the South) the economic life of one of them is capitalist while the economic life of the other is socialist? Certainly no Korean, of whatever political stripe, will consent to the denial that Korea is a single nation. The requirement of a common economic life for any nation entitled to political self-determination as a unit should perhaps be amended to require only potential *economic viability* as a separate state. Even formulated like this, the economic requirement is probably still strong enough to exclude from nationhood the Innuit (Eskimo) people of Northern Canada *at this time* although they do seem to qualify as a nation on most of the other counts. To protest against the injustice of their treatment by the Canadian government it is not necessary to demand formal recognition for them of a right of secession.

The French-Canadian people of Quebec are another story entirely. Here is a sociologically clear-cut case of nationhood, if ever there was one. Another such example is the population of Puerto Rico. It seems clear also, on the whole, that the Israelis now constitute a nation in the sense defined, as do the Arab Palestinians who live in the territory conquered by Israel in its 1967 attack.

But is Northern Ireland a separate nation? Southerners and Northern Catholics argue it is not, on the grounds that it has too much in common with the rest of Ireland, including an actual Catholic majority in much of the Six Counties which make up the Province of Northern Ireland. On that basis, it is not Northern Ireland which would have the right of self-determination as regards unity or otherwise with the Irish Republic, but rather the population of Ireland as a whole. By the same token, the secessionist Confederacy in the southern United States in 1860 (even if we disregard the lack of support for it of the Black population which constituted a majority in large parts of its territory) was likewise no separate nation entitled to secession at will.

It is important to note here that to endorse the secession of any *part* of a nation that chooses to separate, however democratic such a principle can be made to appear, is actually undemocratic because it would in practice enable the interests of the majority of a nation to be adversely affected, perhaps gravely, by the actions of a minority, even if they do happen to be collected together territorially. If the territory in question should happen to be rich in oil or some other natural resource, it is very easy to imagine some imperialist power colluding with a local élite to break the territory away and deprive the majority of any democratic say over the development of that natural resource. That is more or less what Britain did with Kuwait before oil was discovered there, when port facilities were the issue at stake. That is what the U.S.A. did with Panama, which was part of Colombia until the Colombian government showed itself to be insufficiently co-operative with U.S. plans to dig a canal through its territory.

It seems plain that to allot a right of self-determination to any region or locality whatever, regardless of all ethnographic considerations, would turn out to be destructive of the real exercise of self-determination in practice and is thus a highly undemocratic idea in its actual tendency. For its actual tendency is evidently to subvert the democratic right of self-determination altogether. Indeed, one published objection to the principle of national self-determination is precisely that the nation is an *arbitrary* unit to exercise such a right, and, since *no* unit could be credited with such a right without denying it to other units, therefore no population whatsoever should be regarded as possessing any right of self-determination. This argument, however, proves too much. It shows precisely that the nation is *not* an arbitrary choice of unit to credit with a right of self-determination; for it shows that, unless some sociological unit such as that defined by Stalin can be taken as entitled to determine its own political destiny, there can be no meaningful general claim of a right to self-determination at all; and yet, without self-determination at some level or other, there can be no real democracy. If we *start* from a position of commitment to a right of self-determination in the name of democracy, then *the nation*, as sociologically understood, will have to be the only reasonable candidate in sight to credit with such a right. It is not possible to reconcile any alternative position with the requirements of democracy.

Since the criteria of nationhood that are mentioned in the stated definition do all admit of variations in degree, it is not at all surprising that there should be plenty of bona fide *intermediate cases* in the real world of the present day. Is Scotland still a nation? Probably it is. Is Newfoundland still a nation? Possibly not. What about the Turkish Cypriots? Constituting less than one-fifth of the population of Cyprus, they were scattered about the island with no common territory until the 1974 invasion of the Turkish Army and the deliberate forcible resettlement of large numbers of Greek Cypriots. A persuasive case could no doubt be made for the nationhood of the Black population in those areas of the U.S. South where they constitute a majority, but for the demographic fact that the great majority of U.S. Blacks live outside of those areas, and but for the fact, as it appears, that the great majority even of those Blacks who do live in those areas actually consider themselves as belonging, together with their white compatriots, to a single people, of U.S. nationality. That in itself would arguably militate against their possessing a sufficiently separate "community of culture" for distinct nationhood.

How does the principle of national self-determination apply to sub-Saharan Africa? Not very well in those areas where a tribal economy of hunting and gathering or self-sufficient peasant farming still prevails sufficiently to fragment the population and prevent the emergence, as yet, of fully-fledged cohesive *nations* in the sociological sense which we have been discussing. Does that mean that such populations should be ruled by others, by whites for example? Of course not. As this paper has argued, the role played by the self-determination principle is subordinate to the democratic principle. Where the subordinate principle breaks down, the more basic principle may still be directly applicable. It is still possible to differentiate among African regimes as more or as less democratic, as more or else less based on the will of the people, even in those areas where sociological conditions at present rule out full recourse to the principle of national self-determination. Only a superstitious reverence towards man-made principles will insist upon treating them as universal absolutes.

It is, indeed, precisely the *dialectical* merit of the Marxist method to insist on the necessity of approaching politics, just as other subjects, with definite concrete principles in mind, and to insist likewise on the profound folly of taking any such principles as absolutely valid. Orthodox political theory, as taught in our universities today, is most apt to assume that, while it is possible, perhaps, to study society scientifically, and while it is possible—and very human—to pass judgements upon it, pro and con, from a moral point of view, there is no possible way of doing both at once so as to arrive at scientifically based value judgements upon political questions. The Marxist view-point defended here has no sympathy with such an academic outlook. It definitely is not content just to record the doings of men in society, or even just to record them by attaching suitable labels of "good" and "bad" without seeking that deeper understanding of social phenomena and rational justification of moral verdicts for which social *theory* is requisite. At the same time, Marxism has no use for that brand of social theorizing which is conducted at such a stratospheric level of abstraction as not to allow any place for principled scientific attention to the actual struggles of real people and of oppressed nations confronting twentieth-century imperialism. As the young Karl Marx wrote in 1845: "The philosophers have only *interpreted* the world, in various ways; the point is to *change* it."

Selected Bibliography

V. I. Lenin, *Imperialism, The Highest Stage of Capitalism* (1916).

Kwame Nkrumah, *Neo-Colonialism, The Last Stage of Imperialism*, London, 1965.

Pierre Jalée, *The Third World in World Economy*, New York, 1969.

Keith Buchanan, *The Geography of Empire*, Nottingham, 1972.

Vasil Vakhrushev, *Neo-Colonialism: Methods and Manoeuvres*, Moscow, 1973.

V. I. Lenin, *Critical Remarks on the National Question* (1913).

V. I. Lenin, *The Right of Nations to Self-Determination* (1916).

Joseph Stalin, *Marxism and the National Question, Selected Writings and Speeches*, New York, 1942.

Horace B. Davis, *Nationalism & Socialism, Marxist and Labor Theories of Nationalism to 1917*, New York, 1967.

Pierre Elliott Trudeau, *Federalism and the French Canadians*, Toronto, 1968.

Stanley French and Andres Gutman, "The Principle of National Self-determination," in *Philosophy, Morality, and International Affairs*, edited by Virginia Held, Sidney Morganbesser, and Thomas Nagel, New York, 1974.

"Citizens" and "Brutes":
A Philosophical Dialogue

RODGER BEEHLER
GEORGE T. MONTICONE

1ST GENT.: Man is not so unique as he would like to believe. Our ancestry is firmly rooted in the animal world. And if in a time of need we seek a deeper knowledge concerning ourselves we can only come to it by exploring those animal horizons from which, in the course of evolution, we have made our little march. It is time we started thinking of ourselves less as fallen angels, and more as risen apes as Robert Ardrey suggests in *African Genesis.*

2ND GENT.: What could we possibly learn about ourselves by studying the animals from which we have evolved?

1ST GENT.: Well for one thing we could come to appreciate that property, war, and social organization are not human inventions, but are all found in the animal kingdom.

2ND GENT.: Structured societies in the animal kingdom?

1ST GENT.: Not only structured societies, and hierarchy, but morality too. The evidence assembled by the new biology discloses no qualitative break between the moral nature of the animal and the moral nature of man. Evolution has equipped the animal world with innate behavioural commands restraining the interests of the individual on behalf of the species or group, and these commands are every bit as severe—and a good deal more effective—than any handed down by a bearded god to the human species. You should read Robert Ardrey's *The Territorial Imperative.*

2ND GENT.: You speak of 'innate behavioural commands'. Do you mean something like instinct? But if an animal instinctively follows a course of behaviour which works to the benefit of the group or species, isn't this very different from acting out of consideration for justice or right? Can anything which is done instinctively be a case of *moral* action or judgment?

1ST GENT.: I don't see why it cannot be. It is surely obvious that what we call human morality is a series of restraints and demands imposed upon individuals for the sake of the other members of the group; and the same kinds of restraints and sacrifice are observable among other species. The South African naturalist Eugene Marais observed an encounter between a leopard and a baboon troop returning to their lair at dusk. Marais watched two male baboons edge along a rock jutting out above the leopard's passage. The leopard, if he saw

113

them, ignored them, keeping his attention fixed on the screeching, defenseless horde scrambling among the rocks. The two males dropped on the leopard from a height of twelve feet. One bit at his spine. The other tore at the leopard's throat while clinging to his neck from below. In an instant the leopard disembowelled with his hind claws the baboon hanging to his neck, and caught in his jaws the baboon on his back. But the dying, disembowelled baboon hung on long enough to reach with his canine teeth the leopard's jugular vein.

On another occasion a baboon troop left several dead in fleeing from a predator. Among the dead was a mother, whose infant clung to her corpse. A surviving baboon returned, snatched up the infant, and fled. If people shy away from calling this morality, isn't it merely because they continue to be influenced by the Christian myth about the human soul, rules of good and evil introduced by God, and so on? Once we own up to our evolutionary past and learn that there is social control and cooperation among all kinds of animals groups, are we not forced to accept that what we have liked to think was the unique dispensation (or invention) of man is, in fact, an inheritance from our animal origins?

2ND GENT.: In other words morality is instinctive?

1ST GENT.: Not only morality, but also aggression, and the urge to acquire a territory. Studies reveal that virtually every species of animal strives, either individually or as a group, to mark out and defend against others of its kind a space or territory. This is true of birds, fish, mammals, and the primates. Countless children have observed how the red sword-tail introduced into a tropical tank will strive immediately through strength and pugnacity to intimidate and dominate his fellows until there quickly is established an ordered hierarchy in which the most successful and aggressive appropriate the best positions and opportunities. One has only to read a little of the massive documentation of these matters to conclude that aggression, the staking out of a territory, and what could only be called moral behaviour, are not human inventions.

2ND GENT.: Perhaps. But putting aside this question (whether these are the appropriate descriptions for the kinds of behaviour you report) you have not yet shown even that they are instinctive. All you have established is that animals do act as you say. But to show that these things are done is not to show that they are done instinctively.

1ST GENT.: But what else could explain their being done? Consider two cuckoos who fight for exclusive domain above an oak tree beside some English field. Neither will homestead this embattled territory, for the cuckoo is parasitical and builds no nest of his own. Neither will use his conquest to accomplish romantic ends, for the cuckoo is polyandrous, and when the fighting is done these males will share the same bride. Yet they compete for this territory, simply because they must. They compete for reasons of the ancient law of instinct, stern and abiding, forgotten by men and cuckoos.

Consider the rare marsh warbler, who in low, flat osier beds beside some sluggish stream stakes out his claim, patrols his territories, and sings his marvelous song. Vigilant, pugnacious, he cocks his feathers at the breeze. But the female warbler is still winging her migrant way from reedy southern places. So alone is our hero in the scattered marsh-warbler universe in which he performs that it cannot be said that he *competes* for anything—glory, food supply, or wing-tip space. But in a marsh-warbler economy of 'abundance,' he must still play the role of the propertied competitor, fulfilling oldtime laws natural to a world of crowded species, though inappropriate to the contemporary world of the marsh warbler. Surely this shows that what explains the bird's behaviour is instinct?

2ND GENT.: Why should it show that? The mere fact that the behaviour is continued in inappropriate conditions does not show that what gave rise to the behaviour was (and is) instinct. Habit may explain its perseverance. But in the beginning it could have been learned. And it will do no good (if I may anticipate you) to come back and insist that behaviour of this sort is clearly the work of 'natural selection'—the possession of a territory obviously favouring survival, and so on—and so must therefore be genetically transmitted. For a competence or trait can be transmitted other than genetically. The behaviour which favoured survival may have been intelligent, learned behaviour, which was in turn picked up from the parents by the maturing offspring, who *reached* maturity, and had progeny of their own, because of their parents' favouring practices and capacities. The competence or capacity could then be continually transmitted in the group through a growing (genetic) intelligence endowment, or by instruction, or by both. To show (supposing you could) that a piece of behaviour has been naturally selected is not to rule out the behaviour being an intelligent, learned, activity. All you will have called attention to is that animals having this sort of intelligent capacity are better placed to survive than others. You will not have shown that the piece of behaviour in question is instinctively engaged in.

1ST GENT.: But look! Experiment shows that the drive for territory is even stronger and more relentless than the drive for sex. And the drive for sex is a *paradigm* of what we mean by an instinct. I've already mentioned how if you place several male sword-tails in a tropical tank they will rapidly arrange themselves in an obvious hierarchy in competition for food, females, and territory. Now if the water of the tank is cooled, the time will come when the male will lose all interest in sex. *But he will still fight for his status.* Would it not be odd if a drive so tenaciously persisted in, even over and beyond so powerful an urge as sex, were not deeply rooted in the nature of the animal?

2ND GENT.: What exactly do you mean by 'deeply rooted in the nature of the animal'?

1ST GENT.: I mean the animal has these drives or impulses from birth. They are inherited from his forbears. They are a *natural* disposition, and not in any way the result of social experience or learning. They are not the outcome of artifice but of instinct.

2ND GENT.: You earlier mentioned property: According to you, the drive on the part of the animal to possess a territory—which I assume is what you mean by 'property in the animal kingdom'—is something the animal is *compelled* to embark upon. It is not a passion or preoccupation he acquires as a result of developing and seeking to survive in a certain biological and 'social' situation?

1ST GENT.: Exactly. This territorial instinct may, in different species, be fulfilled in different ways. And exclusive possession of territory ordinarily will assure a good supply of food, attract mates, secure against a predator and prevent overcrowding. Nevertheless, while *we* may identify benefits and purposes deriving from the territorial practice, the animal staking out a claim seizes simply for reasons of seizing. If man is so rarely conscious of the ultimate reasons for his actions, it seems highly improbable that the animal should be better informed. And man, and the animal, will fulfill their territorial instinct, as has been spectacularly demonstrated, whether or not benefit will accrue.

2ND GENT.: Be careful. It does not follow that because a man is unconscious of the reasons for which he acts that his behaviour is instinctive. To be unconscious of the reasons for one's actions is still *to have reasons* for acting. It is not to act instinctively. So your remark about men contributes nothing to your assertion about animals.

1ST GENT.: But look: The biology of our century has presented us with the evidence to demonstrate that our attachment to property is of an ancient biological order. Consider the value of a territory to a pair of animals who are mating. Through isolation of the pair on the mutual property, a guarantee is effected that neither will desert the family obligations. In addition, the mysterious enhancement of powers which a territory invariably summons in its male proprietor places energy otherwise unavailable at family disposal. If such enhancement of energy occurs in man, then one cannot explain it as a cultural lesson. On the contrary, the reverse is true: This instinctive enhancement of energy (or lack of it) is what explains particular cultural phenomena. It

116

is here, for example, that we find the explanation of the success of American agriculture and the failure of Soviet agriculture.

2ND GENT.: That in the one case there is private property and in the other there is not?

1ST GENT.: Yes.

2ND GENT.: But suppose someone replies that in the Soviet case there is *group* property?

1ST GENT.: There is; but it is not a proprietorship appropriate to the human territorial nature.

2ND GENT.: Which is genetic and ineradicable?

1ST GENT.: Yes. The materials presented in the new biological and anthropological research just show that there is no reason to accept the central assumption of most human thought about our species, that (with the exception of sex and familial attachment) human behaviour results from causes lying within the human historical experience, and that the direction of human behaviour, therefore, lies within the jurisdiction of enlightened man. This romantic fallacy is no longer tenable. What we now know of animals shows that human behaviour in its broad patterns cannot with any assurance be attributed to causes lying within the human social experience.

To continue to believe that the human obsession with social status and material possessions is unrelated to the animal instincts for dominance and territory would be to press notions of 'special creation' to the breaking point. To believe that the loyalties or animosities of tribes or nations are other than the human expression of the territorial instinct would be to push reason over the cliff. To accept that feminine attraction for wealth and rank, and masculine preoccupation with fortune, power and fame are human aberrations, arising from sexual insecurity, hidden physical defects, childhood guilts, environmental deficiencies, the class struggle, or the cumulative moral erosions of advancing civilization, would in the light of our new knowledge of animal behaviour be to return man's gift of reason to its Pleistocene sources, unopened.

2ND GENT.: But you yourself pointed at the very beginning to the existence of *social* life among animals. And it seems to me that it is precisely the social nature of those practices which interest you— certainly the human practices—that you are overlooking.

1ST GENT.: But I have stressed the social nature of these practices all along, *including* the human practices! Their social nature is precisely their contribution to the survival of the species. This is the implication of what has been observed in birds. The mutual territory of a pair of the species guarantees against desertion, generates energy for the family survival—

117

2ND GENT.: —But you continually assert all this as though it established that underlying this behaviour and explaining its occurrence is instinct. But again, merely to establish that a practice has survival value is not to establish that it is instinctive. The practice of fastening one's seat belt may have considerable survival value, but it is patently clear that it is not instinctively performed. Your remarks about 'energy enhancement' are just as weak. Even supposing there *is* such a thing in animals, and that it is an instinctive response to 'proprietorship,' this hardly establishes either that it occurs in man, or that, if it does, it is instinctive in man. Your argument is of the form: "X can be seen to occur among humans. And X can be seen to occur among animals. Therefore, X is instinctive." But why should we believe that simply because a form of behaviour is observable in animals, it is instinctive in humans?

Even more importantly, I would like to go back to your remark about culture, and what could or could not be a 'cultural lesson'? You have rightly insisted on the importance of something of which many may not be aware: that there is social organization among animals.

But given that animals do have these features, and manifest this behaviour, can we not perhaps explain it differently from what you suggest? Rather than claim that human behaviour is instinctive as it resembles animal behaviour, could we not claim that animal behaviour is, at least in some respects, non-instinctive insofar as it resembles human behaviour?

Rousseau, for one, would wish to claim that most human behaviour is not instinctive. And while no one today (not even someone with as little knowledge of ethology as I) wants to assert what Rousseau asserted—that humans originally lived independent and isolated lives, coming together only to reproduce—this does not detract from what is surely his indubitable insight into the connection between (for example) the institution of property *and social life*: Property is both a social convention, *and* a preoccupation which we have as a result of coming to be raised in a certain 'climate' of values, activities, aspirations, etc. Rousseau's account of the passions and social practices of men as internally related to their developing maturation in an ongoing social life is logically independent of his *a priori* theorizing about how social relations first arise. The important point is his insistence that what men come to desire and value and do is not 'there' from the beginning but comes to be as a result of education and development.

1ST GENT.: 'Comes to be' how, exactly?

2ND GENT.: Well, for example, Rousseau holds that envy, or the desire to be esteemed by others, are human passions which *arise* through living in relatedness to others. They are unintelligible apart from social life. And social life is sufficient to explain their existence, provided we allow as a primitive given what Rousseau calls self-love, or what we might call a shrinking from pain and a seeking of satisfaction and well-being.

1ST GENT.: Which surely are instinctive!

2ND GENT.: Perhaps they are. But the point is that *what gives* pain and *what gives* satisfaction are modifiable, and are modified, through time, as the human animal grows, and attachments, ideals, ambitions, influences claim him, lose their hold, are replaced by others, and so on. Thus, the desire of a human for property is not a necessary desire, in the sense that qua human being with this biological structure, genetic endowment, etc. one strives for property. For one thing, the child has to learn what property *is.* But more importantly: It is at least conceivable that there should be a society in which property as we know it—in land, certainly and in the substances that sustain life—should neither exist, nor be sought after, nor valued. You talk of 'territory' and 'property,' and do not even consider the difference, for example, between 'private' and 'common property.'

1ST GENT.: If I don't, it's only because one cannot say everything at once. In fact, there is a difference in respect of the various animal species as to whether they strive to appropriate and defend a 'private' or 'group' property. It depends on whether they are social or non-social animals.

2ND GENT.: But we are social animals, and yet the territorial drive that you assert is instinctive *in us* is *private* property (witness your remarks about Soviet and American agriculture). This is beside the main point, however, which is that property or aggression do not have a biological origin, but are the result of an intelligent and emotional response to certain social conditions of life.

1ST GENT.: I still don't see what you mean.

2ND GENT.: Well, consider what you call aggression. According to you, aggression, like the drive to acquire a territory (to which presumably aggression is related), is instinctive. But think of an infant human being. The child is from the beginning treated in certain ways. His or her needs are provided for, and, one would like to think, affection is shown the child, not only by attention to the child's wants and needs, but through caresses, play, and in all manner of ways. As the child grows, and becomes increasingly conscious of his environment, he also becomes increasingly conscious of himself, and of others as conscious of him. He also comes to form an attachment to those around him, first, because of their ministering to his basic needs, but in time because their company and attention and affection *become one of his needs.* It comes to matter to him that they include him in their company, and

119

that they care for him. He comes consciously to value standing in a certain way in their eyes and affections. He comes to wish for the esteem and regard of others of his kind.

In the *Discourse on Inequality*, Rousseau speaks of this desire arising in man only after social relations have been entered into by scattered groups of human beings. But the claim survives if we simply translate it into the thesis that it is through living in social relations (of a certain kind) with other human beings that man comes to be concerned with how others of his kind value and esteem him—which is quite different from being concerned about whether or not they will assist one in one's physical labour, or in the defense of one's territory, or whether they are able to force one to retreat to a less fortunate position in respect of food, mates, and so on.

1ST GENT.: Why is it different?

2ND GENT.: Precisely because what is desired and sought in each case is different. The 'drive,' to use your idiom, is for something different.

1ST GENT.: But why can't we say that the drive, or desire, for esteem is merely a manifestation of the drive to acquire property, females, and so on? It is just a different expression of the same instinctive seeking.

2ND GENT.: Because for one thing, the importance to a man of how others esteem him—whether, say, he has their respect—may conflict with his desire to acquire property or to enjoy the favour of some female; so he may refrain from a corrupt practice, or keep from adultery, because to do so would mean that he could not keep his self-respect, and would lose the respect of others whom he admires and cherishes, and whose friendship and affection is one of the joys of his life.

Rousseau at least is able to make sense of such a man. On his story of the human condition, a man may be careless of opportunities to make money, or acquire or extend a proprietorship, or insinuate himself onto the treadway to eminence and power, simply because he is claimed by other things. On your account every man is instinctively on the make. Maybe everyone is, *in our society*. But Rousseau would insist that in these last three words lies the truth about the human condition.

In the case of property, for example, he held that, as the relations of property are in a society, so will the social attachments and projects, and the individual character of men, tend to be. It was this conviction that led him to stress the absolute importance of every citizen having enough land to be self-sufficient economically. Where there are considerable inequalities of wealth, especially in relation to land, the substances that sustain and husband life, some will be dependent for their livelihood on others. From this inequality alone, you get different conditions of life and the possibility of envy on the part of the poor and contempt on the part of the rich—even the possibility of self-disgust on the part of some of those who are deprived, and who value themselves in terms of what the rich have (the ultimate form of subjection). The recognition that one's opportunities are subject to the dispensation of another can lead to feelings of insecurity and to servility before those on whom one depends. But the power of those who have wealth (and so possess the effective cause of other people's happiness or loss) may lead to a lust for power itself. A child may begin by wishing to be the centre of attention because it wishes others to provide what it desires. In time, however, the child may come to delight most in being able to require of others attention and care. So too, the powerful man, who begins by seeking power as the means to the achievement of pleasures after which he strives, may in time come to find in his exercise of power over others his most compelling attraction and lust.

1ST GENT.: But surely Rousseau's insistence upon the need for every man to be economically self-sufficient supports, rather than takes away from, my view?

2ND GENT.: On the contrary, it opposes your view. The central implication of Rousseau's position is that not every property arrangement is conflict-making, but that the utility of property (together with an awareness of what property is) is learned, and that the passion for property is mutable. It is possible that there could be a society in which there was not anything that could be called a passion for property at all.

1ST GENT.: So the predatory man is the product of evil social conditions. Man is neither good nor bad, but society makes him so.

History surely shows that this utopian idea is false; that human nature is far more rigid and unconquerable than you suppose. Look at all the so-called socialist republics. Not one of them (*pace,* Marx) has ever managed to get rid of property, let alone hostility, vice, or misery. This precept, "Change the relations of property, and you will have no state, no war, no aggression," is so much fiction masquerading as science.

2ND GENT.: I'd hardly call your remarks a fair hearing. To begin with, what *is* a change in property relations? Or better, what did Marx mean by such a change? Did he mean only a *legal* change? Or did he mean something nearer to what could only be described as a moral change (to which the legal change was expected to contribute)? To put it differently, did he assert that *only* a change in property relations was necessary? I seem to remember him placing a good deal of importance upon what he calls the consciousness of the population.

Surely we have to distinguish between a change in *the form of social organization*, and a change in what we might call *social judgments or valuations*. What explains the little difference 'socialism' has made in Eastern Europe is that all that has been accomplished there is a legal change.

1ST GENT.: But doesn't the fact that that *is* all that has been accomplished prove my point!

2ND GENT.: By showing that the instincts you allege are relentlessly operative? I don't think it does. It is wholly plausible to argue that what explains the non-preparedness of many of the Eastern Europeans to embrace Socialism is a consequence of their much older traditions of ownership and social life, not to mention their religious allegiances. But to say this is not to say that those traditions are the outcome of instinct. They are *historical* 'artifacts,' which could have been different from what they were. Being what they were, however, they have profoundly affected men's self-conceptions, aspirations, and social commitments.

This difference between social judgments and 'legal' institutions (especially where these last are importantly dependent upon force) is as great as that I drew attention to in the beginning: The difference between acting out of instinct and acting out of consideration for justice. Rousseau has at least this advantage over you, that he allows both for human passion and for human *reason*, which last he sees is importantly a matter of education and experience. What a man thinks, and the reasons which claim his assent, are internally related to the climate of (often conflicting) beliefs, judgments, and aspirations in which he comes to maturity, and is thereafter constantly subject to its influence. Stressing both passion and reason, Rousseau is thus able to allow for human action, for the integration of passion and reason to yield an intelligent and deliberate venture; and for human development—for new passions and commitments and projects succeeding others as the human being's capacities, knowledge and relationships are extended, changed, and transformed. On your account, on the other hand, the behaviour which gives rise to human conflict looks as though it must be regarded as proceeding unreasoningly from the human animal as a fixed repertoire of behaviour. And by 'unreasoningly' I don't mean 'without intelligence.' I mean without any response to or effect upon the human animal of his or her *social life*, and without anything that could be called judgment and intention. So (for example) you insist that we all have an instinctive drive to dominate. But while this assertion may (or may not) be appropriate to a baboon tribe, in respect of the human group it overlooks the commitment which many come to have to justice—justice *not only* for their own tribal members, but for other tribes as well.

122

1ST GENT.: But again the romantic fallacy! The myth of plasticity! You fail to see that so much of human behaviour is otherwise explainable. For instance: Biologists have discovered an interesting relationship foreshadowed in the work of Herbert Spencer and William Graham Summer. Each of these men showed remarkable insight in noting that there exists a relationship between conflict within a group and hazards to which the group is exposed. Each in his own fashion hypothesized that as external hazard increases, so does internal amity. The evidence of human history overwhelmingly supports this hypothesis. Politicians would do well to heed its implications. The continued viability of South Africa despite world boycotts and sanctions, the solidarity of Israel in the face of the Arab League—all attest to this fundamental truth so clearly seen in numerous studies in ethology. Witness the penguin, who becomes the paradigm of benevolence to his fellows during the months of the long, harsh, polar night, huddling close to them, all the while holding a penguin egg on his foot; or consider the blue goose, who is a tyrant toward his aquatic neighbors, yet is a veritable saint to those members of his immediate group.

The implications of this principle of behaviour are far-reaching and crystal clear in outline. Since the invention of the atom bomb, war is an anachronism. The validity of the nation-state wanes. In the face of this, we must create—if we are to live in relative amity—strangers, well-defined subgroups, *in our midst.* The Canadians and Belgians are most fortunate in this respect. The non-destructive hostility engendered by the failure to communicate which is inevitable in a bilingual society guarantees countless amicable future generations. But most societies are not so fortunate. We must strive to create harmless hostility.

But I have strayed from my main line of thought. While I should be the first to congratulate those who contributed to the formulation of what I shall term 'the code of enmity,' I believe they failed to see through the romantic fallacy. For each held that human 'social engineering' could, in time, free men from the harsh demands of the code of enmity.

2ND GENT.: You claim that because the 'code of enmity' holds both for animals and humans, then since animal compliance to the code is instinctive, so must be human compliance. But this is the very form of reasoning which we earlier saw was unsatisfactory in connection with territoriality. You have not made it clear why, in the first place, enmity should be regarded as instinctive in animals. You seem simply to *assume* that because this relationship between hazard, enmity and amity obtains in animal societies, the behaviour which expresses this relationship is instinctive. In the second place, you fail to consider the possibility that such a relationship may in human societies be open to alternative explanations, and that a similar explanation may even be proffered for animal societies. I have strong reservations regarding the claim that animal and human societies do always comply with the 'code of enmity,' but even if we grant that they do, the explanation may be found in the fact of anxiety, fear, and suspicion provoked by experience (or knowledge) of past atrocities received at the hands of other groups.

1ST GENT.: But *why* should such atrocities have occurred?

2ND GENT.: Who knows? Perhaps a severe drought led one group to attack another to secure food. Any one of a thousand explanations of this variety is plausible. The point is that on this account the hostility is the result of the animal's (or human's) *experience* of others of his kind. Such an explanation avoids several difficulties inherent in your account, one of these being your claim that there is an *instinctive* waxing and waning of the *intensity* of two or more passions. (I mean, instead of it being a particular action or desire which is said to occur instinctively, what is alleged to alter as a result of instinct is the relative intensity or strength of the amity or enmity felt. And this is surely an odd suggestion.)

But more importantly, an account which appeals to the animal's experience is free of inconsistency, which is more than one can say for yours. In your remarks about the South Africans, it is clear that by 'enmity' you mean "the (perceived) increased hostility for outsiders." These two are not the same, nor are they connected in any obvious way. (Perceived hostility, for example, may or may not be received with hostility.) Turning to the *relation* you assert holds between enmity and *amity*, whether we take enmity in the first or second sense, your allegation of a relation between the two is not convincing. American perception of the hostility of the Vietnamese for the U.S.A. did not lead to increased amity among the American people, because many Americans judged the Vietnamese hostility to be justified. So far from being provoked to love their fellows more, they came to hate or feel alien to their own community. Similarly, the hostility of many French-Canadians toward English-speaking Canada has not notably fostered amity among the people of Quebec, but has in fact divided them.

Finally: To explain the enmity of animals and humans in terms of their experiences and felt interests does justice to their intelligence and capacities for action in a way that your determinist account does not.

A 3RD GENT.: Forgive me, but sitting here in the sun I could not help but overhear your conversation, and I am unable to keep from intervening upon hearing of the theory of determinism. Determinism, as I learned it at school, is the thesis that every event has a cause. Or, to put it another way, every event can be seen to follow in a law-like manner from previous events. But then a determinist would be anxious to dissociate himself from the First Gentleman's position. For a determinist would insist that what a man or monkey is, is not simply a function of his genes, as the First Gentleman would have it, but rather of the complex interplay between genes (which result in a particular organic makeup) and the environment in which the organism is immersed.

Thus, the genetic component is only one among many factors influencing what one is or does, though we would do well not to ignore it. To insist that the genetic factor alone is operative is to succumb to a fatalism—call it 'genetic fatalism'—only one step removed from the ancients' view that Oedipus could not but meet his tragic end, come what may. We cannot doubt that the genetic factor places some kind of restraint on the possibilities of social engineering, and just what kind of restraint can perhaps be glimpsed darkly in the investigations of animal behaviour. We must, however, exercise the greatest caution in these matters. Because we have evolved from other creatures does not necessitate our sharing all, or even most, of the characteristics of those creatures from which we came. Just what genetic features we do have in common with our immediate evolutionary ancestors will always be, I suspect, a matter for sheer speculation.

1ST GENT.: I am encouraged by your dissociating yourself from my libertarian friend on the issue of determinism. But I believe that you yourself are, in one respect, in the same position as the second gentleman. For you stress the causal effect of what is around the animal, thus emphasizing experience. This implies that if we were to raise the animal in isolation it would not (for example) show aggression *immediately* upon contact with others of its kind. But the evidence accumulated by biology suggests that an animal raised apart from others of its kind *will* manifest the behaviour I have insisted is instinctive. Birds, for example, raised in isolation from others of their kind, sing exactly the song of their species without any contact through which they could have learned the song. They simply embark upon it without any external instruction, so far as can be seen.

2ND GENT.: This may well be true in the case of birdsong. But perhaps we need to distinguish between performances such as song, and behaviour such as aggression or territoriality or dominance. Concerning these last, the writings you are appealing to contradict what you have just said. The research of Harlow with rhesus monkeys, in which the young were raised from birth in isolation—whatever we may think about the brutality or tolerableness of such research—does enable us to reply to you that primates raised in isolation, so far from

125

being aggressive, manifest acute fear and anxiety upon introduction to their own kind.

But there is another point which we've only touched on briefly and which I want to stress against you and the gentleman who has joined us. There is not only a difference between birdsong and aggression. There may be a considerable difference between primate amity and human morality.

1ST GENT.: What difference? Surely you must admit that the action of the baboons mentioned earlier can only be described as altruistic? Or do you want to deny that moral predicates can be ascribed to animal behaviour?

2ND GENT.: It depends what you mean by ascribed. If by calling the baboon behaviour "altruistic' you mean it is the type of behaviour an altruistic person would have performed, all right. (And we may find irresistible the inclination to characterize animal social behaviour in terms of human moral categories.) But this ascription (and inclination) still leaves unresolved whether the behaviour proceeds from anything that could properly be described as a moral consideration, and so can be said to be moral action.

1ST GENT.: But damn it! If the same behaviour can be observed to occur in both species we have *EVERY REASON* to assume that what lies behind it is in each case the same. If observation shows that we share certain characteristics with every animal species, it seems to me to be sheer pusillanimity to shrink from concluding that these characteristics have a common evolutionary basis. It is a fact that *every animal species*—or at least every social animal species—exhibits a triad of needs: for security, for stimulation, and for identity. *Surely* this gives us reason to suppose that these needs are an innate biological constant with which each animal species must come to terms?

2ND GENT.: It may give us reason to suppose it. But does it give us good reason to suppose it? To begin with, what do you mean by a need for identity?

1ST GENT.: The need to know who you are, to achieve identification in the eyes of your social partners.

2ND GENT.: I thought that was what you had in mind. And notice that this is a social need, while the others are not. The need for security, for example, is not logically tied to group existence which is why it is plausible to describe it as 'innate.' Any animal vulnerable in the way most animals are from birth needs, if it is to survive, to be secure from peril. The need for stimulation too is not characterisable as a social need; and the assertion that it is innate says nothing more than what a creature having such and such nature will atrophy, or suffer, or both, without stimulation. *But what explains* this need may be different in different animals. Hegel asserted of the human animal the same thing you do—a need for stimulation. But he linked this need to the self-consciousness of humans, and to their capacity for action. This runs counter to your account of the human story, and shows that solely from the fact of a human need for stimulation we cannot conclude that this need takes the same form in other animals, proceeds from the same capacities, and so on.

In the case of the need for identity, it should be noted first that to describe the need as innate is not to describe it as instinctive. It is, however, to make a claim which raises a question about the distinction between felt and unfelt needs and between innate and acquired needs.

The psychologist Abraham Maslow has insisted, just as you do, that there are innate needs. One of these, Maslow alleges, is the need to be loved. This (like your need for identification) is a social need; and if it is innate, then there are social needs which are innate. Now Maslow's reason for saying that a human being has a need to be loved is his conviction, which he claims to have arrived at empirically, that only human beings who have received love will be capable of that vital, enriching life he calls 'self-actualization,' together with his awareness that a human being who is not received with love, especially in his or her early years, may become psychotic or unfeeling as a result. But it is important to appreciate that Maslow assumes all along that the creatures of whom he is predicating this need to be loved *are in social relations with others of their kind.* This is a crucial assumption.

We can imagine a human infant raised by dogs who, when happened upon by us, is seen to receive affection from the dogs, and to be caring of them in return. Seeing that this human loves the dogs, and is loved by them, we may conclude, reasoning inductively, that deprived of the company of these creatures the human would suffer. (Other humans may in fact remove the human from the dogs; so that we actually see this result follow upon deprival.) "This human being too has a need for affection," we conclude. But if he does—and who would deny it—he has this need *now;* and the affection for which he now has a need is the affection *of the dogs.* If somehow he had survived alone it is perfectly conceivable that we should not be able to say "he needs affection and love"—unless of course in saying this we are appealing to a *possible* state of this human being which we judge is preferable to that in which this human animal now stands. "He needs love" etc., in the sense that he is the worse for being without it. But neither here, nor in the other case, can we claim that his need is innate; unless all we mean by this is that the creature has a potential capacity for love, and for coming to be someone who needs love. In the case of the human who is raised by the dogs, if in time the human comes to need their (or someone's) affection, this may be because he *responds* to the nurture and affection of the dogs, comes to delight in it and in them, to feel secure in their company, and to want (and to experience anxiety and regret apart from) their company and affection. He comes to have this need to be loved. And he comes to have it, notice, *in the company of the dogs.*

Why should it not be this way with us who are raised among our own kind? Why can't it be that, *being in the company of other humans,* and being received and treated by them in certain ways, we come to be a seeker of their regard and affection. Aware of ourselves as an object of their consciousness, delighted, or made anxious by their presence, their attention, their intercourse with us, and so on, we come to love them, and to need their love. Out of our experience and our situation this need arises. But that experience and situation is not innate. Therefore the need is not innate.

This would explain what seems a conceivable possibility: a human being, surviving alone, who experienced no need for love of any kind. If we find this human condition appalling (as Maslow, for example, certainly would), it is because of our implicit appeal to *what could be* the condition of this human. And so, "He needs love!" we say. But just as any animal raised in isolation, so far from instinctively desiring esteem, or a dominant position, responds rather to the 'social contract' with terror, so this human, far from having a need for affection, may experience no such deprivation at all. If *we* judge his condition to be deprivation—a state of being in need—this is simply the operation of our preferred standard.

3RD GENT.: Speaking of standards, may I make a comment? The triad of needs which you have been discussing must be appreciated as not having any direct connection with the matter of survival. Surely it is possible that there should be a species having social arrangements which satisfy these *individual* needs, and yet the survival of the species may be endangered. The great apes—the gorilla, the chimpanzee, and the orangutan—are just such a species, all three being on the verge of extinction, yet their needs, as individuals, seem to be satisfied.

Indeed it is interesting to speculate as to *why* the great apes, with such admirable brain sizes, should be nearly extinct, while their near cousin, the baboon, outnumbers homo sapiens on the continent of Africa, despite severe persecution at the hands of farmer and rancher. A study of the chimpanzee by the British primatologist Vernon Reynolds perhaps gives us a clue. Chimpanzees, Reynolds claims, are amiable creatures, both to members of their group and to outsiders. Chimpanzee society is *not* characterized by the two phenomena the First Gentleman has emphasized—enmity and hierarchy. This fact may in no small way be contributing to the demise of our nearest relatives. Baboons, on the other hand, with a strict hierarchy, appear to have a secure future as a species.

2ND GENT.: Then Reynolds' study constitutes a rather severe indictment of much of what the First Gentleman has been saying. For it seems we have now to acknowledge the existence of a primate psychology different from what the First Gentleman claims is common to all species. The chimp (and the orangutan) neither obeys the code of enmity, nor insists upon rank ordering. Surely this puts a large question mark against the urge to extrapolate from animal to human behaviour?

1ST GENT.: Not so fast, gentlemen: Later studies by Jane Goodall and Adriaan Kortlandt have shown that what Reynolds regarded as the affection and openness of chimps to *other* groups was really affection toward other members of one large group with constantly shifting subgroups. Furthermore, evidence suggests that, at least occasionally, chimp groups are characterized by rank ordering.

But an even more general comment on Reynolds' research is in order. Terrestial man and arboreal ape have been environmentally separated for twenty million years. The chimp is a product of one road of natural selection, we are the product of another. Twenty million years is a long time, even in terms of evolution, and to equate the end-products is a wishful indulgence. Just as one cannot equate the life of the baboon with the lives of the great apes, so even less can we equate the history of that most successful primate species, homo sapiens, with the history of the most outstanding primate failure, the great apes.

2ND GENT.: But doesn't this amount to a sharp reversal in your position? It may be true that chimps are not our ancestors, but we had a common ancestor twenty million years ago, or so you say. Surely this common ancestor is much closer to us than the common ancestor we share with the swordtail, the cuckoo, the marsh warbler, or the countless mammalian species which are alleged to exhibit territoriality, etc. Yet you attempt at length to point to conclusions concerning human moral, social and political arrangements on the basis of studies of *all* such creatures! *Then* you turn around and abruptly declare that even if ethology should justify Reynolds' conclusions about the chimp, *nothing follows about human beings because we are the product of a different evolutionary process.* But this is so contrary to the spirit of everything that you have argued thus far that it is astounding. There can be no doubt; you are caught in a contradiction (and from a contradiction anything follows!). I for one should be most happy to insist, along with you, that the ways of the great ape and hominid diverge, but to admit this is to take the sting out of any claim to the effect that biology, in particular ethology, has a crucial bearing on the problems that vex mankind.

3RD GENT.: Perhaps the first gentleman is merely wanting to point out that xenophobia, hierarchy, and the like are necessary for the survival of a species, and so we humans, with our capacity for self-awareness, should recognize this and arrange society accordingly.

1ST GENT.: Yes, that's right.

2ND GENT.: But to put your point that way suggests that we are dealing with something that cannot be termed 'instinct.' And this seems contrary to your earlier remarks. But this aside, we would do well to ask what evidence we have for thinking that social arrangements incorporating principles of territoriality, rank ordering, the creation of strangers in our midst, etc. *are* necessary for the survival of other species, though even this might be questioned. But why should they be necessary for our survival? Does the mere fact, if it is a fact, that they are necessary for animal survival dictate this conclusion? Is it not possible that developments in technology, and advances in the rearing of children (and in the education of parents), might result in a society of abundance and neutrality?

But even if we were to grant that a society of the First Gentlemen's preferred kind is necessary for species survival, it is entirely conceivable that a people forced to choose between probable extinction and this kind of social life would choose to risk extinction. There are things of value other than species survival; and these may be judged by a people to have greater value. God knows we all hope, or ought to hope, that the social and political arrangements which claim us as right and just will also make possible our survival. But faced with the choice between extinction, or species life on terms inimical to these higher values, there are many who would answer, adapting words from Hardy:

> Between you and I let there be love,
> Even if despair.

Selected Bibliography

Robert Ardrey. *African Genesis.* New York: Dell, 1972.

Robert Ardrey. *The Territorial Imperative.* New York: Dell, 1966.

Reproduction in Democratic Theory

LYNDA LANGE

It is commonly assumed that what is said of "man" by the political
theorist may be applied to woman as well. The twentieth-century male
political theorist, in particular, generally assumes that his subject is the
economic and political life of the human species. But there is growing
scepticism about this on the part of feminist theorists. Much democratic theory (to say nothing of practice) does not withstand scrutiny
very well when the claim of universal egalitarianism is taken literally,
and the full implications of this investigated in detail.

Prior to the twentieth century, it was usual for political theorists
to give some account of the role of women in society. Jean-Jacques
Rousseau is an example of a theorist who wrote a great deal, and very
influentially, about women. Indeed, it was the study of Rousseau's
ideas about women and the family, in the context of his reputed
egalitarianism, that first aroused my own suspicion that the sexist
assumptions of theorists of the past cannot simply be discarded as
undesirable excess baggage, and the "main" theory generalized over
both men and women. The latter belief, common among twentieth-
century thinkers, was difficult to reconcile with the fact that the sexism
appeared at such a fundamental level. In the case of Rousseau, even his
concept of the state of nature in some hypothetical dawn of time could
not really be universalized about men and women. It was not merely
that Rousseau himself unconsciously used the term "man" to refer to
the male sex, maintaining, for example, that "man" in the state of
nature requires only food, sleep, and a female. As the theory unfolded
it became clear that this gendered use of the term was integral to the
theory. This confirmed the suspicion that the sexism of past theory is
not merely incidental, and cannot therefore be excised in such a way as
to leave the rest of the theory intact.

Rousseau went so far as to claim that women have a different
human essence from men. In his book on education called *Emile*,
Rousseau wrote that while reason is the governing principle of man,
that of women was "modesty." It is true that Rousseau was something
of a crusader when it came to the "place" of women. It used to be the
case, however, that even those thinkers who appear to have had no
great personal interest in the status of women, such as John Locke and
Thomas Hobbes, include brief references, or short chapters, on the
structure of the family, and the status of women relative to men. These
thinkers rightly took for granted that the family-form was an important
part of the whole society when viewed as comprising more than just the

form of government. Prior to the defence of women's rights by John Stuart Mill in the nineteenth century, theorists were not embarrassed to prescribe obedience and subjection to women, any more than they were embarrassed to recognize explicitly the existence of an oppressed labouring class. Their complacency was based on the belief that the presence in society of an inferior labouring class and a submissive female sex, was necessary for the very existence of society, and hence inevitable and "natural."

Contemporary theorists who have emerged from the liberal-democratic tradition are not prone to express detailed views on the social role or the "nature" of women. A suggestion such as that they have a different human essence from men does not wash very well in the more democratic climate of the twentieth century, the influence of Sigmund Freud notwithstanding. Contemporary theorists, with a few exceptions, would probably blush to assert, in so many words, that women are different from men in any way that is relevant to their political status. The most usual practice regarding women is not to mention them at all.

This paper is an attempt to investigate the questions a democratic theory of reproduction must face and to show the consequences of a failure to deal with it. The object of criticism is theory usually considered democratic, both liberal (in the tradition of advanced Western capitalism), and Marxist, for it is only here that women should have any expectation of theory that can accommodate them as equals. While sexism, however, is a blemish on Marxist theory to be corrected by further work employing the materialist method, it appears to be a mainstay of non-Marxist theory, because of a fundamental assumption about the family not shared by Marxists, namely that there is a sphere of personal life encompassed by it that is beyond the scope of all political theory.

We may start our investigation by asking why the subject has dropped below the horizon of contemporary theory. A different account of this failure and/or omission must be given for Marxists on the one hand, and democratic theorists in the liberal-democratic tradition, on the other.

In the case of liberal-democrats, it may be partially explained by the widespread belief that the vote is the sum of political power. On this view, the question is closed: Women already have political equality with men; they have only to rouse themselves from the long sleep of their subservient past to enjoy it to the full. I believe this is the political view that underlies the familiar arguments that women "don't want" or "don't need" liberation. If they have it, but are manifestly not using it, it seems to follow that they either do not want it, or do not need it. The important question for democratic theory of reproduction, and the implications for women of the presently dominant way of getting the reproductive work of society done, have not been addressed. Theory about reproduction in human society has been left for the most part to sociology and psychology, a fact which reflects a major theoretical assumption on the part of these theorists that ought to be paid more attention. At bottom, this is a dichotomy which may be described variously as that between the personal and the political, or between the private and the public, or between the "natural" and the conventional. This dichotomy implies a failure or a refusal to see the form of the family from an historical point of view as one of several possible "modes of reproduction," and hence a failure to perceive the social meaning of the relations between its members. It also implies the view that the patriarchal family as the mode of reproduction is fundamentally unchangeable because "natural." As such it is not considered susceptible to basic change after the manner of other social structures.

"Reproduction," as Lorenne Clark has pointed out, includes the whole period which begins with conception and ends with the personal independence of the individual. Only one part of this function, i.e. gestation, is a function naturally done only by women and the rest involves a great deal of real work. The patriarchal family is a family whose head is male in a sense that is more than merely nominal. For most of human history this family in its various forms has been taken as a given, in the sense that it has been thought to be rooted in human nature. The characteristics of this family as it presently exists will form the subject of the second part of this paper. Indeed, when these characteristics are understood, they point to a further explanation for why discussion of reproduction does not appear as a central question in the liberal-democratic tradition. It takes little enough investigation to perceive that there is an inequality between men and women in the patriarchal family! What is generally denied is that this inequality is an expression of profoundly entrenched exploitive practices of which the form of the family is the political expression, and not just a case of "unfairness" or "backwardness" on the part of contemporary societies of whatever economic structure. This awkward position, wherein the role of man as breadwinner, and of the woman as reproducer is on the one hand considered natural (or at least O.K.), and on the other regrettably unfair in its social consequences, is not just one of the mysteries of life so dear to liberal thinkers. There is an explanation for it.

If it appears that the inequality of power between men and women is readily fitted into a political analysis of the sources of power, as I hope to show, then the difficulty of reconciling this family with a democratic political theory, is apparant at once. Liberal-democratic theorists have chosen to ignore this question.

Among Marxists there has been somewhat more analysis of the family, for at least two reasons. The first is the fundamental Marxist view that all social relations, including the family, are ultimately determined by the mode of production, which changes. The second is the denial, at least in principle, of the dichotomy between the personal and the political. Invaluable as the latter insight is in this context, it is, I suggest, very far from fully realized by Marxist theorists. In practice, Marxist theorists have assumed that the structure of the family must be serving the interests of the ruling class. This is undoubtedly true as far as it goes, but that is not far enough. One theory that is fairly popular among Marxists is that the antagonism between working class men and women is a form of false consciousness, further evidence of the insidious ability of the ruling class to "*divide et impera.*" But this leaves sexism within the ruling class itself unexplained, and also assumes quite wrongly that the interests of working class men and women are in fact identical. This is the justification given for the common Marxist opinion that feminism is "diversionary," that it diverts energy away from revolutionary struggles on the part of working class people against capital. Other Marxists have approached it from the opposite end of the social structure, and a number of investigations have been made of the relation between the subjection of women and the institution of private property. The question which has frequently been discussed is: What accounts for the subjection of women by men who have (or hope to have) private property? The answer which has received the widest agreement is that men of private property must be able to control their wives in order to be certain of the paternity of their children. The certainty of paternity enables an owner to pass on his ownings intact to a child of his own. I believe this can be shown to serve the interest of capital in several ways. On the one hand it enhances the rights of absolute control of one's own property and of unlimited appropriation, characteristic of capitalism. This is a stimulus to a capitalist economy, since one may go on appropriating to the day of one's death, knowing that one is free to dispose of one's property as one chooses at death. Were this not so, it would often be more rational to relax after a certain age and enter a period of mere consumption. In addition, holdings are not continually broken up at each generation, so that they get even larger. The right to bequeath property has already been considerably limited in many countries in response to pressure from democratic elements, since it is a right that sharply enhances class-division.

Women are rarely capitalists in their own right, and legislation against full unrestricted ownership by women, equal to that allowed men, has existed, and still exists to some extent, in all capitalist countries.

This case does not in itself, however, prove that there is a power differential in the mode of reproduction as basic as that in the mode of production. Indeed, Engels, in *The Origin of the Family, Private Property, and the State*, argued a similar case for the capitalist class and concluded that in the working class there is no basis for sexual exploitation. His conclusion is often attributed to failure to consider the question of consciousness. I am arguing, however, that it is not a question of consciousness, but of exploited reproductive labour.

In sum, Marxist theorists have for the most part assumed that communism in production will solve the problem of sexism from an objective point of view (presumably by giving women equal access to the means of production) leaving nothing to be done but the tidying up of subjective sexist attitudes. The inequality between men and women which has been and still is present in varying degrees in existing socialist countries is due, I suggest, to the fact that the necessity of democratizing the mode of reproduction has not been recognized as of equal importance to the democratization of the mode of production. While women in socialist countries may make gains as producers, as reproducers they are in practice often still liable to a form of compulsive labour to which men are not, depending on the reproductive needs of the society at a particular time. Even as various services, such as day care, are provided, the remaining residue of reproductive labour continues to be done by women. Furthermore, the policies of socialist countries regarding birth control and the family have in fact varied enormously, not only from country to country but from time to time in the same country. The range of their variation reveals an almost total absence of consistent democratic principle regarding women, to which even lip service is paid. In a recent book called *Soviet Women*, William Mandel attests that women were sent back to wifehood and motherhood after World War II in Russia just as they were in the West, and that this was propagandized as fundamentally right, rather than as a temporary need to raise the birth rate. In *Women in China* Katie Curtin identifies the same lack of consistent democratic principle, and not merely practice in China:

> When the regime is seeking a rapid increase in productivity through a mobilization of labour power, it praises the liberating effects of being a working woman. When it cannot absorb women into production, however, it glorifies the home.

Thus while women *may* make gains in these countries, these gains do not occur of necessity as the revolution progresses, and may even be reversed independently of the democratic trend in production, if there

135

occurs a need for a higher birth rate. Because of the view that the mode of reproduction is wholly derived from the mode of production, exploitation in the mode of reproduction, if it is noticed, is generally blamed on the failure to realize full communism in the mode of production, or it is rationalized on the ground that the economy cannot support the implementation of the measures usually considered necessary for the emancipation of women. This exploitation is therefore not attacked as a basic question on the theoretical level with the consequence that the theoretical problem remains unsolved. Even recent discussions showing how housework and child-care make an indirect contribution to the creation of surplus value end with the same old prescription that women under capitalism must struggle against exploitation in production and identify their interest with that of male workers. They are encouraged to minimize any demands that express a conflict of interest between themselves and working class men. This prescription is made because it is understood that women's wage demands inevitably undermine the wages of men. Direct efforts to emancipate women are supposed to be submerged until after the revolution against capital. In the here and now, where we all have to live and struggle, the super-exploited woman turns out on this analysis to be quite disarmed as a revolutionary. We lack the assurance of a general theory to illuminate direct action on our own behalf.

I want to begin by indicating my own approach to reproduction, and I shall, first, formulate a criticism of liberal-democratic theory, and, secondly, outline a truly materialist theory of reproduction. I shall proceed on the hypothesis that there are two activities essential for the existence of any human society: production and reproduction. That production is a uniquely human activity essential for society is denied by no one. Reproduction, broadly defined to include the labour of nurture and socialization, must be seen to have a place beside production as a primary essential activity of human society, and not a merely "natural," pre-social, albeit necessary, activity. As such, its mode is a determinant, along with the mode of production, of the form of the whole society. My position is different from others in not positing sexual antagonism as even more basic than class antagonism, as Shulamith Firestone claims. Nor do I believe that sexual antagonism has a biological base—the primacy of labour, both productive and reproductive, is central to my view.

The "mode of reproduction" at present is a kind of family which is patriarchal to varying degrees in different societies. It follows that a theorist's views (or his neglect) of this question is as "political" as his views about property or the state.

I have said that the power of men over women is amenable to

political analysis. Since the advent of "sexual politics," the term "political" has become all-purpose when it comes to discussions, and like "Kleenex" it no longer serves to identify the brand which is ours. I believe that the sexism of political theory is rooted in the existence of social units for the performance of reproductive labour (which happen to be exploitive of women) which is taken for granted at the point where theory begins, much as one might say that the existence of raw materials for production is taken for granted when theorizing begins, inasmuch as the belief that there exist raw materials is not thought to have political connotations. But whereas the latter assumption is reasonable, the former is a reflection of a theoretical, political, assumption, whose implications are undemocratic in relation to women. The "material" of society, viz., human persons (and not just organisms of a certain sort) is not "raw." Labour has already been expended on it, else the organisms remain non-human, or they die. This assumption is political on the theoretical level because it is not neutral vis-a-vis the interests of different groups of people, as certain assumptions of a factual nature are. There is also another useful sense of "political," wherein it refers to social practices: By saying that such and such a practice (e.g. law, institution, custom) is "political," is to say that it is a practice that is ultimately determined by the modes of production and reproduction, and in societies where there are internal contradictions between classes and sexes, either serving the interest of those who are exploiting others, or actually opposed to them.

It is easier to understand how reproduction can be given "equal billing" if it is firmly grasped that the reproduction that is essential to society includes more than conception and gestation. It has been defined, not merely arbitrarily, as including the period of time needed to nurture and socialize what begins as a mere organism, into a person in the full-blooded sense. Conception and gestation, i.e. the creation of more people, is a necessary function of society, though in itself less obviously uniquely human than the process of socialization. As to the latter, it seems clear to me that continual socialization of new people is as basic to the continuation of society as production.

My critique of theory in the liberal-democratic tradition will take as a case study the theory of power of C.B. Macpherson in his book *Democratic Theory: Essays in Retrieval*. The charge of fundamental sexism can be upheld against all theorists in the liberal-democratic tradition in a manner which will be clear after the case of C.B. Macpherson is examined. His demonstration of the inability of a society based on "fair" market exchange of privately owned commodities and labour to provide the means to truly human self-development for everyone appears at first as potentially very useful for women.

137

Women, after all, constitute a very large percentage of those who are at a marked disadvantage in the market place, and that for reasons integral to the structure of a market society. The fact that Macpherson, along with the undemocratic contemporary theorists he criticizes, fails to mention women, or the family, is undoubtedly because he shares their assumption that it is unnecessary to formulate the theory about reproduction as a basic part of political theory.

This much appears to be a merely negative criticism, indicating an omission, rather than definite sexist implications of the theory. The status of this criticism will be re-examined after it is delineated. It should be observed that this investigation involves no necessity to impute consciously held undemocratic ideas about women to Professor Macpherson, or any other theorist. Their existence is simply irrelevant to the question at hand. The pervasive belief that the mode of reproduction is a non-political question creates a confusion between sexist *attitudes*, which are thoughts, feelings, and dispositions to behave in certain ways, and sexist *theory*, which has undemocratic implications for women regardless of the psychological states of its author.

If a theorist assumes that the family is outside the political sphere, and that women have, or ought to have, equal political rights, it is difficult to perceive that any sexism which appears is theoretical. But this is just what is claimed.

Macpherson draws a distinction between two concepts of power which have co-existed uneasily in liberal-democratic theory since the middle of the nineteenth century. These are "developmental power" and "extractive power." Developmental power is the effective ability to use and develop one's own capacities under one's own conscious control, and for one's own human purposes. This concept, according to Macpherson, is based on the idea that man is essentially a doer, a creator, an enjoyer of his human attributes, and that these activities are ends in themselves. Ideally, developmental power is complete for each person, so that its extent should be measured down from a maximum by measuring the extent of the impediments to its exercise.

The concept of extractive power is derived by Macpherson from the "descriptive" concept of power found in liberal theory. This type of power consists in one's own capacity to procure utilities, plus whatever capacities of others one has to control, or minus whatever capacities of one's own one has had to give up in the process of procuring what Macpherson calls "the means of life." Extractive power is the amount of the excess of power in the descriptive sense that one person has over another. Its source is the transfer of part of some individual's capacities to the conscious control of another individual, who is the holder of extractive power. The recipient of the transfer is then enabled to use the capacities of someone else for his own benefit. Extractive power, in other words, is exploitive. It is a function of unequal access to "the means of labour and of life," and as a result is necessarily unequally distributed. Within a market (capitalist) economy, the extractive power of a non-owner of land or capital is zero. In addition, the developmental power of a non-owner is negligible, for two reasons. The first is that there is little time or energy left after he has worked the time required to earn a living. Secondly, because his capacities are stunted by the deleterious effect of continuous work that is outside his control. This is true of all non-owning wage-workers, both male and female.

This theory, however, is of man the producer. It has for its ontology only two fundamental categories of people, owners and non-owners of the means of labour. Under this analysis the extractive power of non-owners is zero, regardless of whether they are employed or not. It is certain, however, that the access of non-owning women to the means of productive labour is very inferior to that of men. In Canada, for example, the annual salaried income of female *heads of families* as a percentage of that of male heads of families, has actually declined in the last few years, sinking to slightly below 50%. There continues to be more noise than substance to the claim that women are making great economic gains. In a class-divided society, capitalist and otherwise, marriage has always been, and still remains, the form of access to "the means of life" for the overwhelming majority of women. Male heads of families in these societies are legally responsible for providing a subsistence to their wives and children, a liability which is always correlated with certain legal (as well as social and economic) privileges. His control of the means of life in relation to his family gives him considerable control of those whom he supports. This institution is an example of what is meant by "the patriarchal family." Despite wide variations in the degree of male authority, ranging from the life and death powers of the Roman *paterfamilias*, to the regulated legal powers of contemporary husbands in a liberal-democracy, a significant power differential remains between men and women.

Let us begin by seeing what happens when we apply Macpherson's analysis of power to a family of non-owners. I believe that his is the hard case which must be proved to show that the mode of reproduction is as fundamental as the mode of production. If this is so, it must be seen to result in inequality between men and women who have the same relation to the means of production. This is not the case with husbands and wives in the capitalist class, since these women rarely own or control the means of production in their own right.

If the extractive power of the male non-owner is zero, and his developmental power negligible, what must be the level of power of the woman who is dependent on him for the means of life? Since her power is demonstrably less than his, it appears to sink to a negative quantity! It is not that they are equally bereft of power of any sort since he has power of some sort over her. Macpherson's analysis of power does not accommodate this reality. There is a pervasive form of power which has been overlooked, but what is its nature, and what is its source?

According to Macpherson (and Marx for that matter) only *ownership* of the means of labour is an actual source of power. Those, for example, who have high salaries may have an economic advantage over those with low salaries, yet they do not, strictly speaking, have economic power over them. In any case, husbands in liberal democracies, to say nothing of socialist countries, seldom any longer have institutionalized power to prevent their wives from entering production. This is not to say they have no power of any sort to help maintain their economic and other advantages.

The difference between men and women that accounts for the difference in their power is, I believe, that women are subject to a form of compulsive labour to which men are not subject, namely reproductive labour, as it has been defined. When I say that women are subject to a form of compulsive labour, I mean that they may only resist with great difficulty, and that the majority succumb. The same may be said of non-owners when it comes to wage work. In both cases, it is not compulsive in the sense that one is driven to it with whips and chains (though that happens, too!), but in the sense that no real alternative is generally available to women, and that everything in society conspires to ensure that women do this work. While a non-owner may attempt small independent production, or simply refuse to work and live off begging or state welfare, that is not proof of his freedom. The same is true of women. While a woman may with great difficulty resist doing reproductive work, that is no proof that she is "free" not to do it. This happens to women because a mode of reproduction is established that is exploitive of them. This may be said even though we do not know very much about how that mode was established historically. The sanctions compelling women to perform this work have varied from one society to another depending on the general structure of its assumptions about human purposes and capacities. For the present I shall concentrate mainly on analyzing the sanctions on women in market society.

Freedom of choice is often said to be the dominant ethical value of a liberal market society. For the non-owners this amounts in practice to very little, and frequently means a life of almost total compulsion.

He is free only to make the best bargain he can, but of course his bargaining power is very limited and may actually be nil. His life activity is ultimately determined by the labour requirements of capital. The most important sanction on women coercing them to reproductive work is that their bargaining power in relation to production is even worse than that of men. There are, of course, many other sanctions as well. The sexist ideology arising out of the different relations of men and women to reproductive work must be the most powerful ideology in existence. It pervades the whole of life and often appears, in the twentieth century at least, to be the major obstacle to the emancipation of women. This belief, however, is a mistake. Marriage to a wage-worker remains for most women the best bargain for a livelihood that they can make. Hence it appears as a "free" choice. The terms of this choice may vary from time to time, depending on the reproductive needs of society. When women are needed for production, they are temporarily offered a better bargain or more incentive of some kind for doing productive work. This happened, for example, during World War II. While they do function as a reserve pool of labour, this is not the most basic explanation of their status. The reproductive needs of society may never sink below a certain minimum, and *someone* must perform the reproductive work. The undemocratic assumption that a certain subset of people, namely women, are the "natural" candidates for this, is not undermined by the economic and other gains women make when society does not need a very high birth rate. The reproductive needs of society do change, after all, so that advances made by women on the basis of a temporarily lower demand for reproductive labour, in relation to the demand for productive labour, are superficial, so long as their relation to the mode of reproduction remains the same. The subjection of women to compulsive reproductive labour is largely supported by their inferior access to productive work. Their subjection, *per se*, however, does not consist in this inferior access, but in the necessity for reproductive work, and the existing mode of doing it is exploitive of women. This must be recognized independently of what keeps women from overturning this mode.

It is easy to be misled by the fact that the class of non-owners, male and female, do have in common essentially the same relation to the mode of production. The difference is mostly one of degree. The class of non-owners (as well as that of owners) is, however, further divided into those who are liable to perform reproductive work and those who are not. So long as no *other* means of getting reproductive work done is devised, women will have a fundamentally different status in society from men. The difference is not, by definition, a class difference. It could be called a difference of "reproductive class." More important than terminology is the fact that a non-owning female is at the bottom end of two basic power differentials.

In a market society, the subjection of women to this labour may be termed a liability, because women are not literally slaves in a market society, any more than male non-owners are literally slaves. Forms of coercion considered ideologically acceptable vary from one society to another, and we may expect those applied to women to be roughly similar in type to those applied to others in the same society. Thus, the Roman *paterfamilias* ("*famulus*" is Latin for "slave") had the power of life and death over his wives, concubines, children and other slaves. In czarist Russia in the nineteenth century, when serfs were owned along with land, there was no legal penalty for husbands who killed their wives if it happened in the course of "chastisement."

A woman in our society married to a male capitalist is in a different position from the working-class woman. Her position is clearly not the same as that of the man to whom she is married. Equally clearly, she is not the sister of the working class woman. The explanation for this is simply that capitalists must reproduce the membership of their own class, and it should come as no surprise to anyone that the male members of this class are capable of exploiting the reproductive labour of the female members. The objective fact of this exploitation within the ruling class explains why the illusion of sisterhood in the early phases of the present women's movement could have happened. It was especially likely to happen in the twentieth century when the bourgeois woman has much less assistance from servants, and so may be observed to perform literally the same sort of work as the working-class woman. Reproductive labour *is* labour, its unique characteristic being that it needs to be performed in every class according to the norms of that class. A version of the patriarchal family is found in every class which means, alas, that women are a kind of class servant, their labour being exploited in every class, in the interest of that class, and in favour of its male members. It will in general be in the interest of particular women to demand full member-ship in the class to which their fathers and husbands belong, and indeed, this is exactly what has happened. Inevitably, the demands of bourgeois women. It is working-class women who must compel working-class men to give up their privileges to strengthen the working their aims in a way that makes them totally distinct from the aims of bourgeois women. It is working class women who must compel working class men to give up their privileges to strengthen the working class as a whole. The effects of sexism are very different in each class. The male worker gains certain personal benefits by being free of reproductive labour, but he does so at the expense of being used by capital as a sort of supervisor of the reproductive servant, his wife, for the main benefit, of course, goes to capital. The aim of revolutionary feminism must be to democratize reproductive labour in the working class by such measures as shorter work hours for both sexes, maternity and paternity leave, parent controlled day care, and non-sexist marriage and family law.

There has been considerable speculation, as I mentioned above, about the origin of the patriarchal family and its relation to the appearance in history of private property. For the present purpose, however, the origin of this institution is less important than an examination of the way it functions now. We have seen that women in a market society are liable to perform the essential reproductive work. Child care in a society of private property is not a socialized but a private responsibility. The availability of day care, for example, does not shift basic responsibility from parents. Socialized child care would be inconsistent with the ethical principle of a market society that persons ought to be recompensed according to their contribution to society (be it labour or acquired capital). Children are not productive in this sense. Such measures as universal free education have been introduced largely in response to the needs of capital for more skilled (or perhaps only better disciplined) workers. In general, market societies have always held workers personally responsible for whatever is needed to maintain and replenish their numbers (e.g. health care, education, recreation, reproductive needs) for as long as it has been possible to refuse these services. When they are given, it is largely, if not entirely, because the further refusal to supply them would have worse consequences for owners than the cost of supplying them. In the case of women in particular, the provision of universal day care by a capitalist state could only mean that the productive labour of women was needed by capital more than their reproductive labour. The dehumanizing possibilities of this are enormous, but that question must be set aside for another discussion.

It is not often enough noticed by either Marxists or feminists that keeping male workers legally responsible for the means of life for their wives and children is one of the most important means of curtailing the cost to owners of maintaining a supply of workers. It is therefore in the interest of the owners to perpetuate this personal responsibility of male workers, and this is the basis of the difference between sexism in the working class and sexism among the bourgeoisie. The chief means of perpetuating working class sexism is the correlation of male responsibility with male privileges that cost owners nothing, and at the same time help to ensure that women continue to perform the reproductive work by placing the husband in a kind of supervisory role. Husbands

143

are then in a position of having to give up substantial personal privileges if they rid themselves of the liability.

These male privileges represent the power that particular men have over particular women. In the paradigm case, where the husband has a salary and the wife does not, his control of the means of life gives him considerable power over those whom he supports and enables him to demand that they perform work for his benefit. He may free himself of all work required for his bodily maintenance, such as cooking, washing, and general housework. He may define the conditions of housework and reproductive work. Because of his liability for support of the children, one condition of reproductive work the patriarchal male has always demanded is sexual fidelity on the part of this wife. Though the major economic sanction on women coercing them to reproductive work is not applied by their husbands, it is clear there are many other sanctions he can apply.

Husbands have what might be considered in C.B. Macpherson's terms "non-market extractive power" over their wives. This power is extractive because they may use it for their own benefit. It is "non-market" for two reasons. The first is that his superior access to employment is not the source of his power. Its source ìs the form of compulsive labour to which she is liable, and from which he is free. His superior access to the means of labour is actually outside his control, insofar as it arises from his membership in the male sex. As an individual, of course, there is much he may do to secure his superior access in relation to a particular woman.

Secondly, marriage is not a contract of the market type, wherein a specific exchange is stipulated in advance. It is closer to a feudal-type of contract between lord and serf in being open-ended, and the terms of its fulfillment are decided in an ongoing manner, depending on the circumstances. Most of the deciding, of course, is done by the party to the contract with the most power.

Reproduction, therefore, is a form of labour that takes place outside market relations. The coercion on women that compels them to perform reproductive work simultaneously excludes them from the source of all recognized value in a market society, namely, the market place and the form of political life arising out of it. The same is true of socialist societies, to the extent that the performance of reproductive work hinders the full involvement of women in production and government. Let it be clear that I believe reproductive workers are excluded from *recognized* value, and not from human value itself. That reproductive work is not less valuable than productive work, or less important for human society, is just the point. Where a dichotomy is maintained between the public and the private, however, to be confined to what is private is to be denied the potential of full human development. The social deprivation of women in terms of mainstream values, could hardly be greater. The dichotomy between the public and the private with which we began may now be seen to be an ideology arising out of the mode of reproduction, rather than out of the mode of production.

The argument for male supremacy that from an historical point of view has been most influential, is the argument that men have in fact been the providers of what is needed to sustain life, when women were subject to uncontrolled pregnancy. In more primitive times her liability to become pregnant and her smaller physical frame appeared to be handicaps in the struggle against scarcity. He brought home the bacon and her job was to make it palatable. The argument, of course, is not valid. If it were, its logical conclusion would be the oppression of the physically weak by the physically strong, a division which would surely cut across the sexual division. In any case, that in human societies (to say nothing of political theory) physical strength is never a sole determinant, to say nothing of a justification, of political power, indicates the spuriousness of this argument.

The answers to why this criticism of liberal-democrats and Marxists positively indicates sexism, rather than a mere omission is implicit in what has already been said, and only needs to be mentioned briefly. Reproduction, from conception to the personal independence of the new individual, is an activity essential to the existence of human society. This is not a merely natural, pre-social activity, but in all societies takes on a mode which is of human creation, just as production does. In the absence of a conscious awareness of this, and of the need to democratize both productive and reproductive work, women will continue to be oppressed by a liability to perform compulsive reproductive labour because society must, and does, always ensure that reproductive work is done to perpetuate itself. The omission of a full discussion of this question in a critical analysis of society is therefore equivalent to accepting the mode of reproduction that is most dominant now.

Women have struggled sporadically for emancipation throughout human history. So far, the struggles of men have always outpaced them. Revolutions have come and gone, often representing considerable progress, but always leaving intact a power differential between men and women. What reason is there to think that non-sexist, genuine democracy is any more possible now than it has ever been?

Technological advances in contraception and obstetrical science may be the development that will make it possible for women to make an effective demand for the democratization of reproductive work.

Human control of procreation must be objectively possible before it makes any sense for women to demand control of their own physiological reproductive functions. While the known possibility of the control makes sense of the demand, however, a Brave New World of birth control technology is not a prerequisite for beginning the fight for non-exploitive reproductive institutions. After all, the difference between the diaphragm and the Pill is fairly slight compared to the difference between the diaphragm and no birth control at all. Even more important, the period of reproductive labour on the part of adults, from the birth of the child to the stage of personal independence, has far more impact on the lives of women than pregnancy itself.

The crux of emancipation for women is the non-exploitive organization of this work, along with full recognition of its human and social character and value, regardless of whether such organizations are small circles including children and adults, or larger organizations specifically designed for child care. There is room here for considerable variation, within important limits. "Reproductive work" is always an intimate relation between an adult and a child: Its distinguishing feature among human relations is that work on the part of the adult is integral to it. Because one of its main functions is to transmit the values of the society, this relationship itself must exemplify the values we wish to see perpetuated. It is ultimately for this basic reason that a mode of reproduction which is non-exploitive is not possible in an exploitive, class-divided society, but requires its transformation into something better.

Suggested Bibliography

Margaret Benston, "The Political Economy of Women's Liberation," *Monthly Review*, Sept. 1969.

Katie Curtin, *Women in China*, Pathfinder Press, 1975.

Marlene Dixon, "Women's Liberation: Opening Chapter Two," *Canadian Dimension*, Vol. 10, No. 8.

C.B. Macpherson, *Democratic Theory: essays in retrieval*, Oxford, 1973.

William Mandel, *Societ Women*, Anchor Press, 1975.

Margaret Randall, *Cuban Women Now*, Canadian Women's Educational Press, 1973.

Jean-Jacques Rousseau, *Emile*. (See especially Book V)

———. "*A Discourse on the Origin of Inequality*."

W. Seccombe, "Housework Under Capitalism," *New Left Review* #83, Jan–Feb., 1974.

The Politics of Impotence

MARY O'BRIEN

The question of the relationship of political theory and political action has exercised students of politics and political activists since antiquity. "No practice without theory," Lenin declared unequivocally, a dictum which would have elicited the approval of Plato and Aristotle as readily as that of Karl Marx. Such approval, however, would have been limited to the statement of principle involved. The content of theory, the strategies of action, and the relation between the two have remained the subjects of political controversy over a long period.

In our own time, we have broad and varied approaches to the study and practice of politics. In the academic world, the quarrel as to the actuality and utility of a scientific politics has subsided as the protagonists of the struggle find less and less to say to one another. The North American mainstream, flowing blissfully to its post-behavioural position in post-industrial society—or, some would say, moving a step or two further away from unpleasant reality—remains suspicious of theory, wary of practice and devoted to the development of verifiable hypotheses. Theory, in its traditional sense, is seen as imaginative description festooned with unsupported claims of analytical and practical utility. The total rejection of all theorising has been modified since the grab-bag days when society was defined as a laboratory. The propositions that society can best be understood by analogies with, for example, cybernetic systems or banking practice, are thought to lend sturdy clogs to the bare-footed empiricism of earlier enthusiasms. Such models also provide realistically derived conceptual frameworks for the understanding of social phenomena. While few still claim freedom from values with much conviction, the question of one's personal political position is still thought to be separable from the study of politics in much the same way that classical Liberalism has always insisted on the separation of economic life from social life, and the necessity to separate government from both. "Society," Tom Paine remarked, "is produced by our wants, and government by our wicked-ness." The political scientist objectively analyses such wants and wickednesses as manifested in observable behaviour, dividing the labour with colleagues in sociology and economics. That, which Liberal theory had separated, bourgeois social science attempts to integrate.

A second broad area of political study invokes the philosophy of Karl Marx. Here, practice assumes a relation of equality with theory, and the word *praxis* has been restored to the political vocabulary to

147

represent the unity of theory and practice. The theory here differs from classical theory insofar as classical theory was, as that most bone-weary and dog-eared of disciplinary clichés insists, always a theory of human nature, a 'concept of man' dressed in the raiment appropriate for public life. Marxist theory remains a theory of history, despite the efforts of some scholars to re-interpret it as a concept of man. History, as a matter of record or current observable socio-economic relation-ships, is subject to analysis and verification. It is also subject to criticism, for critique demonstrates the real relation between action and necessity. Critique is precisely the theoretical application of human historical understanding to human events. The exactness of theoretical critique is determined by the correctness of the class perspective: At any given moment in history, only one class is a progressive scocial force. *Praxis* is therefore the unification of an analytical and operational theory of history which compels the correct critical position from which the progressive class in a given society may solve by unified theory and action those problems which history presents to them.

There is a third group of devoted classicists, who prefer to refer to their practice as political philosophy rather than political theory. They insist that theories of politics be derived from contemplation of metaphysical structures which indicate their presence in the order and lawfulness of nature while hiding their awesome essence in the opaque and mysterious character of the natural. This group tends to lack popular appeal and, as their founder, Plato, understood so well, have no impact in democratic societies which distrust the virtuousness of intellectual patricians as acutely as they suspect the good-will of economic elites. Theory becomes eloquent lament and apologetic defence.

Clearly, these approaches to politics are related to political positions which are generally labeled Liberal, Socialist, and Conserva-tive. For practical purposes, Conservatives who prefer progress to lament have joined the first group. They do however, reserve some options, much as those older empiricists who practise Comparative Political Science, and those political theorists who decline to be called normative, but have no other name, attempt to turn their open minds in several directions. There are, of course, complexities and differentia-tions and lots of argument and ideological struggle between these broad groups, but my purpose here is not to examine variations, but to raise the question which confronts women who involve themselves in Political Science or political action. Women have these theoretical paths open to them—well-trodden paths, indeed—but so far political choices have been circumscribed by the urgent need for practical redress of intensely exploitive personal and social situations. 'Man Alone' may represent the dignity and pathos of the philosophically comprehended existential tragedy. Woman alone is a welfare problem. Political action by women has been necessarily issue-oriented. Economic discrimination, abortion, day-care, legal inequality, status in the work-world, political participation: All emerge from experienced humiliations to present practical objectives. Political systems have even been demonstratively if frugally responsive to organized pressure in some of these areas. Broader areas of political activity have not produced a specifically feminist approach. In terms of economic management, foreign policy or constitutional debate, for example, a specifically feminist perspective has not yet developed. In terms of political theory, women have done without, accepting a prevailing ideology or responding with a brand of gut female chauvinism which has served as often to alienate other women as to unite the sex.

Of course, the difficulties presented to feminine understanding and the analysis of lived women's experience posed by the masculinity of theories, concepts, and language itself have been widely recognized. Evelyn Reed, a marxist feminist, lapses into an unwittingly ironical example of the sexist dimension of linguistic expressionism when she writes: ". . . as the liberation movement acquires a stronger thrust and penetrates deeper among working women. . . ."

The imagery is Male and sexual. Clearly, though, women cannot immediately reform language, which is the product of people communicating and not of Commissary fiat. Yet language remains the operative medium of political theory. This vocabulary is interestingly biological. To be sure, this is a result of the remarkable durability of organic metaphors in political thought, metaphors which have dutifully followed biological science through seasonal cycle, teleology, and natural hierarchy to the cosmic clock and evolution. No doubt there are political scientists turning hopefully to chromosomatic analogies. The 'body politic' and 'constitution' are words which draw attention to the life and vitality of political structures. Governments insist on their 'legitimacy' with all the fervour of the bastards of Victorian fiction. Corrupt societies are sick societies, and for Socrates the most fruitful analogy for the statesman was the physician. Jean-Jacques Rousseau panted for regeneration from the state of decay. These modes of expression are something more than metaphor: One crucial dimension of political activity is the creation of stability over time, of permanence beyond the individual life span. Political institutions, at least from the perspective of those who uphold them, are able to do what their human content cannot. They defy death by auto-regeneration. Hobbes called his sovereign state *Leviathan*. Hobbes was a nominalist, and a careful man with a word. Leviathan was the Hebrew version of a monster who appears under different names in a variety of ancient myths. He is a sea-monster, a sea-green incorruptible who comes to cleanse a rotten polity and replace it with a self-regenerating and just state.

The difference between biological and political reproduction has been, historically, sexual exclusiveness. The former is woman's business and the latter man's. Whereas no father can ever look upon a child with the utter certainty that it is his, the Hero who founds the city or the makers of Constitutions whom Machiavelli so admired can look, like gods, upon their work and know that it is good and will continue after they themselves succumb to the natural cycle.

There is some evidence that biological reproduction provided early societies with an experiential principle of human continuity. For some years scholarly arguments have burgeoned over the question of matriarchal social structures, and whether it is not an error to deduce matriarchy from matrilinear kinship arrangements. These considerations provide exciting projects for anthropology, bringing forth another linguistic irony.

It was *anthropos* whom Aristotle famously defined as a political animal. This celebrated declaration is germane to our present considerations. The Greeks who defined the political *persona* as masculine also founded the discipline of political theory. Indeed, it is not without interest that three of the four great founding 'fathers' were not fathers at all. Plato, Augustine, and Aquinas were aggressive celibates unable to distinguish sexuality from lust. Only Augustine confessed to lapsing, a lapse which caused him personal anguish and fortified the myth of that pre-lapsarian temptress, Eve. Not for Augustine those Heroic founders of cities: Secular cities emerge with all their spiritual squalor from the rancid wombs of whores. The Whore of Babylon remained a popular figure in political polemic right through the seventeenth-century bourgeois revolution in England, where ardent Puritan publicists rather curiously metamorphosed celibate popes into Babylonian Whores.

The Greek success in moving public or political identity from blood and kinship to land and property is well-known. Lewis Morgan, the American anthropologist whose researches in kinship structures were greeted with enthusiasm by Marx and commented on extensively by Engels, claims that this historical drama, with its movement from blood to land and from matriarchy to patriarchy, was the informing happening of Aeschylus' *Oresteian Trilogy*. Morgan and Engels agree that Aeschylus has dramatized what Engels calls "*the world historical defeat of the female sex.*" Family centred politics have brought nothing but tyranny and grief which continues generation after generation until

150

a more rational mode of social organization is developed. Thus, the areopagus becomes the first rational public institution, fulfilling the function of maintaining order by law and the exercise of human judgment. It is possible to regard this as a positive step in human history without losing sight of the sexual implications. Athene, who presided over the dénouement of this world historical drama, was fortunately androgynous. According to Plato, Athene belonged to an age when fatherhood was not recognized. She had, however, long been re-interpreted by patriarchal mythologizers as being born directly of Zeus. This eliminated any uncertainty as to her paternal origin, and she was able to be the patroness of the Athenian polis without being its founder. Aeschylus has her listen unperturbed to the male hysteria of Apollo, that faintly hysterical Norman Mailer of the *polis*, who insists that women play no active part in reproduction, but act only as incubators for those sacred seeds:

> The mother is no parent of that which is called
> her child, but only nurse of the new-planted seed
> that grows. The parent is he who mounts. A stranger
> she preserves a stranger's seed, if no god interfere.

Apollo cites Athene herself as a glowing example of the literally motherless child.

The Morgan/Engels thesis is an interesting one. George Thomson, in his *Aeschylus in Athens*, has attempted to add substance to the interpretation in religious, artistic, and economic terms. The overthrow of the chthonic by the Olympian religions is now quite widely documented and accepted. The political reflection of these events appears in the various reforms of Solon and Cleisthenes and the successful career of Pericles. We do not know all the details of these reforms, nor do we have an entirely clear account of the events preceding them. Class struggles, with the ancient calls of the dispossessed for relief of debt and land reform, certainly played their part. What is clear is that a new version of manliness appeared on the scene. Its ideological trappings were contained in the concept of *arete*, embracing civic and military virtue. Man as citizen was born. The parents were landed property and a political Constitution. Men born of women took their social bearings from their situation as sons and brothers of women. Citizens are reborn ceremoniously into the polity, and take their social bearings from the rational institutions created by other men.

This arrangement appears to have worked quite well, until the militarism inherent in the ideal of Athenian citizenship overreached itself in Sicily. The *demes*, or, as we would say, the ridings or geographical districts of Athens, provided a basis for political organization which superseded clan and tribal ties. It incidentally alienated the aristocracy, which is strongly dependent on the hereditary principle. Presumably it made little difference to slaves or women, whose views are not on record. Women did retain a small function, much as the Furies in Aeschylus' play are fobbed off with pious sinecures. To qualify as citizens Athenians had to have an Athenian mother. This is presumably a by-product of the uncertainty of paternity, and in due course the requirement was repealed. Even while it was maintained as a necessary condition for citizenship, it does not appear to have been a sufficient one. By virtue of biological birth the child was Athenian; to become an Athenian citizen required a second birth controlled and legitimated by men. At eighteen the Greek boy, in a curious mixture of primitive rite and bureaucratic efficiency, was registered as a citizen of his *deme*.

Thus, Aristotle's dictum that man was political by nature appears to require some modification. He was in fact political by second nature, by virtue of evolving customs of an artificial, humanly manufactured kind. This presented a theoretical problem, for in Greek thought Nature was the great legitimizer and moral arbiter of human affairs. The natural was the good. This situation led Plato into labyrinthine speculation on the nature of nature. To avoid the Eleatic monism to which such tautological expression logically leads, this phrase can be re-expressed as the Essence of Being. 'Nature' in its material manifestations is, to say the least, a problematic paradigm of goodness. The contemplation of the stately and regular movements of heavenly bodies may attune the receptive soul to the changeless mathematical rhythms of infinity and eternity: Observable nature is, however, also decay, decline, mutation, restless change, and death. This Good which is eternal and orderly also appears to be cyclical and contingent. Locked into the cycle is human life, individually temporal, collectively continuous. By nature, individual man is born helpless and helplessly dies. Unlike later generations, the Greeks did not attempt to subdue nature by mastering her physical laws. They idealized physical nature to reflect an ideal concept of man. This re-interpretation, it is suggested, was made in response to a valid political need. A cycle of birth and decay or a permanent state of revolution is seen by the conservative mind—and these great minds were conservative—as a poor basis for social life. Among the objectives of political life is the provision of communal order and continuity over time. Clearly, the social order which aspires to permanence must attempt to banish contingency and chance from the production of subsistence as well. A rational society attempts to unify these objectives, and political theory has tried historically to identify the dimensions of the Good Society. Modern Liberal theory, of course, endeavours to separate the economic and the political, glossing over the fact that the defence of existing property relations cannot be achieved without active political support. The storms of rhetoric on the necessity of non-intervention in market and property relations cannot obscure the fact that human control over human production of subsistence is fundamental to social life. Aristotle understood this as clearly as Marx, though, as Marx observed, Aristotle's view was necessarily contorted by the empirical fact of slave labour. The need to bring human labour of hand and head to bear upon the necessary provision of subsistence—in other words, the need for a rational mode of production—is basic to social organization. The capitalist mode of production relinquishes rational social organization in favour of rational individual self-interest, and permits the necessary conditions of human life to be surrendered to a theoretically and invisibly benign market mechanism. That this is not a purely theoretical situation is illustrated very well by a current economic situation which is clearly out of human control. Political action is nowhere so patently impotent as in the demonstrable contemporary inability of governments to understand, far less repair, the depradations of inflation.

Even if this is so, what is the significance for women in politics? Clearly, theories of politics are male theories. I want to suggest that the pursuit of understanding of the relation of political theory and political practice can be conducted from a specifically feminine perspective, and that such a perspective may refresh the stalemated condition in which political thought currently finds itself. Feminine scholarship has the task of pursuing a critique of the conceptual apparatus of male stream thought into its most abstruse and sophisticated mazes in moral, political, and analytical philosophy, theology and law. In political terms, the influential philosophy of Hegel is a case in point. De Beauvoir has pointed out that Hegel's celebrated master and slave dialectic may be as usefully illuminative of sex struggle as of the mammoth confrontation of *Geist* with *Geist*, or class with class. However productive this particular metaphor, it is, in the vernacular, but a moment of Hegel's supra-historical vision. There is plenty of factional disagreement about the objectives and success of the Hegelian enterprise, with only a rump 'right wing' accepting Hegel's claim to have systematically embraced and transcended Absolute Knowledge. It seems to me that Hegel's efforts can be usefully understood as a bold attempt to define *Man* as uncompromisingly male, consciously eliminating the claim that 'Man' is a generic and humanistic term. I am quite content to leave to theological ideologues considerations as to whether Hegel's idiosyncratic bi-trinitarian *unio-mystica* is devout, heretical, or gnostic, and philosophers may ponder the question of whether Hegel's massive effort to unite eternal god with mortal man satisfactorily finalizes philosophical thought. What I do want to point out is that Hegel's idealism rests on a total mystification of biological reproduction. Theological thought participates in that bliss in which "Son separates from Father only to be reunited as spirit." Thus, the alienated seed is successfully brought back under male control, but in spiritual terms. The German language does not, like English, provide one word—conception—for what women do actually and men ideally. Hegel, however, was conscious of the connection, and as a young man had pursued the subject. In an analysis of sexual love, he tastes the exquisite knowledge of the irony of fate by which the purest of human relationships—love—is regrettably nonrational. Abraham's ideal of "loving union" is but the unreflective consciousness of the need to perpetuate. The ideal human relationship in reflective terms is that of Father and Son. Later, in the *Phenomonology,* Hegel develops the ideal intra-sexual relationship as that of brother and sister, with Antigone the admirable symbol of womanhood. The mother's womb, young Hegel thought, stands empirically against oneness, "an alive thing." Unifying creativity must thus be expressed in "the concept," according to Hegel, the source of the tragic consciousness in pagan life. Freely interpreted, family life realizes life and love, while political relations realize struggle and finitude. Hegel thought that the development of the constitutional State could mediate these contradictions. One of the practical requirements was the limitation of female activity to the natural sphere. Nature, for Hegel, is space without time and, lacking the creative force of human history, is finally impotent. History, man's sphere, is creative, rational, and right. Rectitude for women is passive; she "has her substantive destiny in the family, and to be imbued with family piety is her ethical frame of mind." This framework is free, and its freedom consists in acknowledging her husband's guidance and actively upholding tradition. Again like Rousseau's Sophie, her freedom consists in willing her own bondage to irrational and impotent nature, while, like Antigone, her work and her only risk was the upholding of the *status quo.* Antigone, that most perfect of women, upheld tradition with an uncompromising particularity, or single-mindedness, or, some might say, pigheadedness. This sealed the terrible tomb to which Sophocles condemned her with the admiring approval of Hegel. She died, of course, a virgin.

Hegel's writings make it quite clear that the paradigm of dialectics is concrete enough, and is nothing but the process of biological reproduction. The search for explanatory models, metaphors, and

154

phrases to elucidate the dialectical process which has engaged teachers and ideologues alike would be much simplified if this were widely understood. The negation of the alienated seed by its fusion with its opposite is negated again by the generation of a higher form of life, a human child. Hegel does not put that quite so clearly:

> The difference in the physical characteristics of the two sexes has a rational basis and consequently acquires an intellectual and ethical significance. This significance is determined by the difference into which the ethical substantiality, as the concept, internally sunders itself in order that its vitality may become a concrete unity consequent upon this difference.

> Thus one sex is mind in its self-diremption into explicit personal self-subsistence and the knowledge and volition of free universality, i.e. the self-consciousness of conceptual thought and the volition of the substantive, but knowledge and volition in the form of concrete individuality and feeling. In relation to externality, the former is powerful and active, the later passive and subjective.

This is much more sophisticated than Apollo's crude protest, but the significant activity is still that of he who mounts. What accrues to the male parent here is power and action. Hegel offers an interesting and perhaps accurate analysis of the origin of the concept of power. The question of power, its exercise, its legitimacy, its differentiation from authority, and, indeed, its definition are questions which have exercised political scientists for a long time. Indeed, for some thinkers power *is* the subject-matter of politics. Some modern pragmatic theorists of democracy have seen the major function of democratic political systems as the packaging, distribution, and re-cycling of little parcels of power, an exercise which is greatly simplified if a large number of legitimate recipients of the parcels are too apathetic to bother about opening them. Power is *the* political reality, and the pragmatic political mind is not concerned with its substance but simply with its exercise. One hopes that by a mechanism similar to the invisible hand of the market-place, this exercise will be in the public interest. The naivete of American concepts of the benign exercise of political power has suffered a painful exposé in the last couple of years.

Pragmatists would scorn the notion of power as human reason's ammunition in a life-risking encounter with universality. Similarly, they wince at the notion of power as the economically based ideological clobber with which the ruling classes manipulate the masses to a satisfactory false-consciousness of their social relationships, or rich nations keep the poor in their place. The important point is that power politics, power, as it were, as the in—and for—itself of political activity, is leading inexorably to a politics of impotence. Politics, once optimistically defined as the art of the possible, is degenerating into the pessimistic categorization of the impossible. Inflation, nuclear control, population control, the ending of internecine and international conflicts, the prevention of famine, and the rational distribution of natural resources—all are realities against which the judicious exercise of rational political power is demonstrably impotent. The fact that the politics of power is the politics of impotence may be abstractly satisfying to the dialectician. It is alarming and increasingly comfortless for the people who live in the world.

It is not suggested that the emergence of women into the political realm will have an immediate impact upon these problems. The pleasant notion that women are naturally possessed of some kind of gift of loving motherliness which can anneal the divisiveness of social struggles is as absurd as the American declaration of the end of ideology. The substance of political life is the residue of centuries of male *praxis*, a grim amalgam of power struggle, ferocious heroics, and material greed. It does not offer women any theory or any strategy for political action other than a choice of tired more-of-the-samenesses. Indeed, Karl Marx attempted to abolish and transcend the spirituality of the Hegelian dialectic by reversing Hegel's abstract confrontation of universality and particularity to the actual conflict of class struggle, the contradiction consisting of particular, individual ownership of the means of production on the one hand, and the universal, or socially collective labour of production on the other. At an early stage, August Bebel assured women that their destiny lay with the proleteriat. Bebel spoke with the same confidence with which John Stuart Mill, or, for that matter, Mary Wollstonecraft had urged women to hitch their wagon to the star of a liberalised middle class. Despite Marx's achievement, there is still a theoretical task for women.

The empirical data for such enquiry are marriage and property laws, the lived conditions of women, the diverse modes of ideological reinforcement of the dogma of male supremacy and the rituals and rites of child bearing and nurture. The active force emergent from the history of human productivity, namely, class struggle, does not have sex-struggle as a necessary corollary. Indeed, the world historical defeat of the female sex appears to have happened in pre-pre-history, and is known only by socio/anthropological residues of a problematic kind and the ability of a great poet to articulate the promptings of ancestral memory. In fact, the material causes of the defeat defeated Engels, as de Beauvoir has correctly said. Neither the division of labour nor the development of class divisions logically entail or dialectically demand the subjugation of women.

At the very least, the world-historical defeat of the female sex has been imperfect. Western history demonstrates an interesting and recurrent phenomenon; periods of crises, Ortega y Gasset's "heights of times," have been attended by prodigious political struggle, class transformations, and ideological shifts, producing great flurries of intellectual and artistic activity. This is true of the rise and decline of Athenian and Roman Imperialism, the Renaissance, the bourgeois revolutions of England and France, and the radical phases of Industrial revolution. The most distinguished contributions to political theory have been responses to these overt socio-economic tensions. A modest accompaniment to such stirring events has consistently been restiveness among members of the subjugated sex. In Plato's Greece, women's liberation was, as Professor Guthrie has rather tentatively put it, "in the air." As the Roman Empire declined, women increasingly declined to reproduce. In Mary Tudor's ill-omened counter-reformation, women were in the front line of the Vestments controversy of 1568, when more than half of the separatists imprisoned in the Bridewell were women. Women were very active in the sectarian activities of Puritanism's Heroic Age. In 1789 Olympe de Ganges was proposing the abolition of masculine privilege in France until the scaffold silenced her. These outbreaks were minor, quickly suppressed and probably class specific.

Breakdown of the political order has as a regular concomitant female revolutionary fervour. This statement will be viewed, of course, as a heresy in some circles and as a grotesquely understated truism in others. The question, though, of the relation between substructure and superstructure in Marxist theory is one which some theorists—Louis Althusser, for example—do feel requires the clarification of further theoretical practice. The structural model seems unduly rigid to explain adequately the momentum of struggle. The relation of the two structural levels is un-dialectical and unmediated. Further questions have concerned the disappearance of the individual ego in the totality of class consciousness. The real epistomological difficulties are not dissolved by sloganized sneers about bourgeois infatuations. This particular issue has often been posed in the form of some kind of Marx/Freud polarization, with much exertion by people like Marcuse and Fromm to close the breach. In simple terms, this is the old problem of the opposing dimensions of individuality and what the young Marx called species awareness. It is suggested here that a new perspective on this ancient dilemma might emerge from a more adequate critique of the social relations of reproduction. For too long it has been fashionable to banish biological reproduction to the realm of animal nature as an activity which cannot assert any superiority of man kind over animal kind. This is absurd. Reproduction is no more and no less an act of pure instinct than production. Copulation and subsistence are equally subject to vast and complex structures of social relationships, institutional arrangements, and economic imperatives, to say nothing of the huge mass of scientific understanding and accumulated fetish. Neither can it be said that reproduction escapes change by technological inventiveness, from the chastity belt through the rubber nipple to the ubiquitous pill.

Perhaps the difficulties which Engels and other Marxists have had in giving an adequate account of the move from matrilinear to patriarchal society arises from the theoretical imperative of relating this move to the mode of production. The necessity of subsistence is only necessarily *social* in terms of mother and child. The weaned male loose among fecund nature could presumably survive without the presence of others. The race could not. Copulation is necessarily social. However transitorily, it takes two and leaves a different dyad.

Furthermore, Hegel and Marx are agreed on the relation of work—Marx preferred the word labour—to the formation of self and social consciousness. Yet labour in childbirth failed to gain serious consideration from either thinker. The labour of bringing forth young is presumably philosophically indistinguishable from the similar efforts of cows or baboons. Women do not think about childbirth, but experience it as 'natural' or, piously, as acceptance and expiation of the guilt of Eve. Hegel's heroes, pregnant with philosophical consciousness or successful conquistadorial militarism, risk their lives to give birth to the ideas conceived in the course of their struggles. Marx's proleterian transcends alienation and hones his class consciousness in the active sociability of mass production and the ensuing revolutionary struggle.

What woman does experience in the course of her labour is the facticity of human continuity in the certainty that the child is hers. It is suggested that continuity is a necessary human experience which men must find elsewhere. It is travesty to characterize the labour of childbirth as immaterial or animalistic. Theoretically, it might be more fruitful to posit a dialectical opposition between the relations of reproduction and production, a dialectic in which Marx's superstructures are not outgrowths but mediative phenomena. To be sure, production has, historically, developed highly complex social relations, but subsistence in its fundamental form is an individual act of eating and breathing, while reproduction is necessarily social, both at the level of conception and the stage of parturition. Dialectical distaste for Pastor Malthus' gloomily algebraic Iron Laws should not blind us to this connection between the production of subsistence and the production of people. Our contemporary world provides as much evidence for it as do the ancient exposures of infants. The fate, which Iphegenia suffered and Oedipus so

158

narrowly escaped is not a mere artistic flourish providing a dramatic logic for more important later events. It represents a stark reality in the dialectic of production and reproduction.

The concrete social form and historical reality of this fundamental antithesis is expressed in each of its poles as human struggle: class struggle on one hand, sex struggle on the other. Both express human resistance to one-sidedness, oppression and alienation. Marx says that the political superstructure is the battleground of the ideological refractions of the real world. Here we may return to a consideration of power. In Marxist theory, power simply signifies human capacity for the mental and physical labour of production:

> The life-process of a society, which is based on the process of material production, does not strip off its mystical veil until it is treated as production by freely associated men and is consciously regulated by them in accordance with a settled plan.

The only power here is physical and mental power, individual capability rationally utilised, the famous "from each according to his ability. . . ." This is quite different from the generalized concept of 'political power,' which is simply dominant ideology. This mystic dimension accounts too for the legendary difficulties of defining power, whether in the theories of Weber, Mao, or community power analysts, or the practical strategic power balancing activities of suave imperialist bandits from Pericles to Kissinger. Power is the "mystical veil" drawn over the irreconcilable paradox involved in treating an abstraction as a commodity. It is fetishistic to regard power as a commodity, yet modern capitalist democracy, like its market partner, insists that power is a commodity which can be bought, sold, voted away, gifted, or traded. In other words it is alienable. That which is alienable, of course, may also be appropriated.

Appropriation as the capacity to lay hold of the powers or products of the powers of others is simple plunder, and its process is one of physical strength, or might. Power is the process by which might is made right or at least legitimate; that is to say it is an ideological and justificatory addition to simple human capacity. I would suggest that its paradigm case is paternity with the associated doctrine of male potency.

'Potency' is a doctrinal extension of the real fertility of men and women alike from the realm of nature and its derivative social relations to the realm of mysticism. Not surprisingly, the development of the concept of potency occurs concurrently with the movement from blood kinship and communal property to locality and private property in Greece. The most sophisticated development is worked out in Aristotle's biology. Aristotle, it will be recalled, regards all final forms as potentially present in formal causes. He asserted that the *telos* of each human being was present potentially in the male semen. The mother's contribution to the child was mere matter, for women lack the "vital heat" necessary to transform material causes to formal causes. This "vital heat" is clearly Aristotle's scientific version of the male potency for which Apollo, fittingly enough for a god, adduced a religious explanation. The difficulty to be met is that male fertility is impotent against time, for the period of gestation renders individual paternity uncertain. Time injects pathos into the fate of the alienated seed. Male-stream thought has struggled for centuries with the perplexities of temporality. To be sure, the inexorability of the march to death has orchestrated much of this speculation. Time has a much more prosaic role in birth than such poetic renderings as the fall from eternity into time suggest. Between the conception and the creation, writes T.S. Eliot, falls the shadow. Indeed—this shadow is precisely that interlude of gestation which deprives paternity of certainty of itself, the shadow of the impotency of potency. Herculean efforts have been made in both practice and thought to close the gap. In practice, marriage laws, marital police, harems, purdah, economic dependence, capital punish-ment for adultery (the adulteration of the holy egg basket), ideologies of female chastity, even the creation of eunuchs—all of these devices have been invoked so that the potent seed, once planted, preserves its donor's potency inviolate. In theory, perhaps the most radical solution is that proposed by Socrates in Plato's *Republic*. For the Guardians it is proposed that clearly unsatisfactorily physical controls be aban-doned. By suitable social arrangements the uncertainty of paternity is to be extended to mothers, even at the high price of permitting the inferior sex to have a shot at elitism. In the proposed community of wives, no parent shall know their child, nor child its parents. This proposition horrified Aristotle, who misunderstood its purpose, and preferred in any case to rely on existing and reasonably effective social controls. Ironically, Plato's ancient dream may find its apotheosis in such unmetaphysical creations as the computerized sperm bank or extra-uterine pregnancy.

The concept of power as defined here is a direct descendent of the concept of male potency, the mystic transformation of the alienated seed to the creative potency which defies uncertainty and legitimates the appropriation of the child as the property of the father, an appropriation without labour. Such an act of appropriation has its defects. Appropriation does not produce the consciousness of continu-ity which women experience practically in labour. The need to create and legitimate a system of social continuity for men may have been a factor in the development of political life, and politics may well have been originally quite literally a man's world. If the need for continuity were merely psychological, it could be and was met by religion. The presence of one's ancestors on one's hearth, however, cannot extend its defiance of lapsed time beyond the family and its communally owned property. The right to appropriate the property of others by an individual requires a much more complex social organization: A principle of continuity and legitimation independent of blood lines and sexuality which fosters "mother right." An artificial creation, this noble lie and splendid fiction requires a powerful ideological defence, ultimately much stronger than the realistic and experiential sense of continuity which women understand as a component of their reproductive process.

If the concept of power is the legitimate child of the concept of potency, then it is clear that power is an idealised chimera vigorously imposed upon human reality. This does not mean that there is no such thing as power any more than the analysis means that there is "really" no such thing as male supremacy. It means that power is both abstract and conceptual while rooted in human reality. Yet at the centre of both potency and power lies the vulnerable artificiality of the whole conception.

What is the purpose of such speculation? It is a necessary component in women's struggle for a political participation which can proceed through issues to the task of the creation of a rational society. This requires the unity of theory and action. Marx's view of "life-process" is correct but one-sided. Human history has now reached a stage when reproduction can be "consciously regulated . . . in accordance with a settled plan." Women are likely to be excluded from the formulation of that plan if they do not engage in the political struggle against the Ideology of Potency. Further, if it is indeed the case that political institutions have emerged in response to exclusively male needs, then women must recognize that they have to reject the conservative ideal of Antigone in favour of revolutionary change. Not only are existing political philosophies and ideologies not sacrosanct, they are probably useless. It may be that women face the enormous task of re-defining humanity, as it were, from the beginning.

In the beginning was the word . . . and the word was made flesh. Thus St. John attempts the early fusion of Attic intellectualism and Judaic mysticism. It is an assertion of male potency, the ability to reverse reality by an act of disembodied mind. Flesh certainly preceded language. Men have been at it ever since, but the perspective has grown narrower and meaner. In our time, man has decided that he makes himself, a device by which the necessary sociability of biological generation leads to the appalled loneliness of autogenesis in a void. As

Samuel Beckett understands, this man in the void is impotent. He has appropriated in thought the feminine creative principle, the female sex hormone. This I take to be the meaning of Estragon's name. Listlessly and without expectancy dualistic man waits for Godot. Godot is Being, or, more prosaically, the child who cannot ever emerge from man alone. In Beckett's grimly comic metaphor, man with his trousers permanently buttoned up has nothing to do but impotently endure the pointless passage of time. Suppose Godot is a woman, what then?

Suggested Bibliography

de Beauvoir, Simone, *The Second Sex*, N.Y., 1961.

Engels, *The Origin of the Family, Private Property and the State*, Introduction by Eleanor Burke Leacock.

Ehrenberg, V., *The Greek State*, London, 1972.

Havelock, A., *The Liberal Temper in Greek Politics*, Yale, 1957.

Hegel, G.F., Fragment on "Love," *G.W.F. Hegel: Early Theological Writings*, Trans. T.M. Knox, Chicago, 1948.

Hegel, G.F., *The Philosophy of Right*, Trnas. T.M. Know, Oxford, 1967.

Pateman, Carole, *Participation and Democratic Theory*, Cambridge, 1970.

Thomas, Keith, "Women and the Civil War Sects," in Aston, Trevor, Ed., *Crisis in Europe*, 1560–1660, New York, 1967.

Thinking about Politics:
An Existentialist Approach

HERMAN TENNESSEN

For the greater part of my life I have been a Socialist, believing in the public ownership of most means of production. Yet, when I recently attended an international congress of philosophy (and pseudo-philosophy) in Bulgaria, I was forcibly reminded of the obvious: The terms "Socialism" and "public ownership" may suggest quite different things to different citizens, Parties, nations, and mistresses of military or naval attachés.

Why should the obvious come as a shock? Some would say that the shock is due, in cases like this, to failure to think hard enough and often enough about politics. They might go on to recommend a Puritanical time-table for rectifying that failure. But these kinds of answers and advice I take to be immature and boring. There need be no particular value in expending more energy and emotion on inner political dialogue if one keeps energetically resurrecting the Olympian and pig-headed absurdities of the past. In what follows I shall attempt to sketch some bare outlines and rough diagnoses of errors in reflection on politics and on man generally—errors that tend to bring us to the nature of the human condition. It should soon become attractive to infer that I have certain sympathies with a number of Existential philosophers and psychiatrists. I say: "By all means infer this! And go on to conclude that what I consider worthwhile in the way of philosophical analysis has next to nothing to do with the ideas of so-called analysts who worship Common Sense and Ordinary English Usage."

1. The Porcine Fallacy:
Utilitarianism and Political Ends

If an eccentric millionaire died leaving me one million and thirteen dollars on condition that "H. T. will bring about living conditions for my beloved hogs which will be as close to ideal as is practically possible at my Medicine Hat Piggery Ranch . . . ," I might well try to earn the sum honestly by making *Happiness for the Pigs* my temporary goal or end. I might try to ensure that the boars', sows', and piglets' food, drink, temperatures, sexual opportunities, electric blankets, medications against fear and depression, etc., were as productive of pleasure and as destructive of pain as I could in that practical context realistically hope to arrange. I would strive to eliminate all anxiety. I would pursue this as an end that constituted the Good Life for hogs.

Unfortunately, something like this model inspired Jeremy Bentham and James Mill in the early nineteenth century when their native Britain was brutalized by the Industrial Revolution, by the enclosing of Common Land (which drove the rural poor to the cities), and by a great many laws which kept power and property largely in the hands of a few capitalists and almost feudal landowners. One result of this situation was the great range of suffering among the majority of Britons: Suffering from hunger, disease, industrial accidents, pollution or overwork; suffering from humiliation, as the reciprocal ties of assistance which feudalism maintained between rich and poor were replaced by relations that gave strength and importance only to those with money, while those without money were stripped of all power and dignity; suffering that arose partly from disappointed expectations of mercy and relief, partly from inability to expect a steady living with any confidence. The understandable, but disastrous reaction of Bentham and the older Mill was to preach reform in terms of The Greatest Happiness (and The Least Misery) of the Greatest Number. I shall call this The Greatest Happiness Principle or Classical Utilitarianism. Classical Utilitarianism helped to secure many social and political reforms that were admirable. But in the long run this Principle encouraged the appalling travesty of good living that we find so often among the economically and technologically advanced countries' better paid citizens.

Before I go into my own (more Existential) reasons for opposing the Greatest Happiness Principle, it may well interest the reader if I mention certain objections which Utilitarians often need to meet if they are to satisfy people who find the Greatest Happiness Principle basically questionable. I shall leave my readers to assess these objections' strengths or silliness for themselves. At least, for what it's worth, the objections show that Utilitarians and Common Sense do not coincide—though Utilitarians talk on many occasions as if they did.

Some Classic Objections to Utilitarianism

Objection I: The Utilitarians talk as if Pain and Pleasure could be *measured* like the heat of a room or the weight of a new born baby. Some may now say that advances in neurology will make this possible. If people were hooked up to some neurological apparatus all or most of the time, however, their freedom of movement and their opportunities to gain pleasure would be ludicrously diminished. Yet if people are only to be hooked up *occasionally*, the needed data about everyday life could not be attained. Others say that we can *estimate* pain and

164

pleasure in terms of Misery Units and Joy Units. But such talk of *estimation* plunges us back into the rough and ready *guesswork* about how others *do* or *would* feel in certain circumstances—the very kind of amateurism that Utilitarians were meant to replace with Science!

Objection II: Idolizing the Greatest Happiness of the Greatest Number is a sure way to justify the neglect or outright persecution of *minority groups* in a society. It may feebly be replied that tolerance of minority groups other than the criminal is clearly conducive to the Greatest Happiness of the Greatest Number. But two things are wrong with this: (A) It is NOT *self-evident* that in all societies the flourishing of minority groups will be conducive to the Greatest Happiness of the Greatest Number; (B) more important is the fact that Utilitarianism tells us what is *fundamentally good, uniquely good in itself—pleasure* or the *greatest pleasure of the greatest number.* (Happiness is equated with minimum pleasure and minimum pain for any species—pigs, humans, snails, or whatever.) Now clearly it is only *right* or *fair* that minorities should be treated kindly because they are composed of other humans—whether or not being fair in this way adds in the short or long run to the Greatest Happiness of the Greatest Number.

Objection III: What Objection II shows is that *Justice* and *Kindness towards Other Persons* are values to be respected as fundamental, just as much as the Utilitarian Principle. In other words, the Greatest Happiness Principle cannot have the momentously basic status its followers proclaim.

Objection IV: Worse still, the Utilitarian Principle does not supply an automatic *Decision Procedure* for choosing wisely between political options. For we have in the Principle two *competing 'variables'*. Let us say that Policy *A*, building another airport near Calgary will result in 260,000 hoggish persons receiving 100,000 Joy Units each over the next twenty years (after which the airport will be closed). Let us say that Policy *B* will result in 100,000 hoggish persons receiving 26,000,000 Joy Units each over the same periods. Policy *A* produces Joy Units for a greater number. Policy *B* produces a greater number of Joy Units. The Utilitarian Principle supplies no Decision Procedure for guiding the politicians. Since it is meant to be *the* fundamental principle to which politicians can appeal, the politicians who believe this are left completely stymied.

Objection V: It occurred to John Stuart Mill, James Mill's much more famous son, that while mere *quantity* of pleasure is all right as a guide to the good government of animals like *pigs*, this will not do for political decisions concerning societies of men. What we must reckon with in the case of humans is the *quality*, as well as the quantity, of pleasure. John Stuart Mill tried to elude the conclusion that if there is *better* and *less good* pleasure qualitatively, then there are higher values than pleasure or quantity of pleasure. He hoped to avoid questions about the verification of which pleasure was of higher quality than another. He hoped to avoid these questions by saying that if anyone reliable tries the two systemmatically and prefers one over the other, then the one preferred is obviously of better quality. But the younger Mill's attempts to find a way out of these difficulties leave the philosophical problems and their political implications no less problematical than they were before. Experts on classical literature, who make their living by lecturing, may well prefer heavy drinking or light-hearted comic strips.

Objection VI: John Stuart Mill also saw that some proof should be attempted by Utilitarians of the proposition that *pleasure is the good.* He suggested the only proof needed of something being VISIBLE is that people see it. Thus the only proof needed of something being DESIRABLE is that people desire it. And certainly people do desire pleasure for its own sake. Unfortunately for Mill, "visible" means "*capable* of being seen" and "desirable" means something very different from "capable of being desired": It means "worthy of being desired," "*good* to desire," etc. Hitler's desiring to exterminate all Jews does not supply the slightest evidence that their extermination would be desirable. Nor would the great majority of men's desiring to exterminate Patty Hearst be in itself a good reason to cut her throat.

2. The Porcine Fallacy: An Existential Critique

Utilitarianism is still very much with us. Happily, a number of philosophers have simply grown bored with it. But an appalling number of politicians, social scientists and even psychiatrists have 'realized' that promoting the Greatest Happiness of the Greatest Number may result in their getting the greatest number of votes to support them, or Trade Unionists and managers to hire them, or patients to keep coming back for more while joyfully paying higher fees.

Alas, such futilitarian frogs are swollen with an antiquarian gas that they believe to be the purest source of realism and insight. They think they are so factual, so 'above it all' with regard to prejudices, so informal, so conscious of how hard reality is actually shaped.

In a Danish Encyclopedia, published around the turn of the century, a highly esteemed scientist wrote an article on "Flying Machines." "It is quite obvious," he concluded, "that none of these fantastic ideas shall ever materialize. Everybody knows that nothing heavier than water can ever float in water; by the same token, it is logically impossible that anything heavier than air can ever fly in the air." And while he jubilantly arrived at his unmistakable conclusion, outside his window birds sailed through the sky. Analogous, and similarly ludicrous, so it has often been argued, was the situation of the dogmatic negativists who, until recently, denied the possibility of human space travel: The deniers were already on board a space-ship, soaring, whirling through an immense, absurdly indifferent vast, vile void, totally vacuous, except for homeopathically sparse excipients of inconsequential motes of dust and specks of light, all blindly blank, deadly deaf, frigidly glaring with sublime apathy. . . .

This image has now become commonplace (appearing even in the inaugural speech of a U. S. president). It is most frequently employed homilectically: to foster and promote human gregariousness. "We are all in the same boat," etc. More intriguing, however, seems to me a question implicitly suggested in the metaphor: What wondrous mechanisms have permitted Man to remain deluded about his own cosmic conditions, and, in face of all the evidence to the contrary, maintained a basically Ptolemaic (if any) worldview?

The shortest, if not simplest, explanation offers a reference to the (a) cognitive and (b) empathetic "disintegrity" of human insights, or "disintegratedness' of Man: The ability (a) to hold cognitively incompatible views or positions, or (b) to prevent knowledge from penetrating "volitional" (etc.) personality layers and thus permitting it to remain purely "intellectual." In this respect, according to Heidegger one of the most effective ontological and eschatological hebetants is man's knack for extracting intervals out of his total term of Being and filling them with work and other pastimes, external sensation (*"Neugier"*), chatter and small-talk (*"das Gerede"*), etc. This, to return to the analogy, empowers the crew and passengers in the space-ship to go on, polishing brass and playing bridge, blissfully unaware of their "cosmic situation." They are all psychologically healthy, content, well adjusted and accommodated—ontologically secure. They have a feeling of integral selfhood, of personal identity, and of the permanency of things. They believe in their own continuity—in being made of good, lasting stuff—and in meaning and order and justice in life and in the universe. In the most fortunate cases, there is a good, healthy, unconditional surrender and submission to the norms of nicety and normalcy of the average, square-headed, stuff-shirted, sanctimonious, middle-class, North-American church-goer and bridge player, with his pseudo-intelligent, quasi-progressive, similicultured, platitudinal small-talk. Happy days, in this the best of all possible worlds! One doesn't notice until too late. In short, all is well (since nobody notices the end of "all that is well") until one night: The day's work is well done and the ship's crapulant fools frantically engulf themselves in a deadly serious game of bridge (till it is time for the night-cap and the tranquillizer). One of the "dummies," a champion brass polisher, suffering from an acute case of uncaused depression, goes to lie down for a while; he doesn't have a dime for the juke box; the room is painfully satiated with embarrassing silence. Instantly and unexpectedly he is struck by an execrative curse of inverted serendipity. He suddenly, in unbearable agony, sees himself as an upholstered pile of bones and knuckles, with the softer parts slung up in a bag on the front side, and his whole life as a ludicrously brief interlude between embryo and corpse, two repulsive caricatures of himself. As for this flying farce, this nauseatingly trivial burlesque in a whirling coffin, and its aimless, whimsical flight through the void: "What is it all about?" The question permeates him with dread and anguish, with "ontological despair" and "existential frustration." "*Angsten*" (Kierkegaard) constrains out of him all his puny, piddling hatreds and petty ambitions in brass and bridge, and fills him with care and compassion for his fellow travellers. In other words, he has become a philosopher, an alienated, nostalgic "cosmopath," and, *eo ipso,* a case for psychologists and psychotherapists, some of whom want to study him and label his "Daseinsweise," others to "unsick" him as well.

"What is it all about?" Mitja (in The Brothers Karamazov) felt that though his question may be absurd and senseless, yet he had to ask it, and in just that way. Socrates claimed that an unexamined life is not worthy of man. And Aristotle assigned Man's "proper" goal and "proper" limit to the right exercise of those faculties which are uniquely human. It is a commonplace that men, unlike other living organisms, are not equipped with built-in mechanisms for automatic maintenance of their existence. Man would perish immediately if he were to respond to his environment exclusively in terms of unlearned, biologically inherited forms of behaviour. In order to survive at all, the human being must discover how various things around him and in him operate: The place he occupies in the present scheme of organic creation is the consequence of having learned how to exploit his intellectual capacities for such discoveries. Hence, more human than any other human endeavour is the attempt at a total view of Man's function—or malfunction—in the Universe, his possible place and importance in the widest conceivable cosmic scheme. In other words, it is the attempt to answer, or at least articulate, whatever questions are entailed in the dying groan of ontological despair—what is it all about? This may well prove biologically harmful or even fatal to Man. Intellectual honesty and Man's high spiritual demands for order and meaning, may drive Man to the deepest antipathy to life and necessitate, as one existentialist chooses to express it, "a no to this wild, banal, grotesque and loathsome carnival in the world's graveyard."

Philosophy and suicide have always been typical upper-middle-class phenomena. Both presuppose some minimum amount of leisure time and a certain level of education. The recent desperate need among psychologists and psychotherapeuts for a "Philosophy of Man and his Fate" arises from the general improvement of living conditions and education. As David Riesman puts it, fifty years ago there was no problem as to what would constitute a cure or at least a step in a more "healthy" direction. Freud's patients were largely suffering from heavy hysteria, dramatic paralyzations, inability to talk or move. The more advanced countries today have caught up with many Utopian ideals concerning economic poverty and unquestionably psychopath-creating authoritarian family structures, while at the same time beliefs in gods and devils, heaven and hell, angels and immortality have almost vanished. In these countries people suffer less from nightmarish misery than from the more subtle disorders previously buried by the harsh and bitter struggle for existence. The clinical psychologists are unexpectedly confronted with patients who by all social criteria are tremendously successful and well adjusted. They have just—prematurely, as it were—anticipated the dying groan, Ivan Ilyitch's three-days-long shriek: What is it all about? Thus, what once was an obviously commendatory endeavour to abolish poverty and ignorance, is slowly raising before us a problem, the severity of which will increase in correlation with increase in leisure time and socio-economic and educational "progress," viz., the most humanly relevant question of all: What does it mean to be Man, what is the Lot of Mankind in cosmos? What once was an object of idle contemplation, has recently become a concern for economists and theologians, for scientists and creative artists, psychologists, psychiatrists, and educators.

The earliest idle contemplators, the so-called Ionian philosophers of Nature, "were rather naive and optimistic . . . they wondered originally at the obvious difficulties," says Aristotle, "then advanced and stated difficulties about the greater matters, e.g. about the moon and the sun and the stars, and then about the genesis of the whole universe." The first severe criticism sets in with Heraclitus who, as everybody knows, became rather frightfully obsessed by the insight that everything changes; and some of his successors were even more upset by the alleged consequences of this observation: "Nothing exists!" (in Parmenides' sense of "exist"). Take for example the oil-capital of Canada, the city of Edmonton. I want to make a statement about Edmonton; but before I have managed to utter or even think "Edmonton," that to which I intended to refer by "Edmonton" has already changed. And since I don't want to use the same proper name to designate different objects, I might as well desist from making use of it altogether, throw up my hands and admit that there is no such thing

169

as Edmonton. The ingenious counter-question is, "But what is it then, this Edmonton of which you say: It does not exist? Clearly you must have had something in your mind." And the answer is: "Yes. That is precisely where I have it: in my mind. The 'Edmonton' in my mind, the concept, the form, the idea of 'Edmonton,' that is the Edmonton, the only Edmonton that exists with an endurance (invariance) that permits a classification." It is quite easy to see how such an attitude, with the assistance of Pauline Christianity, might predispose the philosophers for that radical de-evaluation of all earthly sense-experiences which characterized so many of the most predominant trends of thought during the Medieval Ages and the first centuries thereafter. I shall refer to this type of philosophizing as "brain-philosophy." To a brain-philosopher sense experiences are either of negligible significance, totally irrelevant or represent a more or less serious obstacle to knowledge perfection. Already Zeno of Elea may be used to illustrate a rather typical form of brain-philosophy when he proved the fundamental impossibility of motion. "You claim that you can move?" asks Zeno. "Tell me then: Where does this alleged 'movement' take place?" It seemed to Zeno that there were only two possibilities: 1. Either you "move" where you are, in which case you are not moving, you are standing still; 2. or you do this "moving" where you are not. But how can you do anything, let alone moving, where you are not? Diogenes from Sinope is said to have reacted to this lecture by silently leaving his seat, strolling around for a while and then sitting down again. He undoubtedly meant by this to introduce a counter-argument to the Zenoist standpoint. But Zeno's response is obvious: "Thank you, my dear Diogenes," he would reply, "for this convincing illustration of my point of view. I take it that you all observed Diogenes perform what we have here called a 'motion' which I have just shown to be in principle impossible. So let this be a lesson to you. Don't ever believe your own eyes or any other sense-experience! They are bound to deceive you." The paradigm brain-philosopher is traditionally pictured blindfolded in his ivory tower, meditating on absolute and eternal forms in a world of abstract ideas. Diogenes, on the other hand, may be seen as representing an alternative philosophical attitude, what we shall here call 'the eye-philosophy."

Hippocrates, the "father of medicine," is usually mentioned as its first, most typical exponent. And this is no pure coincidence. It is commonly accepted as advisable for a physician to observe the patient before diagnosing. Few of us, I am sure, would have much confidence in a brain surgeon who performed his operation blindfolded, concentrating on eternal forms. This truism drove Hippocrates to the other extreme. He warned against almost any form of theorizing and advised his students to confine themselves to taking down in their protocols all the observed symptoms of the patient and nothing more. These protocol sentences are the only things that can be known: 10:35 A.M. skin pallid, urine colorless, feces grey.

What a distance to the noble meditator in his ivory tower! And yet, they have one thing in common: Their detachment from the external world, their attitude of "objective," non-commitment, their lack of emotional engagement. The doctor continues unruffled with his protocol: 10:45 A.M. pulse and respiration almost imperceptible. 10:48 A.M. the death struggle has begun. 11:02 A.M.: no pulse, no respiration. The patient is dead. The undertaker can take over.

What thus seems to permit the eye-philosopher to take an equally detached attitude to what he perceived visually, as does the brain-philosopher to absolute forms, is the uniqueness of the vertebrate eye. It is not really a sense organ, as it were; it is part of the brain. Already Augustine points to this exceptional position of our eyes in relation to our more peripheral sense organs. And he goes on to show how all the other senses initiate vision! The whole brain-eye distinction as an indication of two different epistemological attitudes and two different approaches to knowledge perfection—rationalism and empiricism—has thus been reduced to a mere matter of degree. The brain-philosophy dominated up to the Renaissance, in Descartes, Leibniz, Spinoza, Hegel, and others; the eye-philosophy broke through with the Renaissance (and its stress on bodily lust and sense-experiences) with Leonardo da Vinci, Galileo, etc., and later the British empiricists from Bacon to Locke, Hume, and Mill.

3. Existentialism as a "Heart Philosophy": The Alternative to Porcomania

More conspicuous than the brain-eye distinction is the ethical and epistemological distance from brain-eye-philosophy on one hand, to what one on the other hand might call "heart-philosophy." Generally speaking, heart-philosophy presents itself as a romantic reaction to the "existential lethargy" which allegedly characterized the attitude of brain-eye-philosophers. It is a plea for a dynamic, Heraclitean world view in which human life is more than a mere puppet show, and is a plea for freedom, initiative, decision, responsibility, novelty, adventure, risk, chance, romance—a world which, with effort, we can fashion to our purposes and ideals, a world where anything is possible. The existential "heart-philosopher" refuses to submit to any external or internal forces demanding his obedience, such as "logical truths," "factual truths," "sense-data," "the structure of language," etc. They may all be worth considering, but the choice, the decision is the individual's alone. And he must be thoroughly deprived of any pretext to avoid this responsibility.

I once gave a course in logic for high-ranking NATO officers during which I suggested a possible procedure according to which one first has to make clear what the choice is all about, then evaluate (in some systematic manner) the consequences of various possible decisions, and then make the choice. I took a concrete example of a commander on board a Norwegian torpedo boat, who, in a war with Russia, discovers a huge Russian battleship helplessly cooped up behind a neutral tanker in the end of a narrow fjord in Greenland. I asked the officers first to map out the various possible choice-alternatives. But, to my surprise, they protested violently. I had, they claimed, attacked the problem from the wrong end. It turned out that what they resented was that they were going to make the choice. They did not like it a bit. And here is how they managed to avoid decision and responsibility: (1) There are, it seems, such things as "militarily relevant data." (2) With each torpedo boat follows what one might call a "direction for usage."

What the commander is trained to do is just to compare direction and data, and the only correct course of action emerges more or less automatically out of this activity.

The commander was, the existentialists may contend, a victim of brain-eye-philosophy. It is the task of the existential philosopher to break this spell, and awaken us all to come out and face our choice situations instead of cowardly hiding behind natural and logical "laws" and ratio-empirical "data."

An important obstacle here, however, is the ordinary language, the everyday prose. The heart-philosopher needs an extraordinary language, a poetic-dramatic transmitter, in order to adequately convey to himself or fellow beings what the choice is really about. Ordinary language, "*die Umgangssprache,*" "*das Gerede,*" represents "the public worldliness," "the intersubjective world," "*das Man*" (in Heidegger's terminology). It lulls us into this platitudinal world of small talk where everything is taken for granted: Life, death, the world and man's fate in it, society, language. No reason to wonder or worry; everything is what it is and not another thing. The world is what it seems to be—a dry, unimaginative, down to earth, square-headed, stuffshirt-about-mid-morning-after-a-good-night's-rest. And as for such questions as what it means to live and die—there's nothing to it, it is commonplace, almost everybody does it. We are thrown into an absurdly indifferent world of sticks and stones and stars and emptiness. Our "situation" is that of a man who falls out of the Empire State Building. An attempt at "justifying" our brief, accelerating fall, the inconceivable, short inter-lude between our breath-taking realization of our "situation" and our inexorable total destruction, is bound to be equally ludicrous, i.e. whether we choose to say: 1. "This is actually quite comfortable as long as it lasts, let us make the best of it;" or 2. "Let us at least do something useful while we can," and we start counting the windows on the building. In any event, both attitudes presuppose an ability to divert ourselves from realizing our desperate "situation," to abstract, as it were, every single moment of the "fall" out of its irreparable totality, to cut our lives up into small portions with petty, short time-span goals.

So much for the heart-philosophical concepts of "true" and "truth." As for "value," we are confronted with the chasm between an authentic life worthy of man, lived in clear and penetrating awareness of its utter absurdity, and a fraudulent, illusory life, lived in pleasant self-deception, essentially indistinguishable from the life of any other self-complacent, giddy-witted pig with some sense of cleanliness and indoor plumbing. The choice implies the unconditional acceptance of the value of human dignity at the cost of traditional, axiological objectives such as adjustment, success, happiness, peace of mind, etc.

The heart *vs.* brain-eye philosophical controversy is rather inter-esting in that the analytically oriented philosophers accuse the existen-tialists of not knowing what they are talking about because of their exotic, imprecise language (cf. Carnap's famous critique of Heidegger). The existentialists return the compliment: Analytic philosophers do not know what they are talking about, because of their lack of engagement, commitment. . . . And this dimension of knowledge imperfection not only prevents the analytic philosophers from realizing what "man's lot" is like, but has a direct ethical relevance. A brain-eye-philosopher, so say the existentialists, may have worked out the clearest, strictest set of moral rules and norms, and they may have no impact whatsoever on the philosophers' moral behavior.

A professor may not feel ethically obligated to follow his norm system. It does not engage him except in the most exterior cortical centers, which in his case have little or no communication with the deeper, action-determining mechanisms. His ethical convictions are not interiorized, not internalized, not sufficiently integrated. They have no existential validity.

The existentialists, however, may be said to be in another predica-ment. They over emphasize existential validity, the exotic, poetic-dramatic, through-bones-and-marrow conveyance of their messages, to such an extent that they lose sight of, or ignore the tenability of, the "objective truth," if one wants, of the cognitive, epistemic content of these messages. Thus, during the reading of say, Sartre's celebrated *Le*

Mur, one can become deeply impressed by the wasteland and extreme distance between human minds, which has often occupied authors and dramatists through the years, and not least in the twentieth century. One is possessed by a terrible vision—"the loneliness of man," "lonely as a ship in a starless night"—and by a prophetic premonition—"and thus it will always be . . . ," until one day one renews one's acquaintance with Leonid Andrejev's "The Seven Who Were Hanged," and the mind is suddenly opened to a new insight, one diametrically opposite, it might seem. Andrejev forces one to conclude that human beings are indeed able to understand each other, feel for each other, identify themselves with each other, and this to such an extent that Andrejev's seven rebels cannot, as it were, be hanged apart and individually on the gallows.

If such types of literary descriptions as Sartre's and Andrejev's are persistently emaciated by rational and ruthless analysis, the ready-peeled, objective skeleton will say something about the impossibility or possibility of human contact in stress situations or during extreme circumstances of all kinds. It is clear that these dry, peeled-off formulations make it simpler for the cool and detached analyst to find effective methods for controlling the rules which apply to interhuman contact, the identification with other people, people-orientation, etc., and even enable the analyst to draw practical inferences of value for applied psychology—the "counseling" psychologist. The dilemma remains, however, not as a logico-philosophical paradox, but as a mere heuristic-didactic predicament: Is it practically possible usefully to communicate the course-of-life-suggestions which such "precise" formulations may have been intended to transmit, without lowering the precision level, and stressing empathy rather than clarity? Rather than "precising" language, we may have to "break through language in order to touch life," and turn the communicants involved into "victims, burnt at the stake, signaling through the flames."

Men are not angels, living in an eternally stable paradise where their eyes are opened to all possible mysteries of the world. Human beings are only on the threshold of the most preliminary steps to the mysteries of man and cosmos. There is not a single sentence among what we today should look upon as adequate transmitters of our most important, surest, and most indisputably significant assertions, which may not at another stage of our insight become an object for ridicule and painful shame. Thrown into an eternally changing universe, human beings cannot be tied by a set of rigid rules for language, thought or action. Assuming that we, and most of our fellow beings, choose to exist, and to increase our insight, perfect our knowledge about ourselves, our fate, and our cosmic situation, we should never express any judgement of value or truth without carefully considering the status of present relevant research. It seems that only the incorrigible knowledge we have ascertained so far is that there is no incorrigible knowledge. Let's grant the existentialist that, given all available insights, *anno* 1976, it is hard to see that man's lot in the universe is not totally absurd. It is clearly important that we realize this and do not intend to small-talk ourselves out of our insight. We may, however, most certainly still improve our language, our conceptual tools, our methodological approach and add to the quantity and quality of our present information about the mechanism within and around us. It is hard to predict today what we may not be able to predict with the coming millennia. This seems in itself fascinating. Without man in the universe, any later state of the universe might at any given time be predictable with a maximum of certainty to a LaPlacian superscientist—at least on the macroscopic level. With man in the world, anything is possible. There is no conceivable cosmic catastrophe which could not either be produced or prevented if man put his mind to it for a million millennia or so. Hence the battle cry sounds: Man, let's go on!—not because we have a mission in the world, not because it makes us happy or proud, but merely because we are different. We are accidentally thrown into this world as its sole principle of uncertainty. That's all.

4. The Fallacy of Succumbing to Super-Talk

A fellow Norwegian will be my target in what follows. Perhaps I shall appear a little harsh in singling him out for a philosophical beating. What I mean to single out, however, is a certain *a priori* brand of paternalism that creeps nonsensically into political as well as philosophical, anthropological, and theological pontification. We try to think about men and their cultures as if we could 'transcend mere human limitations.' Grotesque political theories are likely to result from the Fallacy of Succumbing to Super-Talk—the fallacy of thinking we can leap up from an ivory desk to some absolutely correct level of thinking and pronouncing, whence we may assess objectively the sense and relative merits of terms, beliefs, ways of talking, etc., of peoples with very different cultural traditions.

A set, untypical liberal, whose idealogy is properly derived from the seventeenth-century writings of John Locke against absolute monarchy, presumes to be able to discern which modern states are really *democratic* and *free* and *on the right track*. He ascribes to himself no less power of certainty about whether a tribe of natives in New Guinea or Alberta is *tyrannically governed* or not, whether a society in the Amazon jungle or a new nation in Africa, recently left to itself by a colonial power, really *believes in justice* and *treats persons as persons* or not. He can discern whether any society's structure really is or really is not based on a proper 'analogue' of Locke's, or Rousseau's Social Contract.

There are some Marxists who would claim, after studying such societies and nations, to be able to tell us whether or not the common people in each are really at the *m*th or the *n*th stage of development in the Marxist developmental scheme of Super-Talk. (Marx himself might shudder.) There are other Marxist theoreticians who are convinced that they can tell for sure whether Brezhnev's conception of Communism is *more perfectly free of imperialism and deviationism than* Lenin's, or Trotsky's, or Stalin's, or Khruschev's or Mao's, or Dubcek's. Marx developed his theories in response to the sufferings of certain peoples whom he knew well at a certain time; he, himself, changed his mind concerning the indispensibility of violent revolution in Britain as Britain changed in his later years through the growth of strong Trade Unions; Mao had to act for the well-being of humans cast in a total situation far different from that experienced by Marx or Lenin, far too difficult to be captured by the scheme of *primitive tribal communism/ancient slave economy/feudalism/capitalism/Socialism/Communism*—such facts make nonsense of supposing that the Absolute Overview and Super-Talk of political theoreticians should weigh heavily in the forming of political theories and proposals for concrete action.

What I am attacking, then, is a certain mentality whose appearance makes rubbish of speculation not only on politics but also on a good many other subjects as well. Since my intended victim exhibits that mentality in so deliciously clear a manner, although he is not a political theorist, I proceed to the attack without further apology.

Can there be, or are there in fact, different concepts, 'true' or 'truth'? And if so, can they be compared? Both questions are—with blue-eyed innocence and sincerity—answered in the affirmative by (linguist, classicist, and theologian) Thorleif Boman, in a monograph, which in 1960 had seen three German and two Japanese editions and, finally, an English edition entitled, *Hebrew Thought Compared with Greek* (*The Library of History and Doctrine*, published by the Westminster Press, Philadelphia, 1960. English translation from German by Jules L. Moreau). Boman's reflexions on the allegedly different truth concepts of "*amen*" and "*alethes*" are philosophically interesting only insofar as they inadvertently expose the fatuous absurdity of all attempts at a so-called "*outline*" of various—more or less (dis)similar—philosophical systems (Political Theories of Man), syntheses of total or near-total world views, comparing say, Aristotle, Descartes, Spinoza, Hobbes, Locke, Leibniz, and Marx.

The psychological difficulties in relinquishing the grand surveys of philosophy and political theory are obvious: There is something so frightfully elegant, fastidious, intellectually delicate, and refined about the literary aesthete who flauntingly displays what pretends to be a perfect command of our total cultural history. He conveys the impression of possessing a miraculous capacity for placing and classifying philosophers, political theorists, and schools of thought in a wondrous way that makes them altogether amazingly comprehensible, transparent, obvious, plain. It is, however, most unfortunate that only after having (unashamedly) made the concession to oneself and others that no survey has been achieved, that the entailments of the various "philosophies" are vague and bewildering—only *then* does it become possible to enjoy a tiny, tentative touch of a deeper understanding, to sow the seed of more subtle and perceptive philosophical insights. Without discontinuity, crises, blind leaps, creative internal decision, it is supposed to be possible for a reasonably intelligent stuff-shirt—at least at mid-morning, after a good night's rest—to close in one, "approximate," as Kierkegaard would have said, a steadily deeper, fuller and more precise comprehension of all philosophies.

This is a heinous, pernicious, and extirpatory underestimation of the worlds of thought. The perpetration of surveys in philosophy and political theory is nothing but an atrocious object of wise men's derision that makes a parodic mockery of the individual thinker and his work. It represents "the real-estate view of philosophy": Philosophies and political theories of man (as total or "semi-total" world views) are regarded as a number of houses open for inspection. The prospective buyer visits house after house, taking notes of everything—advantages, disadvantages—making his evaluations and comparisons, totally unruffled that the function of a *philosophy* is *inter alia* to furnish the criteria, the parameters, the conceptual framework in terms of which *any* evaluation and comparison may conceivably be made.

A rather well known psychologist, concerned with perception, Jimmy Gibson of Cornell, once sent me a reprint where he generously offered new reasons for a philosophy he referred to as "realism." I did not even bother to read his article, before I wrote him the following note:

> *Either:* your argumentation takes place within a realist frame of reference, in which case the reasons arrived at are reasons solely to someone who is already well within that frame. *Or:* your argumentation *transcends* a realist frame—and presupposes *eo ipso* the acceptance of a *non-* or *a-*, or *un-* or *sur-*realistic philosophy.

The point is that while "*scientific* results" *may* affect our *philosophy*, insofar as we have one, or, in a more esoteric way, our existential *mood*, and circuitously modify our "*Lebenswelt*,"—again, *If we have one*, which may itself be rather a curious claim—*a change in philosophy alters absolutely everything.*

Let us repeat: The only justification for looking at Boman's pollyannish attempts at comparing '*amen*' and '*alethes*' rests on the supposition that it will reveal—and, I shall suggest, quite neatly so—the scatter-brained naiveté and pernicious fatuity that characterize in general the "real-estate attitude" to philosophy and political theory as demonstrated in attempts at comparing total or near-total systems said to have cognizably different truth-concepts (which are themselves only cognizable *within* those very systems).

The basis for Boman's exposition may roughly and tentatively be sketched as follows: Were a representative of a philosophy, a philosophical system, or Political Theory of Man, *A*, to have reached the conclusion that a proposition, *x*, is true and a proposition, *y*, false, whereas a representative of a system *B* had found *x* to be false and *y* true, then any conclusion to the effect that they actually disagreed would rest on the presupposition that the *words* "true" and "false" were similarly used within the two systems. Or, to use Boman's terminology, that, within both systems they have identical, or, at least, similar (related) concepts 'true' and 'false' respectively. And *vice versa*, of course, for a terminological *agreement* between representatives for the two systems, were they unanimously to consider, say, *x* true and *y* false. Hence, if there were something to Boman's claim that the *truth concept* in Hebrew thought is different from the Greek, then any possible Hebrew-oriented system would necessarily be incommensurable with any possible Greek system, *viz.* with regard to all conclusions as to what is true and what is false.

But what if the metatheoretician has a deeper and more extensive system, embracing both Greek and Hebrew systems? He would then undoubtedly, Boman suggests, be in the position to map out the two sub-systems within his own wider field of possibilities. The Greek and Hebrew systems may then become commensurable and lend themselves to the following type of observation:

"For the Greeks", Boman maintains "truth—is that which is unveiled ('*alethes*' = '*a*'— privative + '*lethé*' = 'hidden';—) therefore, that which is revealed, clear, evident, or that which is to be seen clearly.... The corresponding *Hebrew* concept of truth is expressed by means of derivatives of the very '*aman*—'to be steady, faithful,' '*amen*—'verily, surely,' '*omen*—'faithfulness'; '*umnam*—'really'; '*emeth*—'constancy'—trustworthiness, certainty, fidelity, (to reported facts, truth'; cf. '*omenah*—pillar, door-post)."

In short, "*the Hebrews really do not ask what is true in the objective sense,*" Boman continues, "*but what is subjectively certain, confidence-inspiring, what is faithful in the existential sense.*"

Within Boman's meta-system it now becomes possible, at least in principle, to compare Hebrew and Greek philosophies. For every proposition, p, which explicitly or unexplicitly is accepted as "true" (*amen*) in a Hebrew text within a Hebrew system, H, the crucial question to be asked is: Would p within a Greek system, G, be considered "steady, faithful, reliable . . . ," or whatever? Is the answer *yes*? Then a *concordance* is formed between H and G. Reciprocally the question may be asked as to whether a proposition, p, which in a Greek text, within system G, is regarded as "true" ('*alethes*'), within a Hebrew system, H, is seen as "revealed, clear, evident . . . ," etc. Should the answer be *no*, then a *dis*cordancy is alleged to have been established between the systems H & G.

Let us grant Boman the necessary assumptions of a sufficient cognitive similarity within H and G with regard to such locutions as the suggested translations of "unveiled," "revealed," "clear," etc., as well as "to be steady," "faithful," "reliable. . . ." Nonetheless, there is something rather rummy about Boman's comparison of Greek and Hebrew truth concepts within a presumably superior Norwegian, German, or Germanic frame of reference. The mere problem formulation—"Is the truth concept in Greek thought identical with (resp. different from) the truth concept in Hebrew thought?"—is itself quite problematic. For one thing, what *concept* 'truth concept' would Boman—had he ever thought of it—intend to employ in the above question? Is the *locution* "truth concept" there designed to denote something which would have been less misleadingly conveyed by "the truth concept in Germanic thought," or "the truth concept in Hebrew thought," or "the truth concept in Greek thought"?

Only scholars are blissfully unaware of the amazing fact that *they themselves are actually thinking*, are the most pollyannish in reporting radical differences in modes of thinking between ethnic groups, cultures, historical epochs, philosophers, or schools or systems of philosophy. They take a non-participant, spectator attitude towards humanity. Or a position not dissimilar to that of a rat-psychologist towards the rats in the maze: *He* sees *everything*, the rats see only a fraction, and each of them sees something slightly different from the others. In contrast to this 'non-participant' mentality, there is one which I commend: The Existential mentality of the philosopher or political theorist who realizes that he, too, is speaking as a person (thrown into the world) from a particular point of view, with commitments of his own that are personal.

The frame of reference implied by Boman does not offer itself as a third *possible* system—e.g. a synthesis of Greek and Hebrew thought—but as *reality itself*! Firmly based on reality he is now in the position to determine that this is where the two different modes of thinking originated: They have their basis in *reality itself*.

There are still too many political theorists who believe that anything precise enough to justify a rational standpoint, can, or is likely to be conveyed by means of the formulation: "How to compare two systems with different truth concepts." Such assurance reveals nothing but a reckless semantic optimism. It is unclear what could be meant by the claim that systems have or can have different truth concepts, as well as what this claim—if it could be understood—presupposes and entails. Boman, for one, apparently wants us to accept that not only is the different truth-concept-claim intelligible, but "it" transmits a ture proposition: *That there are in fact different systems with different truth concepts*. And this difference in truth concepts, so the claim goes, may be seen and actually shown, established, *demonstrated* by (and to) representatives for one or both systems, or by (and to) representatives for a third system, or by (and to) someone who does not represent any system whatsoever. The demonstration, I suppose, is intended to show that *something* (which is true) *is true*—in which case alleged differences in truth-concepts would entail differences in demonstration-concepts.

Sartre has pointed out that it is the limitations placed upon us by our physical and historical context, together with the limiting commitments we accept ourselves in response to that context, which make us personal agents. The project of leaping above all contexts and commitments to think with Divine objectivity reflects man's desire to be God! But the project is absurd. And so the philosopher and political theorist must aim at what it makes sense to attempt within the reality of the human condition.

5. Concluding Remarks

I have largely concentrated in this essay on trying to convey the Existential approach and attitudes which political thinkers should seek to adopt when they think about the human condition. Some will react by criticizing the proportion of polemic to argument. A Zen Master would see no reason to apologize for the proportion of slaps and jokes and riddles to the number of explanations he offered his pupils. I too see no reason to apologize: One must learn not just to see how Utilitarianism may be challenged in argument, but also to perceive and to feel in the heart how false that ism is to the potential dignity of man. One must learn not just that an 'investigation' like Thorleif Boman's generates a host of paradoxes and contradictions. No, one must be moved to realize that such an Olympian way of discussing human institutions is a form of bad faith, of self-deception about the kind of beings we humans really are.

I began by saying that for the greater part of my life I have been a Socialist. This I remain. Of course, I want all citizens in my society to be well fed and housed, to have many educational and working opportunities, to have leisure and freedom to philosophize for themselves. But, unlike Plato, I believe in no "paradigm laid up in Heaven" of the Just State. There is no True Form of the Just State which ought to be realized concretely by humans in all places and at all times. At one time and in one particular place we may find our own reasons for committing ourselves to this rather than that form as "more nearly right in our context." The rather Platonic view that Science will soon demonstrate what all men's political habits should be like is a very *dangerous* idea, even though it remains an *absurd* one. It is the seed of a new and possibly worse growth of Fascism. Dear reader, if you do not believe me, you had better read this essay again.

Utopia: The Tomorrow that Never Came

ROBERT H. KEYSERLINGK

Man is the only animal to plague himself with ideas. His own existence is a real problem: He cannot escape from it, and he cannot finally solve it. He just happens to find himself on this tiny unit of the universe. Though he can trace some of the stages of his development, he does not know by himself how or why he originated or where he is going. He sees that the processes of life involve features which are scandalous to the human mind. Life feeds on life, and men are hostile to men. It blooms imperfectly and dies so suddenly. Life is complex and infested with various forms of evil. What are we doing here? Some men cannot bear to leave the unanswerable question unanswered. They want to assert. Indeed, their very natures drive them to assert.

Man's ideas about his purpose and future reflect this dilemma. Part animal, man is driven by irrational herd instincts. Men are also, however, part reason. From the depth of their nature, men attempt to understand their apparently accidental span of existence and connection with nature and their fellow man. They find themselves somehow tied to nature and other men, but at the same time deeply feeling their separation from them. They yearn to restore some sort of unity within themselves and with external life and time. Through devotion to a diety or an ideal, and through the process of living and acting, men demand as their reward an experience of the sense and unity of life. Their very best and very worst expressions can be seen as more than mere striving for physical satisfaction or comfort. If they reject religious traditions, they fall back on do-it-yourself insights composed of scientific fact, biblical nostalgia, and synthetic myth-making. Such utopian ideas are chiefly interesting as documents about the minds of men who could not rest in the state of unknowing.

Utopia poses the important question: Despite man's unfolding intellectual capacities and ancient history, has he come any closer to the dream of understanding and perfecting himself? The question is as embarrassing as the answer is painfully clear. Men still know little about themselves and how human beings live together except what they have learnt painfully and empirically in the course of some thousands of years. No perfect or permanent healing answer to man's disasterous relapses into crisis and suffering has yet been found. Old ways are sometimes gradually, and sometimes suddenly, put aside by new forms, which in turn spawn their own families of disharmonies. Our Western answer to the age-old problem of scarcity, what Lewis Mumford is pleased to call our "megatechnical society," has produced its own types of mediocrity, frustration, and anger. Rapid change, material accumulation, and secularization have not brought the completely adequate life promised by them. As a result, our society has grown increasingly impatient with human incompetence and fearful that today's life might be projected into the future.

Most men come to terms with the society they live in. In the West, most decide for a benign and non-violent view of what is possible historically. Others seek release and redemption from incomplete mortal existence. If unable to find some progressive ideal, they fall into disgust and rejection. They stand rooted in horror and dispair before impending doom, haunted by the terrible cries of the victims of wars and injustice, persecutions and concentration camps, which seem to have sealed the fate of mankind. No paradise in heaven or on earth can be found in which to believe. As Sartre, the (almost) complete sceptic once put it, man in the atomic age is merely a useless passion. The best one can do under the circumstances is muster one's courage, confront triumphant evil, and look unscathed into the terrible abyss of the human spirit.

But men have lived under the threat of evil and annihilation before. The early Christians were convinced that the world was soon coming to an end, but beyond the dark horror of nothingness and destruction there stood the vision of a paradise of supreme beauty and goodness. This belief in a place which the angel refused to describe to Moses because the human mind could not comprehend it is still very much alive today. Western man has generally turned from despair or passivity to a search for salvation. This article focuses upon his search for earthly salvation and redemption following the loss of belief in divine transcendence. It aims to be a rapid survey of Western man's god who fell from heaven to earth, of his flight from cultural despair into a new redemptive history.

These beliefs are not only interesting documents about man's search for redemptive meaning, they are also facts which help to shape reality. This is the meaning of the self-fulfilling prophecy about which Robert K. Merton and others have written. Measured despair expressed publically can warn us against catastrophe and rouse us from lethargy. Extravagent despair, on the other hand, leads to a withdrawal from political and cultural action deemed justifiable by a society into helplessness, utopian dreams, or cults of destruction. It contemptuously rejects the potentials for non-violent change which exist. These decisions or beliefs are practical questions as they will be acted upon in real life. They provide not only interesting material for scholarly discussion, but also inspiration for present behavior. Behind most human acts lies more or less buried a calculation about utopia. Is civilization grossly imperfect? Can man be redeemed on earth?

If utopia is ubiquitous, it is also ambiguous. Like some primitive nature god, utopia has many faces but few clear meanings. At one time it appears as a mere literary fantasy or imaginative play. At another, it sweeps in as a revolutionary passion for immediate and total destruction in the name of human redemption. What in one place may be a literary virtue becomes elsewhere a political vice. Why is one man's fancy another man's logic? And what about the man caught in the middle, who knows what he wishes to avoid better than what he wishes to follow? Yet utopia's ambiguity illuminates more meanings than many fundamental clarities. Its very ambiguity permits it to range freely about the whole gambit of human hopes and contradictions. It underlines the uneasy association between revolutionary categories of the perfect and the practical imperatives of living. It speaks of man's morally difficult task of living between ideal and reality. It highlights the tension between prudence and passion, abilities and ambition, pessimism and optimism, loneliness and sociability. It poses an extraordinary number of basic questions: Can man ever become truly moral and virtuous? Is utopia only a warm sentiment, or a positive ideal and call to revolution? What are the differences between religious and secular apocalypse? Does the pursuit of utopia aid or hinder the critical analysis and reformation of the existing world?

Politics have been termed the art of the possible. But what is possible? For the ordinary, myopic philistine, the answer is: Nothing very different from what is happening already. Someone has to keep the old ship of state afloat, and most of the time fairly competent navigators somehow appear to take over the task. Occasionally, it is true, some upstart from the lower deck will try his hand at it and temporarily throw everything out of order. But sooner or later he comes to the end of his tether, and a sort of normality is inevitably restored. The Anglo-Saxon tradition of political comment is reflected in this sturdy, down-to-earth commonsense. Its practitioners are wary of abstract ideas, quarry history for illuminating precedents rather than principles, and interest themselves in what is practicable as opposed to what may be desirable. Its vocabulary belongs not so much to the world of intellectuals as to that of practical men of affairs and state.

Unfortunately for this comfortable and confident view of life, we are living in a century of political upstarts, the most successful of whom do not think in terms of the possible, but of translating dreams into reality. In pursuit of these visions, they have been willing to accept overwhelming challenges—and have sometimes won. The very essense of life is for them revolutionary and visionary. They aim to alter the very conditions of existence, and to lay the foundations for a radically different type of man and society. They employ a will to social transformation which is self-conscious, planned and guided by closed doctrines. Their methods are to undermine, combat, and tear down traditional social orders. Institutions are unjust, experimental, and reformable in accordance with human intent. Man himself is infinitely malleable and changeable. Happiness or destiny can be conquered against all odds by the introduction of true reason, discipline, and leadership into life. By their great flashes of intuition, these men have pointed to earthly republics of a rationalist, ahistorical, socialist, nationalist, or racialist utopian nature. While sceptics can justifiably treat with cynicism the utopian claims of these men once in power that they have kept their visionary doctrines pure, it would be foolhardy to ignore that they came into existence, continue in existence, and attract supporters because they promise to actualize utopian hopes about man and his future.

The sturdy pragmatism of our society has proven to be no absolute obstacle to the propagation of utopian ideas among us. Because we manage to ignore or outgrow these doctrines ourselves is apparently not reason enough to prophecy their early death. Over a century ago John Stuart Mill analyzed the writings of Auguste Comte and the Saint-Simonians and outgrew them as he perceived the despotism that was latent in their schemes. More recently, thinkers such as Sidney Hook, the first philosopher to advocate and explain Marxism in the learned American journals of the 1930's, rallied against and surmounted Marxism. Neither example, however, stopped the growth of the positivistic authoritariansim of the right nor of the Old and New Left in the twentieth century. Each generation discovers anew the allures of utopianism, and in some cases even combines the moral courage to act with the achievement of intellectual conviction. The problem is surely as much a psychological as a philosophical one. In ideology, almost anything is possible.

Every future begins in the past, no matter what or how new its claims. Utopia speaks of the future—the very idea of present and past time is viewed as the product of repression. Time, claims utopia, is neurotic. But utopia too has a past and cannot spring outside of history. The utopian tradition in Western political satire, literary fantasy, romantic creation, and even academic research is a long and beguiling one. Utopia has become a fashionable study, and it is not difficult to see why. The study of utopia is the study of a host of relevant topics including radical politics, avant-garde culture, sexual experimentation, futurology, and totalitarianism. The search for the ideal earthly home, however, did not begin with this generation.

The roots of the dilemma over the association between the revolutionary catagory of the perfect and the imperatives of real life lie far back in history. From the historical point of view, one can begin almost anywhere at will. For the sake of brevity and as a comparison with later utopian ideas, we can enter the stream with Joachim of Fiore, a Cistercian monk who lived from 1135 to 1202. From the eleventh to the fifteenth centuries, heterodoxy, in its various forms, was endemic in Western Europe until with the Reformation the universal authority of the Roman Church, under stress for two centuries, finally broke. Numerous groups sought to return to first apostolic principles which they felt were not represented in the church, by following literally Christ's teachings in the Bible. Religious utopian views of this nature continued to emerge through the centuries, and are represented in the many spartan, fundamentalist communities still established in North America today. The appeal to an ideal religious past received perhaps its greatest impetus from the writings of Joachim of Fiore, admired universally in his time by kings and popes. His was the first comprehensive historical interpretation of the world which sought to explain its development in terms of universal laws. Past, present, and future were part of a continuous process of development, which had a definite goal in the world. He transferred many of the happenings reserved for the next world to this one by interposing a thousand-year age of gold on earth between the present and the Final Judgement. He gave a goal of human history in the culmination of the future age of gold on earth. The future lay at once in the consummation of all history and within the grasp of the present. He thereby generated a sense of apocalyptic expectation, which owed its power to a similar inspiration as that behind modern utopian movements, namely, that the golden future lay in the present's hands.

Neither Joachim nor his followers regarded themselves as interpreting history as such, but rather as trying to understand God's purposes through the events of the world. His new outlook, however, although judged fully orthodox at the time, became a source for outlooks which he would doubtless have disavowed had he lived to see them. Not the least among these subsequent, secular followers was Adolf Hitler, who employed Joachim's idea of a thousand-year Reich to disasterously different ends. As secularization took place following the religious wars of the sixteenth and seventeenth centuries, hopes previously focused largely upon an other-wordly eternity began to switch to this-worldly objectives. This process began to climax in the age of the Enlightenment, when Helvetius turned Locke into a complete utilitarian. The ultimate message of Thomas More three centuries before in his famous *Utopia* had not been that utopia should be practiced on earth, but only that men should draw moral lessons for their own personal reformation from it. When he later realized that some interpreted his moralizing as a secular fantasy to be acted upon, he made his historic retreat, an intellectual withdrawal which has left a disfiguring question mark on the whole story of simple utopian innocence. In his *Confutation of Tyndale's Answer* he fulminated against the infection of heresies, which were springing up out of essentially good works, including the Bible, Erasmus', and his own writings: "I would not only my darling's books (i.e. Erasmus') but mine own also, help to burn them both with my own hands, rather than folke should (though through their own fault) take any harm of them, seeing that I see them likely in these days to do so." But the process of bringing dreams down to earth was not to be so lightly halted. Some, such as More and others after him, suddenly realized that something new and rather terrifying was being said, which if accepted, would destroy the traditional religious basis of life, morality, and society. According to the new theory, men were now supposed to be guided only by the hope for earthly happiness to be measured by the desire for reasonable pleasure and moderation and by the fear of pain. Eighteenth-century salons refined and distributed the idea, and Bentham developed it into a working philosophy in Britain. The *Encylopédie* embodied this view, and was thereupon (weakly) condemned in pre-revolutionary France as decidedly antisocial.

Something like a new secular religion began to emerge. The great victories of the French Revolution over traditional Europe created luminous visions of a perfect humanity through which the individual man could save himself as an individual lost in a great work. If traditional bonds could be so thoroughly disposed of, the road to human perfectibility could be cleared. Condorcet, the youngest of the encylopedists, clearly saw the new outlook which man needed to possess if he was to have an inspiring, human religion without transcendental religious doctrines. The old biblical stories and promises were remodelled. The Noble Savage, Republican and later National, Proletarian, Ayran, or Person became an alternative for the story of Eden. The sensationalist psychology of Locke as interpreted by the new prophets of progress and earthly salvation indicated a future to be reached through education, scientific knowledge, and human endeavor. Turgot outlined a philosophy of history which inspired the individual to feel that he had a noble part to play in creating the better world. Facts and individuals no longer hovered chaotically in the air. They could now be judged against the new philosophy of history and thereby became clues to something, some law, beyond themselves—nature's or history's mysterious meaning. Diderot inspired the idea that working for posterity was man's role of service. Posterity came to play the same role for him as the next world

187

did for the religious. Condorcet, in the shadow of the guillotine, dreamt of a new world of truth, virtue, and happiness, where consolation would be found for all the errors, crimes, and injustices which men had suffered and which had so long soiled the earth. In contemplation of this luminous future, man could find his true compensation for virtue. As he wrote in his well-known passage:

> The mind of the philosopher rests with satisfaction on a small number of objects; but the spectacle of stupidity, slavery, extravagance, barbarity, afflicts him still more often; and the friend of humanity can enjoy unmixed pleasures only by surrendering to the sweet hopes of the future.

Against a background of loss of spiritual roots and of rapid change, Condorcet set up the emotional-imaginative model of a naturalistic utopia, which has since exercised an immense attraction for other secular men seeking a redemptive human history.

As the eighteenth century closed, the doors were opened to the most extravagant hopes for the future of mankind. Spurred on by dreaming moralists such as Jean Jacques Rousseau, the sentiment arose that culture in general could be radically reformed *via* the child and educational revolution. Since Rousseau, more new systems of education have been developed than in all the previous centuries. "Impure" (Rousseau) or "decadent" (Nietzsche) culture could be saved only by freeing education from traditional social and restrictive paths. Only in this way could the essential confrontation be brought about between the renewed spiritual soul of youth and the corrupt adult world. Freed from the responsabilities and values of the adult world, encouraged to enter into opposition to the loveless and hateful stereotypes of a cruel, exploitative society, youth has since been sheltered and led to dream of renewing this world. Human existence is, it was claimed, both knowable and malleable. Neither Rousseau nor the other educational revolutionaries could foresee that not the future, but the divine present would, in fact, become youth's main hold on reality.

Yet the demand raised by Rousseau in *Emile* for a carefree, child-like enjoyment of life and the hope of replacing institutions by the community exercised a vast influence down to the romantic young rebels of our own day. Even a spartan philosopher like Kant, whose life was dedicated to duty and punctuality, did not escape Rousseau's call. In his simple room only one portrait was hung—that of Rousseau. He himself has recounted the deep, abiding influence Rousseau's writings had on him. He was so fascinated by his reading of *Emile* that in his absorption he gave up temporarily his familiar punctuality and daily walk. He described later the unforgettable crisis precipitated within himself by Rousseau's writings and his consequent desire to start his life and work anew, rebuilding himself and humanity, as it were, out of nothing. Despite the obvious differences between the two personalities, ways of life or thought, the nature of the tie which bound them was a similar and sincere belief about man's vocation on earth. These were the dreams spun out by two men prepared to keep their distance in different ways from society. As Rousseau repeatedly assured his readers, he never loved men more warmly than when he seemed to be drawing away and fleeing from them.

This form of misanthropy or withdrawal from the stubborn, contemptible, glittering suffocation of real life to rely on one's private insight has continued to be a trait of utopian thinkers. "There is only one great adventure," wrote Miller in *Tropic of Capricorn,* the hippies' Bible, "and that is inward towards the self, and for that, time nor space nor even deeds matter." Men must go forwards (backwards?) to that life of childhood, which seems "like a limitless universe." The hipster, wrote Norman Mailer, lives "in that enormous present which is without past or future, memory or planned intention." Violence and obscenity, typical of childhood scatology (and of their adult protagonists), become permissible on the grounds that adults are "things" exterior to one's own world. Suddenly there is to be no Time. The Worst has come. Total Evil is about to triumph. Every soul must Rise Up. Any Means, however impure, is justified by the Pure End. The sheer toil, anxiety, and worry of adult society can and must be replaced by one of creative play and unity.

As the political, industrial and intellectual revolutions after 1800 speeded up the cruel process of secular change, the politics of paradise became progressively more dominated by visions of revolution and renewal, of the fiery death of the old and the rebirth of a new man and society from the ashes, by the legendary, metaphorical imperatives of fire and blood. Revolution became the creative fire of all time, the great incendiary cliché, the Promethean stereotype of salvation. Classical metaphors were re-discovered which spoke of the instability of all things and of the motion and flux of life under the surface. Heraclitus, the subject of Marx' doctoral thesis, had believed in periodical conflagrations. Apocalytic portions of the Bible assisted translation of the metaphor into political terms. The modern age of disarray, despair, and defiance revived mythological and biblical hopes for a flaming sword which could usher in a better world and primordial freedom.

Although they sometimes balked at the need for violent revolution, most post-revolutionary philosophers and prophets were satisfied with views of secular and unlimited historical evolution or progress. August Comte and his "scientific" followers, including J. S. Mill, dreamt of a new, more rational, and well-ordered universe achieved by peaceful means. By harnassing man and science, a happy if hierarchical society could be created in which the individual would fit and find his niche and social sense. The new secular collectivity would be called Humanity and was worthy of deepest devotion and service. Man would be happy to follow without questioning nature's and history's law as interpreted by the wise ruling elite.

Whether the means to arrive at the bright new future were to be violent or non-violent, true progress awaited man only if he could somehow abstract himself from the present and fathom nature's and history's law for humanity and the world. This progressive attitude was accepted by leading secular thinkers of the last century. The essential drive was to identify the individual with history, the natural dynamic of the universe, and the natural evolutionary law behind things or an age. If man could just get himself into harmony with history's and the world's naturalistic movement, he might begin to look forward to a happy and fulfilled future—or at least his children might. That which had previously been assumed to be beyond time and to be extra-worldly was brought into this world and subjected to human expectation. That this expectation was only to be possible by co-ordinating humans to what was considered to be nature's dynamic—and often cruel—law was not, at the time, seen as a danger but as a promise.

Today we can identify two broad types of utopian thought—the scientific naturalism of "experts" and the intuitive naturalism of their ideological or artistic critics. The first group includes mainly scientists, technocrats, and social scientists who represent "modernity," and who see the hope for mankind in science and its methods. Throughout the first half of the twentieth century, the key terms for these philosophers of science, as in theoretical sociology and anthropology, were "structure" and "system." All the way across the field of human knowledge, from logic and mathematics to the human sciences and the fine arts, the task was defined in static, structural, ahistorical, non-representational, and wherever possible, mathematical terms. By the early 1920's, it was an unquestioned truth that the intellectual content of any truly scientific system like that of Russell and Whitehead formed a timeless "propositional system." Logical models and analyses continued to distract from the urgent problems of social and cultural change. When T.S. Kuhn first suggested in the early sixties in his *The Structure of Scientific Revolution* that there might be an historical sociology of science, cries of indignation were heard from those who held to the logical coherence of science as to a god. The second group of utopians includes writers, artists, theologians, and academics, intellectuals who generally are not well versed in the scientific side of modern life nor in the direction of practical affairs. While the scientific utopians promise to transform the present system to its optimum through their own effort, their utopian critics tend to replace modern life by ideal systems run, strangely enough, by intellectuals who also resemble closely these critics themselves. In both cases, however, the illusion is shared that the social process will soon be fully explained and controllable, even if the analyses radically differ. Academics, marxists, artists, social scientists, futurologists, and politicians preach that it all depends on discovering the right method or key to the secret of life and society. Both groups believe it is possible to break nature's secret code. And both believe in their own ways that it is a matter of attitude and information: The former through cybernetics or better information models, the later through a more consistent and rigorous use of their ideological tools for criticism and practical renewal.

Despite some recent and fairly severe setbacks, the belief still abounds that the practice of science has by an inner necessity an elevating influence on those who cultivate it. The scientist belongs to an international community and is morally committed to an ethical code which regards the messy reality of greed, nationality, and politics as immoral. Furthermore, the scientist is committed to truthfulness in the observation of his data and his reports to other scientists. Even if some of the fraternity have sometimes sinned by attaching themselves too closely to corrupting power, the benevolent theocracy of scientists, the moral guides of society, should lead because they control a method which enables them to think more rationally about human society than those who lack such methods. Utopian scientific naturalism has a blind confidence that the inadequacies of actual historical knowledge and praxis of human society can be replaced by the application of the natural and social sciences. It deliberately narrows the scope of what we can— and therefore should—know to what can be measured experimentally and mathematically. The central preoccupation of Descartes and Locke, Hume and Kant—scientific and philosophic alike—arose out of a similar, basic intellectual concern. Their common aim was to explain the fundamental implications and presuppositions of the New Science and to perfect its intellectual procedures. Through this work, science moved from the stage of a geometrical manifesto to that of transcendental critique. Since that time, interest has centered upon the internal logical relationships within ideal systems, promising that soon a universal generalization, a so-called unified theory, would be found. The quest today is as powerful as the quest for community is in human behavior. Then the stubborn complexity of nature and society will be fundamentally changed. The new scientific lay theology not only reduces man and society to manageable proportions but fulfills another powerful function as well: It helps to earn its keep by convincing policy-makers of the rectitude of their policy decisions when taken on other than scientific grounds in much the same way as one previously consulted oracles, theologians, or historians.

Unfortunately, there exists a grass-roots prejudice which expects thinkers to deal not only with objective facts, but at the same time with moral issues. It is easier in some senses, however, to resort to vague generalizations and conceptualizations, escaping the particular through dealing only with larger contexts and complexes. The great weakness of this abstract and well-mannered attitude is that it creates equally abstract men and worlds free of individual characteristics and variety. It is in constant danger of falling into vague, bland clichés through its inability to seek out individual insight or character. Even more insidious is the masking of a strong moral position behind feigned objectivity. Perhaps more seriously, in both sociological theory and philosophy of science questions of historical change were set aside at the turn of the century in reaction to the massive, directional historical systems of the great nineteenth-century ideologues and historians. There can be little doubt that science and its concepts, too, have a history and a sociology. Normative standards are brought into scientific enquiries by the scientists themselves from the outside. Science too has passed through—and will continue to pass through— historical transitions in which one set of tentative scientific concepts succeeds another. The final or even temporary revolution in scientific knowledge is only a more dramatic fashion of describing a much more evolutionary and continuing process of knowledge collection. But it is not necessarily one in which knowledge accumulates towards an ascending, unbroken line, unidirectional and irreversible. We often detect behind a cool scientific exterior the same sort of providentialism found in the great nineteenth-century ideologies of Comte, Spencer, Marx, or social Darwinism. Other serious scientists such as René Dubois readily admit that even the more physical problems, let alone "social problems" are destined to remain ambiguous. Certainly social problems cannot be "solved" by economic and social measures. Pollution, urban crowding, and social mobility, for instance, remain messy problems. They are not beautifully scientific; they are not clean scientifically. What do we really know of man after all these centuries? There is still, for instance, no general psychological theory which is accepted or compatible with the remainder of science; only an array of more or less related theories.

The apparent failure of scientific rationality to decode nature's secrets and open the door to a perfect earthly future leaves the field wide open to the second type of utopianism we are considering—intuitive or ideological utopianism. The same belief detected behind scientific utopianism is present here too; the belief that organic human evolution is not merely irreversible but unidirectional. This unidirectionality is a measure of progress towards the final happy goal. Both recent types of providentialism distracted attention from detailed study of real social and cultural change, in this case by the dazzling and sweeping doctrines about the All-Embracing March of History. Dominated by the notion of cosmic system, by the temptation of knowledge of the past and future, and by the desire to plumb the universe's secret, thinkers of this ilk also sought to escape religious uncertainty or social confusion. The ability to "step out of time" and see everything simultaneously—past, present and future—is only permitted to a chosen few, who then attempt to assemble followers for their vision and find them. This sort of intuitive naturalism permits man to float away on deep oceanic feelings, convinced that he has at last captured the secret of life and of the cosmos. Imagination and intuition, the tools employed, do not mean illusion in this context, but the felt ability to pierce the flat externals of civilization and institutions in order to grasp the reality behind. The door to the perfect future can be opened only through this type of insight. The lonely artist or philosopher-hero then aids his contemporaries and followers to break through to man's and nature's deeper existence. He criticizes the present according to his insight and thereby creates the future. Patterning himself on Prometheus or Antigone, he preaches the recreation and resurrection of man, if only others will listen and adapt to nature's real, dynamic law.

"History" is distinguished from "nature," even if the talk sometimes is of nature. The modern physics of Descartes and Newton accounted for the physical world as understandable in terms of mechanics and without final cause. But immediately questions arose about how man, who was part of nature, could have the freedom to know it and decide about good and evil. Those thinkers who were unwilling to reduce man to nature or forego morality, and who at the same time agreed with the new explanations of nature, showed that man lived on two levels—that of nature and that of freedom. It was this crisis, this attempt to conceive a nature without final purpose but with human purposefulness, which produced the modern conception of history around 1800 in the persons of Kant and Hegel. History described the realm of human action in which collective humanity functioned not only because of the cause and effect of science but as a free, moral creature as well. Man alone creates and suffers "history." Man is seen as part of evolution, but also as its director, consciously pointing the very process from which he sprang. Man is the creator of his own future in this sense, if he will only stop, look, and listen to history. Time is tamed by submitting it to a known historical process. Those who study history in this way—time as history—are turned to what will happen in the future. Whatever the differences in content between the three major ideologies of our time—Marxist socialism, liberalism, and national socialism—they all demanded that their followers be strong in their mastery of the future. On Marx' tomb in London is inscribed his most famous maxim: "The philosophers have only interpreted the world in various ways. The point, however, is to change it." Greek heroes were summoned to noble deeds but not to changing the structure of the world; we are called to master the world and make it what we want.

This is not to claim that all naturalists or secularists are activists of "struggle." Lucretius, Hobbes, and Santayana were scarcely this type of world-changer. Vilfredo Pareto, the naturalist sociologist, William Graham Sumner, the social Darwinist, and many others are hardly cosmic confidence men, but exude rather a mood of acceptance. Not all atheists are looking for a substitute earthly immortality. The great philosophical novels of Ignazio Silone and Arthur Koestler are condemnations of this sort of apocalyptic naturalism. Other naturalists such as Adolf Hitler who aver that power, struggle and racial supremacy reflect the most basic law and needs of men and nature are of obviously quite a different cut of cloth. Those who attach themselves to a monistic, naturalistic, ethical absolute and are willing to sacrifice for one supreme end all other ends of life, create a collective sadism possible only for the fanatic. On the contrary, many naturalists worry deeply about the problem of the freedom of the will. A fully informed man, they realize, might still not be a free one. This question was certainly an important factor in the mental collapse of John Stuart Mill, Russell's suicidal broodings, and William James' bouts of neurosis.

In the conception of or insights into history now prevalent among those creative or artistic men who plan to change and master the planet, however, changing and mastering become ever more ends in themselves. They are undertaken more and more for the sheer sake of the creation of novelty and hope in the artistic insight. Adolf Hitler at the end of his life excused himself for the bloodshed by claiming that he was, after all, only an artist. Lukacs, Gramsci, Garaudy, and Marcuse, heroes of the radical left, developed artistic insights into the historical world that had to ignore too detailed an account of the world as it was. That elitism was, no doubt, partly a response to the non-revolutionary character of the mass. The artistic, creative totality of the dialectic became more important than the empirical thrust of Marxism. Issues of bureaucratic power and elite manipulation of power, the institutionalization of conflict and economic opportunities, common to all societies including those of the non-free world, disappear behind radical secular expressions of the hopeful path of history.

Is there really no choice between meekly accepting everything or destroying the whole system? Certainly, many of the modern utopians claim that one must choose one or the other. Simone de Beauvior refers in her autobiography to Raymond Aron as a despised moderate. "We (Sartre and herself) are temperamentally opposed to reform; society, we felt, could only change as a result of a sudden cataclysmic upheaval on a global scale." Persons who dwell in the world of political fantasy, where the fact-fantasy ratio has become unbalanced, are apt to be characterized by great cruelty. The rejection of reality and the search for a surrogate world is fraught with frustration and aggression. Maxim Gorky, who had known Lenin for many years, wrote during the revolution that Lenin "has no pity for the mass of the people . . . Lenin does not know the people." Hitler's contemptuous statements about the Germans fall into the same catagory. All human thought partakes of fantasy; the tension between fantasy and reality is a healthy one. When, however, solace is sought solely in yearning for a new national class or racial world, when dream takes the place of reality, hate of the existing knows few bounds. Artistic creation has won over human values and realities. Nothing is so certain as a tautology. By linking the undesired with the definition of evil, the hated must perish. Though rejecting Einstein and Freud, Lenin was convinced that his "scientific" knowledge of the world's progress justified his harsh sentence upon capitalists and those included in this definition. Whatever the present cost, utopians of the right and of the left are determined to look at reality through their ideological generalizations, then push to revolution so that humanity can make the qualitative leap into a new society.

The ideology of nature's true law of freedom fulfills the desire to know all, feel all, and be united with something deep, powerful, and permanent. This knowledge and its morality, however, is tied at least in theory to a radical opposition to traditional cultural, artistic, or social forms. These artistic or intuitive critics of modern industrial society and its technological elites dream of new forms or action which will push man into the future. Any accompanying crudities or cruelties are excused as historical necessities, whether they be cultural nihilism, collectivization, monolithic ideological myth, racial extermination, fraudulent trials, or imperialism of the most naked sort. Besides the glorious goal to be achieved, what weight should be given to the loss of tradition, or abrogation of individual rights, democratic process or free thought?

The leadership of the New Left in the last decade, composed mainly of social scientists, historians, and philosophers, never demanded the end of the one-party state or the return of freedom inside Russia. The monolithic political structure created by Lenin and Stalin was not brought into their debates of the 1960's. On the other hand, it was claimed that the cultural and political imperialism of the West caused the Berlin blockade, Stalin's represions in East Europe, and the Korean and Indochinese wars. Lenin remains beyond criticism. Despite the New Left's selective disquiet about Stalin's exterminations of the thirties, the Soviet invasions of Hungary in 1956 and Czechoslovakia in 1968, violence and revolution are still touted as the routes to the future. Claiming to be a youth movement, when in fact it is no more one than were the Childrens' Crusade or the Hitler Youth, the New Left was created by middle-aged intellectuals like Adorno, who later complained, "How was I to know that they were to realize it (his lectures on theoretical methodology) with Molotov cocktails?"

Just as the utopia of the scientific type flees from the individual into huge uniformities and rational (because man has constructed them this way) collectivities, the intuitive utopia assualts the dignity of the free individual by making man the puppet of vast, implacable cosmic (national, international or racial) laws working themselves out through history. Both sets of narrow, dreary determinisms make life and man easier to explain and contain a deep emotional reward for their adherents. Both act in our age of secular uncertainty as sources of certainty about human affairs and the future. By ignoring the complexity, mystery, tragedy, and potentiality of open social situations, the human person and leadership disappear into great scientific or radical collectivities. Scientific or ideological, right or left, these revolutionaries see the world and man in the present under essentially pessimistic terms. Social, cultural, or national decadence is everywhere. Struggle is needed for creative transformation. The aching loneliness of the loss of old certainties and community of an organic nature can only be eliminated by an absolutely forceful human will to jump into a better future.

These utopian programmes suffer from the two ills of either remaining empty if satisfying rhetoric, or worse still, of being put into practice. In the first case, they suffer from the weakness of all preaching: With all their certainty about sin, virtue and redemption, they are notoriously vague about the mechanism for substituting the new man for the old. Their very vagueness and abstraction indicate both the reason for their popularity and their limitation. They have no idea how to get rid of the old system, or what would happen if they did, or what we would have to envisage if we did. Their only resort is to the preacher's well-known proposal for a complete change of mind or conversion. On the other hand, the practitioners have achieved human suffering, loss of productivity, and destruction on a scale not seen until now. Instead of loosening the bonds of life and history, they have made them heavier and more oppressive than ever, reducing in the process intellectuals to functionaries of the state and the people to servitude.

196

Yet, even if one rejects the prospects for human perfectibility as a practical goal on earth or an excuse for tyranny, it is difficult to avoid sharing the hope that man can become superior to what he is now. It is here that common-sense rationality linked to ideals can help man to analyse his real life and his deficencies and help make life a little more civilized and humane. Despite the great forces of technological renovation and social change visible in the last two hundred years, there is no need to abandon oneself to the process of change in its extreme form in order to tame change. More study and concentration on the forces of stability and order and the ability of men to ride out change is also necessary. In many ways, societies are amazingly continuous. Man is more than a mere wisp completely at the mercy of change or to be reconstructed according to some simple plan of science or accelerated historical change. The yearning to rush towards a fabulous historical goal and to become godlike must be recognized for the false dream it is. A completely harmonious or rational world is impossible, and attempts to reach it are made at the cost of abandoning what little humanity man had so laboriously achieved over the ages.

Selected Bibliography

Feuer, L.S., *Marx and the Intellectuals: A Set of Post-Ideological Essays* (Garden City, New York, 1969).

Hertzler, J.O., *The History of Utopian Thought* (New York, 1950).

Kateb, G., *Utopia and Its Enemies* (New York, 1963).

Koestler, A., *Drinkers of Infinity* (London, 1968).

Levin, H., *The Myth of the Golden Age in the Renaissance* (Bloomington, Ind., 1969).

Mannheim, K., *Ideology and Utopia* (New York, 1959).

Manuel, F. (ed.), *Utopians and Utopian Thought* (Boston, 1966).

_____. *French Utopians* (New York, 1971).

Molnar, T.S., *L'Utopie: éternele hérésie* (Paris, 1973).

Mumford, L., *The Story of Utopia* (New York, 1968).

Nelson, W., *Twentieth Century Interpretations of Utopia* (Englewood Cliffs, N.J., 1968).

Plath, D.W., (ed), *Aware of Utopia* (Urbana, Ill., 1971).

Plattel. M.G., *Utopian and Critical Thinking* (Pittsburg, 1972).

What is a Free Society?

ANTHONY M. MARDIROS

Freedom

In the history of Western civilization and now in the twentieth century throughout the world, freedom is high on the list of things that men value. (Sexist terms are unfortunately embedded in the English language so that it is difficult to avoid them unless one resorts to unwieldy phraseology. In this essay "man" means "man and woman" and male pronouns stand for both male and female ones).

The history of the Western world is often described in terms of the struggle for and the successful achievement of freedom, and in the present century, colonial, semi-colonial, and ex-colonial countries have dedicated themselves to the same struggle. Rival forms of society in the modern world confront each other, each claiming that *they* are free and that their opponents are essentially unfree; and everywhere men proclaim that they are prepared to *die* for freedom—many have done so.

Freedom, therefore, seems to be among the first and greatest of our values. Yet of its nature and conditions, we are far from sure. To understand it is, therefore, one of the most important tasks of philosophy: The prevalence of contradictory views and confusions indicates the need for a fresh analysis, even though so much has already been said and written about this topic.

Although sometimes denied, it seems clear to me that freedom in the political and social context depends upon a prior foundation which involves the recognition of human beings' power to choose between alternatives—in a primary or metaphysical sense—before the matter is complicated by interaction with other human beings who seek power over their fellows.

In his novel *Free Fall*, William Golding, describes the experience which lies at the basis of our conviction that we have freedom of choice:

> When did I lose my freedom? For once, I was free, I had power to choose. The mechanics of cause and effect is statistical probability yet surely sometimes we operate beyond or below that threshold. Free will cannot be debated but only experienced, like a colour or the taste of potatoes. I remember one such experience. I was very small and I was sitting on the stone surround of the pool and fountain in the centre of the park. There was bright sunlight, banks of red and blue flowers, green lawns. There was

no guilt but only the plash and splatter of the fountain at the centre. I had bathed and drunk and now I was sitting on the warm stone edge placidly considering what I should do next. The gravelled paths of the park radiated from me: and all at once I was overcome by a new knowledge. I could take whichever I would of these paths. There was nothing to draw me down one more than the other. I danced down one for joy in the taste of potatoes. I was free. I had chosen. How did I lose my freedom?

Although Golding says that freedom cannot be debated but only experienced, it has in fact been debated for centuries, and it has been argued that the experience he describes is an illusion and that we live in a world in which every action and every event is determined by previous events. It has been argued that the development and success of modern science has conclusively shown that determinism is true, and that free will is a superstitious fallicy.

It is easy to see how the growth of science led to this view. As people, through the development of the natural sciences, began to learn more about nature, they found that such knowledge gave them increasing control of the natural environment. Thus *scientific knowledge* of the operations of the laws of nature, rather than the pronouncements of oracles and prophets, was conceived to be the means of controlling present and future events. It became an assumption of science that nature was completely determined by natural laws and that those events which appeared not to be determined were merely those whose connection with natural law had not yet been discovered. With the advance of science, these would be subsumed under natural law and become controllable. Hence determinism seemed to be the necessary condition of a knowable and thus controllable environment.

People, however, wished to control not only their natural environment but also their feelings, actions, beliefs, and values which led to the development of psychology and the social sciences. Since the attempt to gain knowledge and control of the natural environment assumed a determinist nature, it was argued that the knowledge and control of persons in society depended upon determinism there as well. Indeed, it was argued that if man is to *make* himself, if he is to rise above the determining influences of his natural environment and to shape himself and his society, then he must discover the deterministic laws of human nature and society. Only this discovery could free him from either the determinism of the natural world or the vagaries of chance. This was expressed in the famous phrase: Freedom is the recognition of necessity.

If we understand how human nature and human society work, we can set in motion psychological and social forces which will bring about the improvement of human nature and the reform of society. We must know how to educate the next generation to produce the right kind of people for the right kind of society. We must discover how to prevent the development of criminals, delinquents, and other misfits in our society and how, on the other hand, to produce skilled, intelligent, and well-behaved human beings. Determinism of both man and nature is necessary if man is to gain control of his own fate.

Now this modern determinism involves a paradox: The role played by the social engineer, the reformer, or the educator in using their knowledge of human nature and society to change and redirect them is at odds with the basic deterministic assumption. For the initiator of change—if he really does initiate it—must be conceived as standing outside the deterministic stream, changing its course by outside intervention—a stance which assumes that the initiator himself is free from the deterministic process. If the future is really predetermined, i.e. fixed beforehand, then no matter how well I come to know it (whether by consulting oracles or by scientific prediction), and no matter what I do, nothing will be altered. The paradox of social and psychological determinism is its implication that the future both *can* and *cannot* be altered.

It might be argued at this point that I have refuted an inconsistent attitude which some people hold about the nature of change and determinism, but that this does not do away with the fact of determinism. The knowledge of necessity may not lead to freedom, nevertheless we *may* still be subject to that necessity. Well, we *may* be, but the burden of proof lies on the determinist. How can he *prove* that all events are conditioned by specific previous events and in turn give rise to specific consequences? It is possible to produce evidence that *some* events are determined by previous events, but not possible to produce evidence that *all* are. It is possible to *imagine* a world in which indeterminism prevails. In such a world chaos would prevail: Babies would sometimes grow up to be boys, sometimes to be cabbages, and sometimes cats, but never the same thing twice. It is also possible to imagine a world that is completely determined and is the working out of a complex but rigidly unchangeable pattern.

The world we inhabit is unlike either of these worlds, we know from experience that it is not chaotic and without pattern, but we can also be reasonably certain that it is not rigidly determined—that there is room in it for a certain degree of spontaneity and initiation of change. It is upon this premise that all our actions are based. A completely indetermined world would be beyond our control, since we could not have any reliable expectations concerning the results of our actions. Likewise, but for a different reason, the *completely determined* world would be beyond our control, for nothing in it could be other than it is. In neither would it be possible for man to *make* himself. In our world, on the contrary, human beings are a source of novelty, and the future is not just an unfolding of what is inherent in the past. A person's actions are partly but not wholly the result of the previous forces and influences brought to bear upon him, they are at least partly the result of his own spontaneous and uncaused choices. Otherwise, a person would merely be a machine for grinding out actions which were determined before his birth.

Man's freedom of decision is not, of course, unqualified or unconditional. Limits of time, space, and circumstances, of ability and of social pressure circumscribe his choices, and the degree to which these choices are circumscribed is also a variable. Indeed, a person may lose his freedom of action through a series of wrong choices, as in some cases of alcoholism or drug addiction, disease may rob him of his ability to make free decisions. But short of such disasters, people normally have a range of choices between which they can freely decide.

By exercising a series of such choices a man may be said to *make* himself—to choose in effect what sort of person he is to become. Thus he may be said to be *free* in a very important and real sense of that word.

In a wider context, it is argued that since decisions made in concert can change a given society for better or worse, its future is not closed or predetermined, but open to a greater or lesser degree. Unless people are free in this basic sense, then all talk about political liberty and free societies is mere flag waving. The individual's freedom, whether exercised singly or in collaboration, may be lost as a result of his own actions, through natural causes, or through the restraints placed upon him by others, particularly when they are imposed by social institutions. Therefore, people born free may yet live in social chains. Hence, the demand and struggle for political liberty and free societies.

Two Concepts of Liberty

Two main lines of thought have been pursued by those thinkers seeking to define the kind of liberty which it is possible or desirable for an individual to enjoy in a social framework. The first, which may be called the negative concept of liberty; views the opposite of liberty as restraint or coercion exercised by other human beings. An individual is free only to the extent that he is not restrained by others. Any limitations which he may suffer from non-human causes or circumstances, or innate disabilities do not count as restrictions upon his freedom. Liberty concerns only the relations between men.

201

Now liberty conceived in this fashion clearly has to be subjected to severe limitations, and equally clearly this kind of freedom if it is a good is only one good in competition with others which may in certain circumstances be preferable to freedom. It is easy, of course, to name the general limitations upon freedom which nearly all of us would accept. For instance, your freedom to wave your arms falls short of the tip of my nose which means, of course, that man's freedom falls short of encroaching upon the freedom of others. This sounds acceptable, but there are difficulties when one looks more closely. It assumes that for each person there is an area of activity which is private to himself. But this is true only in the very special circumstances of a sparse and scattered population in which individuals live in semi-isolation. When there are large numbers living in close proximity, nearly all actions effect the interests of others, and no clearly defined area can be regarded as the exclusive concern of the individual alone. There are times, furthermore, when even inaction by individuals cannot be allowed. In time of plague, drought, famine, or war, the demands made and the restraints placed upon the individual increase enormously, even in those societies which claim to have achieved a high degree of liberty. Thus the hardships and disasters to which both ancient and modern societies have been and are subjected inevitably lead to the erosion of a liberty conceived as absence of direction or restraint. On the other hand, even some of the great social advances of our time have been equally inimical to liberty thus conceived: The growth of education has led to compulsory attendacne at school; concern for public health has multiplied laws and regulations aimed at protecting the community; improvements in the means of transport have brought with them the necessity for traffic regulations. The whole apparatus of modern society has so developed that we are tempted to see freedom from restraint only in the few, isolated pockets of primitive society that remain.

These are some people, of course, who have in fact retreated to the desert island or the primitive jungle in search of a life of freedom from restraint. But this is possible for a few only, and not a solution we can seek en mass. Nor would most of us enjoy the freedom thus obtained—a few weeks of unrestrained struggling with the forces of nature we would be glad to hurry back to the amenities and the restrictions of modern society (which also emphasizes that there can be non-human restrictions on liberty).

It seems clear, therefore, that there is something inadequate in the conception of freedom or liberty as mere absence of human restraint. If liberty is to retain its place as one of our cherished ideals—is to be something more than a shibboleth—then we must give some other account of its nature and justification.

202

We have available another traditional conception of freedom which defined not in the negative sense of absence of restraint, but positively in terms of the conditions which promote the well being and further development of the individual. The existence of restraints does not count as a loss of freedom provided these restraints do lead to the development of the individuals who suffer them. For example, we may well say that the child forced to attend school in North America is by this very compulsion rendered freer than the children of exploited and under-developed countries where education is available only to a few, but where children may be said not to suffer the restraint of compulsory schooling. Again, the child subjected to a reasonable form of discipline may well be said to emerge freer than one who has in the name of freedom been subjected to few or no restraints.

What criteria are we using when we define liberty in this positive sense? I think that we are judging in terms of power and control, and that we are implying that anything which increases the powers of an individual—which gives him increased means of controlling his destiny—are, no matter what their nature, increases in his freedom. It would only be a seeming paradox to assert that certain kinds of penal institutions and mental hospitals might be instruments of freedom, although they apparently exist to constrain their inmates. (This would be the case only if these institutions succeeded in reforming or curing those consigned to them. I hasten to add that more often than not such institutions fall short of this achievement, and when this happens they are rightly regarded as mere means of restraint.) The positive conception of freedom conceives of liberty as essentially a good and never as an evil. It is the goal of life: The improvement and development of man's powers by whatever means.

The negative conception of liberty sees freedom as only a good in some circumstances and on some occasions, and it thinks of the struggle for freedom as necessarily placing the individual in conflict with society. Social life is thus regarded as a competitive enterprise in which each individual tries to preserve as large an area of his life as he possibly can free from outside restraints. The result of holding this view of liberty is the wide-spread sense of alienation from society. The State and other social institutions are considered something other than and not belonging to the individual; the necessary demands placed upon him are complied with reluctantly, until with relief the individual returns to the area of private life which he has marked out as really and essentially his own. It is this conception of liberty which has diminished the active participation of people in the democratic process, even though the formal means for this participation exist and command respect. Thus, people pride themselves on having the right to vote, while simultaneously giving minimum thought and attention to what they vote on, even to the point of failing to cast a ballot.

On the other hand, the positive conception of liberty accepts society as essentially an area of cooperation in which a man increases his powers, and hence his freedom, by coming to agreements with and adapting his behaviour to others on equal terms. Society is, thus, not an enemy from which we retreat to a desert island, or more commonly to our private homes, but a means to increase our powers and improve the human condition by participating with others. The positive conception of freedom has its dangers, however, for it may degenerate into tyranny and regimentation: Constraints may be placed upon us in the name of the positive conception of freedom which, while promising to increase our powers, in fact limit them.

A similar distinction can be made between formal and material liberty. We may be said to have formal liberty when we have the right to act in a certain way established and secured by law. But it has often been noted that many of our legal rights are frequently impossible. We have the right to express our opinions freely on a wide variety of matters, yet we may lack the effective means. Clearly, the publisher of a newspaper has more effective freedom of this sort than do most newspaper readers. Yet publishers are few and readers many. Formal freedoms are clearly necessary, but to become actual freedoms they need to be supported by material freedoms—the availability of the means by which the freedom is put into practice.

To sum up: A man may be said to be free in a social and political sense if four conditions are fulfilled. 1. If he *chooses* his own goals. That is, if he has received the kind of training and education which make him able to see the possibilities that are open to one with his capacities and if he is able to make a reasonable choice between them. This is a condition which is frequently not fulfilled for women, native peoples, and the poor in general. 2. He must have available to him the *means* of fulfilling these goals, i.e. a man is not free if he has the capacity and ambition to be a doctor, but cannot afford the expense involved in a long course of training. 3. One must be *free of formal or external restraints*. In some parts of the world, for example, people are excluded from professions, not from lack of ability or lack of the material means to develop that ability, but on grounds of colour, creed, or sex. 4. In the final analysis a person's freedom is to be judged, over and above the three previously mentioned conditions, by the extent to which it is possible for him to participate in and develop within the society in which he lives.

This brings us to the fundamental question: What then is a "free society"?

A Free Society

Since society is necessarily a system of law and order and hence a system of restraints placed upon the human beings who compose it, we may well have difficulty explaining to ourselves just exactly what the oft-used phrase "a free society" means. Would it be correct to say that a free society has the fewest restraints, and therefore is closest to that condition where a society can barely be said to exist? Certainly John Locke, the seventeenth-century English philosopher thought so. He and thinkers like him envisaged a period in the past when men lived in a natural state without law and society and therefore free of all social restraints. They further conceived of society as the price we paid in lost freedom, in exchange for the security that life in society offered to us. Although no men have ever been discovered living in such a state of nature, some primitive societies do approximate this condition, and many of the men who first journeyed west across the North American continent, the so-called "mountain men" certainly lived a life which lay largely outside of society and social restraints. Such a life, however, has its own restraints imposed by circumstances and the limited range of choices open to the solitary man. It would be more reasonable to think of the change from natural to social living (if ever there was such a change) as the exchange of one set of restraints for another, *different* set. An exchange, however, in which men gained new capacities and new powers and, therefore, a *gain* in freedom.

Men like Locke thought of society as the trading of freedom for security, rather than as the gaining of new freedoms, because they lived in periods of social revolution when men were in rebellion against the social restraints placed upon them by a comparative minority of other men.

In fact, our present ideas of a free society often arise from the period when our ancestors strove to free themselves not from social restraints as such, but rather from the restraints of a despotic monarchy and a semi-feudal social system. The institutions which were shaped during this time have thus been identified in our minds with the possession of freedom, and the subsequent growth and development of these institutions has become for us the history of the development of freedom. As a result, we tend to think of the growth of freedom as, on the one hand, identical with the limitation of the power of the state, and on the other with the existence of certain specific institutions— parliamentary government, the two party system, free elections, etc.

Many of our ideas of freedom spring from the period of the English Civil War and rebellion against the despotic monarchy of the Stuarts. Yet although Elizabeth I was more despotic than any Stuart dared to be, we do not regard her reign as a dark period for British freedom. Rightly or wrongly, we consider the Tudor despotism in its context as a freer society than what preceded it, that it represented an advance for the British people, even though at a later date, the very same institutions were judged an obstacle to freedom.

We must also distinguish between the end arrived at and the means of achieving that end. The particular institutions which we cherish as "free," have often been the result of a long historical development which included violence, rebellion, and intrigue, and these institutions are now possible because our society has attained a relative stability. That is, our society may rather be said to have free institutions because it is stable, than to be stable because it has free institutions. In fact, democratic institutions work best in those societies where, for one reason or another, there is no radical process of social change, and as soon as a society begins to suffer major social change the democratic institutions begin to feel the strain and start to deteriorate. This is true of all countries during war-time, but it is equally true in other periods of social crisis.

As we all know, many countries have adopted the forms of democratic government without the underlying reality, in every case either because they are undergoing social change or because they are experiencing major social tensions. Even though it would be foolish to expect such countries to be models of democratic government, we may still ask—and sometimes answer—whether or not the changes they are experiencing are advances in freedom.

Democratic institutions are delicate plants—they may suffer from being in a society where there is too much change or too little. In a society where there are no major differences between the contending political parties, where new parties find it hard to establish themselves, and where a change of government makes no significant difference, the forms of democracy may remain unaltered, but their vitality may well have vanished. Unless the members of a society are really thinking and making rational decisions about significant problems which concern them, then democracy does not really exist, despite the presence of democratic apparatus.

It is, therefore, no simple matter to decide whether a society deserves to be described as "free" or not. One should only judge in the context of its development, and one should take all of its characteristics into account and not merely the nature of its political institutions. A society which, all things considered, is making an advance in the welfare and human development of its members therefore deserves to be called free.

We may, of course, imagine as our model of a free society an ideal in which people live under the most favourable conditions conceivable.

In this absolute sense I think that no existing society has the right to call itself free since all fall short in one way or another of the set of conditions which would prevail in the ideal, free society.

The first of these conditions is *tolerance*. No society can claim to be really free if restraints are placed upon any of its members because of their race, colour, creed, or sex. Any society which is intolerant of dissent, whatever form this takes, is placing obstacles in the way of enquiry, and thus in the long run doing more harm to itself than even the most evil of dissenters.

The second foundation of a free society is *equality*—not only as a more equal distribution of goods, but in the sense of each man's freedom being as important as that of every other man, so that no freedoms will be recognized or allowed which clearly and fundamentally harm the welfare of others.

Cooperation is the third condition of a free society. Insofar as a society is anything other than a system of constraints, it consists of opportunities for cooperation between its members. Certainly a society is moving towards freedom as it increasingly substitutes forms of cooperation for competition. The true individualism is that which fulfills itself by cooperating with others, so that one person's good is not a restriction upon another's but, on the contrary, the good of each is part of the good of all.

Finally, a free society is a *rationally planned* society. A haphazard and unplanned life for an individual would hardly be claimed as the best way of his securing freedom. It is hard to see the difference for a whole society. To take just one example: The relatively unplanned growth of cities in the twentieth century has led to mass ugliness, traffic-jammed streets, and the other innumerable frustrations of living in a modern great city. This applies to all the major areas of modern life—merely to allow things to happen without control is to court disaster, and the gradual loss of freedom of action.

It should be noted that all the conditions I mention as necessary to a truly free society—*tolerance, equality, co-operation* and *rational planning*—are expressed in a general way without specific mention of the kinds of institutions or social forms which may embody them. I do this deliberately because I do not think that we can tie these various conditions of freedom to any specific set of social institutions. It is a grave mistake to think that the particular forms of social life which we have found useful in the past and which have embodied freedom in one or other of its aspects will necessarily continue to function in the same way. The free society is another name for the good society, and this we have not yet attained.

In our admittedly imperfect societies, what can we do to promote, not a mere negative freedom, but a positive freedom conceived as the sum of all those conditions which give men power to improve themselves and their lot? We should look at our own society critically to make sure that our freedoms have not become mere empty forms devoid of life—we should consider how, if necessary, we may change or revitalize these forms. We should also look with a critical eye at the political and social processes going on in other countries and try to assess the degrees to which they are moving towards or away from a free society. Those who are moving towards a free society require our support and encouragement (let us hope that we deserve their's). We should not, however, expect them all to be working through the political and social institutions to which we have become accustomed. A tolerant and understanding attitude is necessary towards those who are achieving freedom in *their* way even although it may appear very different from *our* way.

Selected Bibliography

Berlin, Isaiah. *Four Essays on Liberty.* London: Oxford University Press, 1969.

Golding, William. *Free Fall.* Harmondsworth: Penguin Books, 1968.

Macpherson, C.B. *Democratic Theory: Essays in Retrieval.* London: Oxford Clarendon Press, 1973.

Mill, J.S. *On Liberty.* New York: The Liberal Arts Press, 1956.

Radcliff, Peter. *Limits of Liberty: Studies of Mill's "On Liberty."* Belmont: Wadsworth Publishing Co., 1966.

Notes on Contributors

RODGER BEEHLER read politics and history at the University of Manitoba, where he graduated. He then studied at Oxford where he received the B. Phil. in politics. After teaching at Dalhousie University, Halifax, for two years, he undertook philosophical studies at the University of Calgary and now teaches at the University of Victoria. He has published papers in *Analysis, The Canadian Journal of Political Science, Dialogue,* and the *Canadian Journal of Philosophy.* He is the editor with Alan Drengson of *The Philosophy of Society* (Methuen, forthcoming).

CONRAD BLACK was born in Montreal in 1944. He lived in Toronto from 1945 to 1962, before attending Carleton, Laval, and McGill Universities, obtaining the degrees of B.A., LL.L., and M.A., respectively. The arts degrees were in history. In 1966–1967 he was a consultant to the Canadian Council of Resource Ministers, in which capacity he prepared research and policy for several people, including the then Prime Minister of Quebec, Daniel Johnson. At the same time he was an editor of a weekly newspaper in the Eastern Townships. He made an extensive tour of South Vietnam and other countries in the Far East, partially under the auspices of former U.S. President Lyndon B. Johnson. He was in 1971–1972 a correspondent on Canadian affairs with the Hudson Institute. In 1969, with associates, he purchased the *Sherbrooke Daily Record,* which has become, with further acqusitions since 1970, Sterling Newspapers Limited, the seventh or eighth most profitable newspaper company in Canada, with eight daily and eight weekly newspapers in four provinces. Black is the Chairman of that company and is a director of a number of other companies in different industries. His articles and opinions on various political and historical subjects have appeared in Canadian newspapers and journals, as well as on the English and French radio and television networks of the CBC. Since 1970 he has worked on an extensive biography of Maurice L. Duplessis based on unique documentation. It will be published next year. Black is a vice president of "Le Cardinal Léger et Ses Oeuvres" and a director of the Canadian Press. He is a known critic of several aspects of contemporary liberalism.

LORENNE M.G. CLARK was born in Vancouver, graduating from U.B.C. in 1962. She completed her graduate work in Philosophy at Somerville College, Oxford, in 1965, and returned to Canada in 1966, where she has remained in the Department of Philosophy at the University of Toronto. She has been an active member of the Canadian Women's Movement for many years, having first become active in the area of day-care, moving from there to work on abortion and rape. Her main interests are political and legal philosophy. Motivated partly by her interests in the latter, and partly because of her involvement with the women's movement, she attended Osgoode Hall Law School, York University, during 1970–1971, and the fall term, 1971–1972. Following this, she was also appointed to the Graduate Faculty, Centre of Criminology, University of Toronto, and began research into rape. In conjunction with Debra J. Lewis, she completed an examination of all rape complaints made to the Metropolitan Toronto Police Department in 1970. The results of this work are to be published by Canadian Women's Educational Press, Toronto, early in 1976, under the title, *Rape: The Price of Coercive Sexuality*. She is currently completing a second rape project, an analysis of all cases of rape going at least to Preliminary Hearing in the Province of Ontario, 1970–1973, and in-depth interviewing of rape victims whose cases went at least as far as Preliminary Hearing in Ontario during that same period. This project was funded by the National Law Reform Commission, and she has been assisted by Ms. Margie Barr-Carley and Ms. Mary Ward, who are completing M.A.'s at the Centre of Criminology. She and Ms. Lewis have just begun a large rape project in Vancouver, funded by the Donner Foundation, which will exactly parallel the work already completed in Ontario. Because of her research interests, and her commitment to fulfillment of a reproductive as well as of a productive function, she is currently teaching only part time at the University of Toronto, devoting the remainder of her time to rape research, and to the care and nurturance of children and vegetables at her farm in British Columbia in company with Earl T. Clark.

Born in Toronto in 1940, DAN GOLDSTICK is old enough to remember vividly a high-school Empire Day Assembly where the (Canadian-born) teacher addressing the assembled students and staff on the theme, "Why I am Proud to be British," emphasized that in his youth, if a British subject living in a "banana republic" were to be placed under arrest "on a trumped-up charge," a Royal Navy gunboat would be promptly dispatched and the arresting government informed that unless they released the prisoner at once their capital would be blown off the face of the earth. Today Goldstick teaches philosophy at the University of Toronto. He has published technical philosophical contributions on a variety of topics, as well as such articles as "Do Religious Believers Mean What They Say?" (*Freethinker*, Volume 90, No. 19), "Lenin on Truth and Duty" (in two parts, *Communist Viewpoint*, Volume 3, No. 3 and Volume 3, No. 4), "Disobedience" (*Canadian Jewish Outlook*, Volume 10, No. 9), "Four Modern Forms of Intellectual Religion" (*Queen's Quarterly*, Volume LXXX, No. 1), "Philosophy and Decadence—and what must be done" (*Communist Viewpoint*, Volume 5, No. 2). He is currently working on a book, entitled *A Practical Refutation of Empiricism*. He maintains that the general decline in people's confidence in reason observable throughout the Western world in this century ("stupidity by choice") is only another ideological symptom of the general decay of the capitalist system. As a Communist parliamentary candidate in the 1974 general election in Canada, he advocated a new pact between Canada's two nations to regulate their common affairs constitutionally—on a basis of strictest equality between them—in the light of a formal recognition of the right of either of the two nations to secede from Canada should it choose to do so.

ROBERT KEYSERLINGK was born in Berlin and came to Canada as a child. He received his B.A. from Loyola College (Montreal), his M.A. from Toronto, and his Ph.D. from the University of London. He also studied in Fribourg, Gottingen, Bonn, and Munich. From 1956 to 1962 he was a Foreign Service officer with the Canadian government and was stationed in Bonn and

210

London. In 1964 he joined the University of Ottawa as a professor of history. Dr. Keyserlingk is a past president of the Canadian Catholic Historical Society and the editor of the Humanities Research Council of Canada. He is the author of several articles on the teaching of politics, French and Canadian relations, German student politics, and theories of nationalism. He has recently completed a manuscript on Bismarck and the press, and he is the author of a booklet on the history of the Knights of Malta. His present research centers on the history of fascism and fascist ideologies.

JOHN KING-FARLOW is Professor of Philosophy at the University of Alberta. Born in London, England (1932), he studied at Westminster, Christ Church, Oxford (M.A.), Duke (A.M.), and Stanford (Ph.D.); he also attended courses at two universities in France and served as an officer in the Royal Air Force. John King-Farlow has held faculty appointments at the University of Liverpool, U.K., the University of California's Santa Barbara campus, Amherst College, the University of Pittsburgh, California State University's San José campus, the University of Guelph, the University of Ottawa, and Australia's University of New England. He has held post-doctoral awards from the Mellon Foundation, the Leverhulme Foundation, and the Council for Philosophical Studies. The author of *Reason and Religion* (London, 1969) and co-author of *Faith and the Life of Reason* (Reidel, 1972), he also contributed several dozen articles to philosophical journals and books of many countries, in both English and French. He is co-editor with Yvon Lafrance of the French Canadian series *L'UNIVERS DE LA PHILOSOPHIE* (1973-) and co-editor with Roger Shiner of the volume *New Essays in Philosophy of Mind* (1975). His work of verse *The Dead Ship* was published by Advent Books of London in 1968 and other poems have appeared in a number of literary magazines. John King-Farlow is Secretary of the Canadian Philosophical Association, Executive Editor of the *Canadian Journal of Philosophy*, Counsellor of the Association of Philosophy Journal Editors, member of the Editorial Board of *Philosophy Research Archives*. He is a former Officer of the Oxford Union Society and a member of the London Athenæum. With William R. Shea (McGill) he is Co-Editor of the series *Contemporary Canadian Philosophy*.

LYNDA LANGE was born in Winnipeg in 1943. She received her B.A. and M.A. from the University of Manitoba, and is at the present writing a dissertation entitled, *Women and Democratic Theory: A Study of Jean-Jacques Rousseau* at the University of Toronto. During the past five years, she has been an active participant in the women's movement in Canada, writing and speaking on women's issues, and helping to organize such services as Abortion Referral, A Women's Place, and the Toronto Rape Crisis Centre.

LOUISE MARCIL-LACOSTE was born in Montreal and received her education at the Ecole Normale des Soeurs Grises, the Université de Montréal, and McGill University where she received her Ph.D. in philosophy in 1974 for her dissertation on the common sense doctrines of Claude Buffier and Thomas Reid. Dr. Marcil-Lacoste taught at the elementary and high school levels for several years and worked for a while for the C.B.C. For many years, she acted as Vice-President of the Québec Teachers Corporation, and she was until recently a member of the Superior Council of Education, where she served as

President of the Elementary School Commission. She is also a member of the "Conseil franco-québécois pour l'innovation et la prospective en éducation" and co-author of a forthcoming book entitled *Ecoles de demain?*. Dr. Marcil-Lacoste holds joint appointments in the Departments of Philosophy of McGill and the Université de Montréal. She is the Joint-Secretary of the Canadian Philosophical Association. Her interests in philosophy centre on epistemology, ethics, and education. Her articles have appeared in *Dialogue, Philosophiques, Canadian Journal in Philosophy, Education et développement, Education Canada, Les Cahiers du Québec* (HMH), *L'Univers de la philosophie* (Bellarmin), and *Dix-huitième Siècle* (Garnier). She belongs to the Civil Liberties Union of the Province of Quebec and acts as an advisor on problems of rights in education.

ANTHONY M. MARDIROS is a Canadian citizen. He was educated at the University of Melbourne, Australia, and Trinity College, Cambridge, and is Professor of Philosophy at the University of Alberta, where he teaches Aesthetics, Ethics, and Social Philosophy. He has published some 40 articles and reviews in such journals as the *Canadian Journal of Philosophy, Canadian Dimension, Canadian Forum, Dialogue, Queen's Quarterly, Mind*, and *The Philosophical Review*. He is at present completing a political biography of William Irvine (one of the founders of the CCF in Canada) and is preparing a monograph on *Art and Imagination*.

Born in Detroit in 1942, MICHAEL McDONALD did his undergraduate work in Philosophy and English at St. Michael's College in the University of Toronto (Honours B.A. 1965). He then went to the University of Pittsburgh and received an M.A. in 1967 and a Ph.D. in 1972. His doctoral thesis was entitled *Duties to Oneself* and was done under Kurt Baier's supervision. The main argument of this work was that the content of morality has self-regarding as well as other-regarding aspects. Since 1969 McDonald has been at the University of Waterloo. He has taught a wide range of courses in political and moral philosophy and, recently, in the philosophy of law. One of his major concerns has been to apply the methods and insights of political philosophy to Canadian social and political problems. The essay "Aboriginal Rights" originated in McDonald's "Canadian Problems" course. Other papers on such topics as the October Crisis and Canadian identity are likely to follow. Currently McDonald is preparing papers on the quality of life and on vainglory in Hobbes. Outside philosophy, McDonald has been active in the pursuit of due process in decision-making regarding the employment of academics. He is a member of the Board of the Canadian Association of University Teachers and past president of the University of Waterloo Faculty Association. Off campus he has two main, but carefully separated, avocations—sailing and the enjoyment of good food and wine.

GEORGE T. MONTICONE studied at Washington State University in the United States and completed his graduate work in Philosophy at the University of Calgary in 1973. Since then he has taught at the University of Alberta and Laurentian University and is currently teaching at the University of Victoria. Monticone wrote his doctoral dissertation on *The Linguistic Critique of Religion*, and he has presented papers at meetings of the Canadian

212

Philosophical Association. He is currently interested in problems in the philosophy of religion and in moral philosophy.

JAN NARVESON was born in the American State of Minnesota, and was educated at the University of Chicago, Harvard, and Oxford Universities, receiving his Ph.D. in Philosophy from Harvard in 1961. He has been at the University of Waterloo since 1963 where he is presently Professor of Philosophy. He has been a Canadian citizen since 1973. Among his principal writings are a book, *Morality and Utility* (Johns Hopkins Press, Baltimore, Md., 1967) and numerous papers in philosophical periodicals. Among them are "Pacifism: A Philosophical Analysis," *Ethics* 1965, "Utilitarianism and New Generations," *Mind* 1967, "Silverstein on Egoism and Universalizability," *Australasian Journal of Philosophy* 1969, "Promising, Expecting, and Utility," *Canadian Journal of Philosophy* 1971, "Aesthetics, Charity, Utility, and Distributive Justice," *Monist* 1972, "Moral Problems of Population," *Monist* 1973, and "Three Analysis Retributivists," *Analysis* 1974. Professor Narveson's principal avocation apart from philosophy is music. Besides being an avid collector of phonograph records, he is the founder and president of the Kitchener-Waterloo Chamber Music Society.

MARY O'BRIEN was born in England, in 1926, raised in Scotland, of Irish descent and a Canadian Citizen. A political activist long before she was a political theorist, she worked for the Labour Party in Glasgow, Scotland, during the tumultuous post-war electioneering of the late forties and fifties. At the same time she pursued a career in nursing. Like many of her generation, O'Brien found the bright promise of post-war European politics tarnished by the twin disillusionments of Hungary and Suez in 1956. She emigrated to Canada in 1957, just in time to cast a cynical eye on Diefenbaker's Northern Vision. Concentrating on her nursing career, she held the post of Director of Nursing at two Montreal hospitals in the sixties. She completed a part-time B.A. in sociology first at Sir George Williams and then at York University's Atkinson college. In 1970, she abandoned nursing to undertake graduate studies at York, with a major concern with political theory and politics in literature. To both of these she brought a consciously feminist perspective. Currently, she is working with two other Canadian philosophers, Lorenne Clark and Linda Birchill, in the production of a collection of *Essays in Revolutionary Feminism*.

WILLIAM R. SHEA was born in Gracefield, Quebec, in 1937. He was educated at the University of Ottawa, the Gregorian University in Rome, and Cambridge University where he was Chairman of the Students' Association of Darwin College and obtained his Ph.D. in philosophy. Before going to McGill, where he is the Chairman of the History and Philosophy of Science Program, Professor Shea taught at the University of Ottawa, and was a Fellow of the Renaissance Center of Harvard University, a Senior Fellow of the Canadian Cultural Institute in Rome, and a Visiting Professor at the Institute for the History of Science in Florence. Professor Shea is the Chairman of the Canadian National Committee for the History and Philosophy of Science and a Consulting Editor of *Dialogue*, the journal of the Canadian Philosophical Association. He contributes regularly to philosophical and historical journals and is the author of *Galileo's Intellectual Revolution* (New York and London, 1972), and the co-editor of *Reason, Experiment and Mysticism in the Scientific Revolution* (New York and London, 1975) and *Values and the Quality of Life*, which appeared in the same Series as this volume. He is currently editing a book entitled *Basic Problems in the Philosophy of Science* which will also be published in the *Canadian Contemporary Philosophy Series*. Professor Shea is mainly interested in the history of the scientific method from the 17th century to the present day and he is preparing an English translation and commentary of Descartes' *Le monde*. He is also collaborating, with his colleague Jonathan Robinson, on a translation and commentary of Hegel's early dissertation on the nature of science and the motion of the planets. Prof. Shea is married to Evelyn Shea Fischer, a lawyer and criminologist, and they have three children.

HERMAN TENNESSEN received his M.A. from the University of Oslo, Norway where he taught for many years. (During the war he was a member of the Norwegian Resistance against the Nazis). As a student and later a colleague of the leading Scandinavian philosopher Arne Naess, Professor Tennessen made original developments and applications of Naess' foundational work on Empirical Semantics and the concept of *preciseness*. U.N.E.S.C.O. awarded him a Fellowship for advanced research in Paris. He later taught for five years at the University of California, Berkeley where he championed the methods of Empirical Semantics against the more introspective "Ordinary Language Philosophy" of such colleagues as J. L. Austin, Stanley Cavell, and J. R. Searle. Since 1962 Herman Tennessen has been Professor of Philosphy and Senior Research Professor at the Centre for Advanced Study in Theoretical Psychology at the University of Alberta. Professor Tennessen has served on the Editorial board of *Inquiry, Methodology and Science*, and other philosophical journals. His articles have appeared in *Analysis, Theoria, Synthèse, The Journal of Philosophy, The Philosophical Forum, The Danish Philosophical Yearbook, The Journal of Existential Psychiatry, The Monist, Inquiry, Universitas*, and numerous periodicals in several countries. His published books have been mainly devoted to the philosophy of language. The author, a Canadian citizen, is married and has four children, two of whom recently graduated from the University of Alberta.